SuQAr

GREG & LUCY MALOUF

Photography by Alan Benson

Hardie Grant

BOOKS

CONTENTS

PASTRIES AND TARTS

FRITTERS AND PANCAKES

CONFECTIONERY

PRESERVES

DRINKS

INTRODUCTION

A lifetime of working in restaurants has taught me that nothing makes people's eyes light up the way desserts do. For all that we chefs like to focus our energies on the savoury components of a meal, we know, in our hearts, that a significant number of diners will skip straight to the pudding menu before choosing.

I've often wondered whether this is simply habit, or if it is somehow innate, this desire to finish a meal with something sweet – even if it's just a few small bites of pleasure. Because make no mistake about it, sweet things are purely about pleasure! They are the fun stuff, the fripperies, the indulgence. When they follow on from a savoury course, any real hunger has already been satisfied, but I do think that desserts satisfy a different kind of hunger: they nourish the soul, if not the body.

For many of us, our first hands-on experiences of cooking involve flour and butter, eggs and sugar. Rolling out cookie dough and stirring cake batter is perfect busy-work for little hands, and there are few joys in later life that match licking the frosting spoon!

In truth, my own mum never baked a biscuit in her life. When my brothers and I asked for pudding, she would push over the fruit bowl – and this is still the way that most Middle Eastern families will end a meal. Nonetheless, my earliest food memories do revolve around sweet things. In my own case, there was a brigade of women – my grandmothers, aunties, great-aunties, cousins and family friends – who descended upon our kitchen at various times of year to prepare monster batches of cookies for family celebrations and religious holidays. From these women, I discovered the camaraderie that comes from communal cooking and learnt the simple lesson that preparing food for others is love. The other lesson I learnt was about generosity: because abundance and extreme over-catering is definitely the Lebanese way!

The next stage of my dessert education came in France, where I spent six gruelling months as a junior in the pastry section of a busy Michelin-starred country restaurant. Here I learnt a harder truth: that cooking is mostly about repetition. I spent many weeks picking mint leaves for garnish, many more whisking egg whites, then more, still, making custard. How I longed to get into the real stuff: the ice creams and sorbets, the fancy gateaux, the petits fours, the elegant tarts and pastries. But with time I realised that this repetition – this practice – is what hones technique. And nowhere is precise technique more important than in the pastry section of a fancy restaurant.

While I've not spent a large part of my cooking career actually in the pastry section (and, being a dreamer rather than a technician, my food is far from the tricked up, fancy fare of that French restaurant) it's still one of the areas that gives me the greatest pleasure – both in thinking up dessert recipes and in eating them! Perhaps even more than savoury dishes, desserts offer such potential for playing with texture, temperature, and, above all, flavour: imagine the honeyed sweetness of a perfectly ripe mango, the melting tenderness of a shortbread cookie, or the mouth-filling silkiness of a delicate milk pudding; think of the soft chew of nougat, the snap of chocolate or the shattering crispness of a flaky pastry. When it comes down to it, there are few things in this life that offer one as much opportunity for making people happy as desserts and sweets do.

The other thing I have come to understand about dessert cooking – more, I think, than any other kind – is that there are always, always things to learn. And this appeals to a certain kind of cook – let's call them the perfectionists. These are the people who thrive on the exacting demands of their profession – the precision, the chemistry, the mastery of the thing. In my restaurant kitchens, over the years, I've been privileged to work with several of these extraordinary chefs and have been bowled over by the skilful way they've been able to interpret – and make real – my wildest (or vaguest) imaginings.

People often ask where Lucy and I get the ideas for our recipes and of course there are many inspirations: it might be a mound of perfect apricots at the market or a hedgerow laden with purple blackberries. Our imaginations are frequently sparked by dishes we've eaten in restaurants around the world (because who better to inspire you than your peers?); other exciting ideas turn up on our travels – and I've been lucky enough to broaden my knowledge of the Middle East in recent years, gaining a wealth of new inspiration along the way.

And then there are one's memories ... For me, expressing my Lebanese heritage is always paramount, and while planning this book, it's been thrilling to find out just what long roots Middle Eastern desserts and sweets have. Many of the ingredients and dishes I remember from childhood – the chewy fruit leathers and sticky dates, the flower waters, the fruit molasses, the nutty pastries – have their origins thousands of years ago and remain largely unchanged to this day. More surprising still has been the discovery that many European desserts have a Middle Eastern influence: when you choose your favourite sorbet, eat a hot doughnut, a slice of fruit tart or a spoonful of rice pudding, these are all culinary concepts that can be traced back to the Persian, Arab and Ottoman empires. This is less surprising, perhaps, when one understands that sugar has been around for much longer in the Arab world than in Europe. After all, *suqar*, this book's title, is the Arabic origin of our English word.

It's a bold move putting together a book of sweet recipes in these health-conscious times, and Lucy and I acknowledge that sugar, as a foodstuff, bears a heavy burden. The history of its cultivation and trade is stained by association with slavery and, today, with its link to obesity, sugar is demonised by many as the devil's work. Like many of us, I have a complicated relationship with sweet foods: I have a sweet tooth (as do many Middle Easterners), but I have health issues that restrain me from over-indulging. I like to think that having to exercise self-control means that I appreciate sweet things even more when I do actually eat them. In truth, this is the way Middle Easterners have always consumed them: as special and occasional treats, rather than standard daily fare. And it's also important to note that when you prepare recipes yourself at home, rather than buying commercially manufactured sweets, cookies and cakes, you will be in control of exactly how much sugar you are consuming.

A few words about the practicalities: with some exceptions, most of the recipes in this book are simple to prepare and require little in the way of truly specialist equipment, other than what I'd consider to be a pretty standard kitchen kit. We've also tried to limit the number of overly expensive or esoteric ingredients. Thankfully, the range of Middle Eastern products available has hugely improved from when we started writing cookbooks twenty-odd years ago, which means that you can source nearly all you need for our recipes from major supermarkets. Try adopting the mindset of a pastry chef and aim for precision and accuracy as much as possible – key requirements for all dessert cookery. And most important of all, invest time in organisation and planning. Always read the recipe through from beginning to end before you start and ensure you've got all the equipment and ingredients required.

The following desserts are a coming together of many influences. Some sprang from menus past and cried out to be included, others have been dreamt up specially for this book, but, as is always the case with our cookbooks, they have all been tested many times in our home kitchens. All chefs' recipes reflect personal prejudice and there are many ways of defining deliciousness! But while you might spot the occasional hint of English hedgerows (reflecting Lucy's home in the Kent countryside) most of the recipes in this book are firmly rooted in my own Lebanese background. They are absolutely the things that I love to eat myself and they never stray too far from my soul.

I'm a firm believer in the human need for joy – and, let's be honest, life would be very bleak without a touch of sweetness from time to time.

This book is for those times.

Greg and Lucy Malouf

FRUIT

Chilled watermelon with halva, crushed strawberries and lime syrup **11**

Classic citrus-date salad with cinnamon dust **12**

Stone fruit 'fattouche' with sweet lemon dressing **13**

Roasted apricots with cinnamon brioche and toasted almond cream **16**

Slow-roasted quinces with chantilly-yoghurt cream **17**

Arabic five-spice pineapple with saffron ice cream **18**

Baked figs, sweet curd, honey and thyme **21**

Plum soufflé with cardamom and orange **22**

Strawberry-rose pavlovas **26**

Dates in cardamom coffee **28**

Date tiramisu, Middle Eastern style **28**

Pomegranate-lime jelly **29**

In truth, more often than not, Greg will elect to have fresh fruit at the end of a meal: a slice of chilled watermelon, a few perfect figs, a small bunch of perfumed muscatel grapes – even a humble apple, which he'll peel and slice into segments with as much care as he gives to preparing any fancy dessert. No doubt this is the result of growing up in a Lebanese family where it was just never a tradition to eat dessert after a meal.

Fruits are nature's sweet treats, of course, and Middle Eastern countries produce an abundance of them. Apples, citrus fruits, stone fruits, grapes, figs, pomegranates, melons and bananas – to name just some – have been grown in these lands for many thousands of years. Grapes and orchard fruits were some of the earliest crops to be cultivated in the Fertile Crescent. Stone fruits spread from China along the ancient Silk Road and some of the world's best apricots are still grown near the Iranian city of Isfahan to this day. In the Arabian Gulf countries, of course, the date has always unquestionably been king.

You'll soon notice that a preference for fruit seeps through into other chapters in this book, too, and this is not just to do with fruit's natural sweetness. Fruit-based desserts tend to be naturally refreshing; they offer a wide range of colours and textures (from creamy to crisp, from firm to juicy or softly yielding); some fruits are perfumed, while many have a pleasing tartness. They all offer a desirable counterpoint to rich or creamy cakes, pastries and desserts, and generally provide a lighter finish to what might otherwise be a heavy meal.

In this chapter, though, we've selected some of our favourite recipes where fruit – often fresh, sometimes cooked – is the star. Many require very little by way of preparation; others involve some simple cooking to intensify and enhance a fruit's natural flavours. We've tried to offer dishes for all times of the year, so do your best to choose recipes according to what is seasonally best.

You'll need very little in the way of special equipment to make the fruit desserts detailed here. In addition to the usual range of mixing bowls, kitchen utensils, saucepans and baking trays, a food processor will come in handy for blitzing nuts and spices. You'll also need a large soufflé dish (or a set of small ones) for the plum soufflé, an attractive mould for the jelly, and perhaps a piping bag for the pavlovas.

CHILLED WATERMELON WITH HALVA, CRUSHED STRAWBERRIES AND LIME SYRUP

Often, chilled fruit is all that's offered as dessert in Middle Eastern households, and, to be honest, is there anything more refreshing on a baking hot summer's day? A smiley wedge of ice-cold watermelon is Greg's idea of heaven, and this is only a slightly more elaborate way of serving it.

Greg often has versions of this summery fruit salad on his menus, and they nearly always include nuggets of crumbly halva – the Middle Eastern sweet made from sesame seeds. They add lovely textural contrast and an intense nutty flavour.

SERVES 6

1 small seedless watermelon, chilled
250 g (9 oz) blueberries
300 g (10½ oz) ripe strawberries, hulled
100 g (3½ oz) pistachio halva, broken into large chunks
handful of viola flowers, petals only (optional)

LIME SYRUP
80 g (2¾ oz) caster (superfine) sugar
100 ml (3½ fl oz) water
½ vanilla bean, split lengthways and seeds scraped
juice of 1 lime
1 teaspoon rosewater

EQUIPMENT
melon baller (optional)

To make the lime syrup, combine the sugar, water, vanilla bean and seeds in a saucepan. Heat gently to dissolve the sugar, stirring from time to time, then bring to the boil. Lower the heat and simmer for 5 minutes to slightly reduce the syrup. Remove from the heat and leave to cool to room temperature. Fish out the vanilla bean and save it to perfume your sugar canister. Stir the lime juice and rosewater into the syrup and chill until required.

Cut the watermelon in half crossways. Use a melon baller or teaspoon to scoop out the flesh and transfer to a large mixing bowl. Add the blueberries, along with half the strawberries and half the chilled syrup, and toss lightly.

Put the remaining strawberries in another bowl and add the rest of the syrup. Mash roughly with a fork to make a chunky sauce. Add to the bowl with the fruit and toss everything together lightly.

Divide between pretty serving bowls or tip onto a serving platter. Sprinkle with chunks of halva and the viola petals, if using, and serve straight away.

+ ALSO SERVE WITH
Rose jam ice cream (page 57)
Mini meringue kisses (page 194)

CLASSIC CITRUS-DATE SALAD WITH CINNAMON DUST

The classic Moroccan salad generally showcases oranges, but we like to mix things up a bit with a variety of citrus fruits. It is a simple dessert – and none the worse for that – and makes a refreshing end to a rich meal, or one that is heavily spiced.

SERVES 4–6

2 large oranges (or 3 blood oranges)
2 tangelos
2 clementines
1 ruby grapefruit
1–2 tablespoons rosewater, to taste
6 medjool dates, pitted
handful of small mint leaves
50 g (1¾ oz) icing (confectioners') sugar
¼ teaspoon ground cinnamon

Use a very sharp knife to slice away the peel from all the citrus fruit. Slice the segments out of their skin casings into a mixing bowl, making sure you catch all the juices. Also take care to remove all traces of bitter white pith and membrane. Add the rosewater and toss gently. Chill until ready to serve.

When ready to serve, tip the citrus segments and juice into a shallow glass bowl or attractive serving platter. Slice the dates into slivers and finely shred the mint leaves. Scatter both over the salad. Sift the icing sugar with the cinnamon and dust over the salad at the last minute.

+ ALSO SERVE WITH
Cream cheese ice cream (page 61)

STONE FRUIT 'FATTOUCHE' WITH SWEET LEMON DRESSING

Fattouche is the familiar Lebanese garden salad jazzed up with crunchy bits of fried pitta bread. Here, we replicate the idea in a sweet fruit salad. After trying various crunchy elements, the ones we liked most were shards of chocolate wafers (page 92), but you could substitute any thin, crisp wafer that takes your fancy.

Use a combination of the best quality seasonal stone fruits available. We like to blanch and peel peaches because their fuzzy skins can be a little bitter, but wouldn't worry about doing the same with other fruits – unless you are feeling particularly refined.

SERVES 4–6

2 white or yellow peaches
1 white or yellow nectarine, pitted
2 apricots, pitted
2 blood plums, pitted
handful of sweet ripe cherries, pitted
few sprigs of small mint leaves
edible flowers, to serve (optional)
Chocolate arabesque wafers (page 92),
    broken into shards, to serve

SWEET LEMON DRESSING
80 g (2¾ oz) mild-flavoured honey
juice of 1 lemon
½ vanilla bean, split lengthways and
    seeds scraped

To make the lemon dressing, combine all the ingredients in a small saucepan and bring to the boil slowly. Lower the heat and simmer for 5 minutes to slightly reduce the syrup. Remove from the heat and leave to cool to room temperature. Fish out the vanilla bean and save it to perfume your sugar canister. Chill until required.

To blanch the peaches, bring a saucepan of water to the boil. Add the fruit and cook for 2 minutes. Transfer to a bowl of iced water and, when they are cool enough to handle, cut them in half, remove the stones and peel away the skins with a sharp paring knife.

Cut all the larger fruit into chunks of roughly similar size. Keep the cherries whole, unless they are very big. Combine in a large mixing bowl and toss gently with the chilled lemon dressing.

Transfer to a serving bowl and decorate with small mint leaves and flowers, if using. Tuck shards of wafers in among the pieces of fruit and serve the fattouche as is, or with something creamy on the side.

See photo on pages 14–15.

+ ALSO SERVE WITH
    Middle Eastern clotted cream (page 32)
    Chantilly-yoghurt cream (page 48)
    your favourite ice cream or sorbet (pages 55–64)

ROASTED APRICOTS WITH CINNAMON BRIOCHE AND TOASTED ALMOND CREAM

This versatile dish is ideal for a special Sunday brunch, and just as lovely for dessert. And you could also serve it with your favourite ice cream, instead of the almond cream, which would make for a lighter and more refreshing accompaniment. That being said, the toasted nut cream is intensely almondy and not overly sweet, making a lovely counterpoint to the tangy roasted apricots and crunchy brioche. It's based on a fabulous nut-infused milk pudding we enjoyed during our travels around Anatolia. Make it ahead of time, as it keeps well in the fridge for a day or so.

To ring the changes, Roasted star anise plums (page 42), or even poached cherries, would also make a successful threesome with the toasty nut flavours of the cream – actually, the brioche makes an excellent vehicle for all sorts of poached fruit.

SERVES 4–6

600 g (1 lb 5 oz) ripe apricots, halved
100 ml (3½ fl oz) fresh orange juice or water
1 tablespoon amaretto, or to taste
100 g (3½ oz) golden caster (superfine) sugar
juice of ½ lime

TOASTED ALMOND CREAM

80 g (2¾ oz) whole blanched almonds
400 ml (13½ fl oz) thick (double/heavy) cream

CINNAMON BRIOCHE

200 g (7 oz) brioche loaf
generous knob of unsalted butter
50 g (1¾ oz) caster (superfine) sugar
1 teaspoon ground cinnamon

To prepare the almond cream, first preheat the oven to 180°C (350°F) fan-forced/200°C (400°F). Scatter the almonds on a small baking tray and roast for 10–15 minutes, shaking a few times, until a deep golden brown.

Transfer the nuts to a heavy-based saucepan along with 300 ml (10 fl oz) of the cream and bring to a simmer. Turn off the heat and leave to infuse until completely cold, then tip into a blender or food processor and blitz until smooth. Pour through a fine-mesh sieve and discard the solids. You'll be left with a taupe-coloured, intensely flavoured almond cream; don't worry if it's a little grainy. Let it cool. Add the rest of the cream and whip to soft peaks. Refrigerate until ready to serve.

Preheat the oven to 170°C (340°F) fan-forced/190°C (375°F).

Arrange the apricot halves, skin sides down, in a single layer in a large roasting tin. Pour in the orange juice and splash the amaretto around. Sprinkle with the sugar. Roast for around 25–30 minutes (depending on how ripe the apricots are), or until the apricots are tender and lightly caramelised on top and the liquid has reduced to a sticky syrup. Once the apricots are cool enough to handle, gently prise out the stones. Squeeze on the lime juice and keep in a warm place while you prepare the brioche.

Increase the oven to 180°C (350°F) fan-forced/200°C (400°F). Cut the brioche into 4–6 slices, around 3 cm (1¼ in) thick.

On your stovetop, melt the butter in a large ovenproof frying pan or a roasting tin large enough to accommodate all the brioche slices. Sprinkle in the sugar and cinnamon in an even layer. Add the brioche slices to the pan and bake in the oven for 3–4 minutes, or until they start to colour. Flip them over and return to the oven for another 3–4 minutes. They should be golden brown on both sides. Remove from the oven and leave to cool slightly in the pan. They will crisp up as they cool.

Serve the warm brioche and apricots with the chilled almond cream.

+ ALSO SERVE WITH
Honeyed yoghurt sorbet (page 55)

SLOW-ROASTED QUINCES WITH CHANTILLY-YOGHURT CREAM

The knobbly, fuzzy quince is not nature's prettiest fruit, but it is adored in Middle Eastern countries such as Iran, Syria and Turkey, where it has been widely cultivated for more than 4000 years. It has an elusive tart-sweet perfume that lends itself to both desserts and savoury dishes, and, when cooked, its pale, intransigent flesh magically transforms to a glorious deep and yielding garnet. The fruit's slightly musty flavour is greatly enhanced by the spices and herbs in this cooking syrup. The actual length of oven time will depend on the initial ripeness of the fruit and how tender you want them to be. And given how rock-hard quinces can be, we don't bother about peeling or coring them, as we find this is just a battle too far.

Serve with soft spoonfuls of Chantilly-yoghurt cream (page 48); its slight sourness is the perfect foil to the quince's honeyed sweetness. They're just as good with Cream cheese ice cream (page 61), Honeyed yoghurt sorbet (page 55), crème fraîche or softly whipped cream.

SERVES 6–8

5 medium quinces, de-fuzzed with
   a soft cloth
300 g (10½ oz) caster (superfine) sugar
100 ml (3½ fl oz) runny honey
300 ml (10 fl oz) verjuice
juice and strips of peel from 1 orange
juice and strips of peel from 1 lemon
3 bay leaves
10 black peppercorns
2 cinnamon sticks
6 cloves
2 star anise
Chantilly-yoghurt cream (page 48),
   ice cream, crème fraîche or whipped
   cream, to serve

Preheat the oven to 140ºC (275ºF) fan-forced/160ºC (320ºF).

Use a very heavy-duty knife to cut the quinces in half and arrange them, cut side up, in a roasting tin or baking dish just large enough to hold the fruit snugly. Scatter with the sugar, then drizzle on the honey. Pour on the verjuice and citrus juices, then tuck the strips of peel in among the quinces. Add the bay leaves and the remaining spices to the tin. Cover the surface with a piece of baking paper, then cover the whole tin loosely with foil.

Bake for 2 hours, then remove the foil and bake, uncovered, for a further 2 hours, or until the quinces are very tender. The cooking liquid should have greatly reduced to a perfumed, thick and sticky ruby-red syrup and the surface of the fruit may be lightly charred.

Serve the quinces in their syrup, warm or at room temperature, with your choice of accompaniment. If you don't want to eat them straight away, they will keep in the fridge quite happily for a few days, but bring them to room temperature before serving.

+ ALSO SERVE WITH
Honeyed yoghurt sorbet (page 55)
Cream cheese ice cream (page 61)

ARABIC FIVE-SPICE PINEAPPLE WITH SAFFRON ICE CREAM

Sweet spice blends are popular in the Middle Eastern kitchen and this Arabic five-spice, with its heady notes of aniseed and cinnamon, works wonderfully well with pineapple, especially when infused into a warming rum caramel. As ever when using spices, for maximum impact we'd encourage you to make this from fresh whole spices and grind them yourself.

Although we usually serve this spiced pineapple compote with a simple ice cream – saffron is our favourite, but good-quality commercial vanilla would also be fine – it's surprisingly versatile and can also be used in sweet tarts and pastries or to accompany rum babas (page 174). For a slightly more elaborate 'composed' dessert, we will often add a crunchy component, such as cardamom fritters (page 170), or the orange-cardamom wafers suggested here.

SERVES 4

25 g (1 oz) unsalted butter
2 tablespoons light brown
    muscovado sugar
2 tablespoons honey
80 ml (2½ fl oz) dark rum
½ vanilla bean, split lengthways
    and seeds scraped
1 teaspoon Arabic five-spice
    (see below, or, at a pinch, use
    Chinese 5-spice powder)
400 g (14 oz) ripe pineapple flesh
    (around ½ pineapple) cut into
    2.5 cm (1 in) dice
Saffron ice cream (page 64), to serve
Orange-cardamom wafers (page 91),
    to serve (optional)

ARABIC FIVE-SPICE

1 tablespoon ground cinnamon
seeds from 10 cardamom pods
15 cloves, coarsely ground
4 star anise, coarsely ground
1 teaspoon fennel seeds,
    coarsely ground
1 teaspoon caster (superfine) sugar

To make the Arabic five-spice, tip all the spices into a small frying pan and cook over a medium heat for around 2 minutes just until warm to the touch. Tip into a mortar with the sugar and grind everything together further, to achieve a fairly even, powdery consistency. Sieve to remove any fibrous bits and store in an airtight container. It will keep well for a couple of weeks before the potency of the flavour begins to fade.

Combine the butter, sugar and honey in a small saucepan and cook over a medium heat, stirring occasionally, until the butter has melted and the sugar has dissolved. Increase the heat and cook for 8–10 minutes to a deep chestnut caramel.

Add the rum, vanilla bean and seeds and five-spice powder, followed by the pineapple chunks. Cook over a high heat for 2–3 minutes, tossing frequently, until the pineapple is thoroughly coated in the glossy caramel, but still holding its shape. Don't cook it for too long, as this mutes its intrinsic, sweet-sharp pineapple-y tang.

Remove the pan from the heat. Fish out the vanilla bean and save it to perfume your sugar canister.

Serve the hot pineapple and caramel sauce with saffron ice cream and orange-cardamom wafers, if you like.

+ ALSO SERVE WITH
    Crunchy cardamom fritters (page 170)
    Baby babas (page 174)

BAKED FIGS, SWEET CURD, HONEY AND THYME

If you are lucky enough to have ready access to a fig tree, then, come late summer, one of life's simplest and most exquisite pleasures is within your reach. The fig flourishes in hot climates – it is thought to have its origins in modern-day Anatolia – and has been celebrated for millennia in the myths and legends of many Middle Eastern and Mediterranean civilisations.

While it's hard to beat the pure sensory joy of a perfectly ripe fresh fig, baking them does intensify their honeyed sweetness. Thyme and goat's cheese are a natural and popular match, and both add a savoury note to the fruit's honeysuckle sweetness. This not-too-sweet dessert is ideal for people who like a more savoury finish to a meal, and, at a pinch, it might even do service as a cheese course! If you're feeling adventurous, you could use feta or a soft blue cheese instead of the goat's curd.

SERVES 6

6 perfect figs
25 g (1 oz) caster (superfine) sugar
juice of 2 oranges
juice of ½ lemon
few sprigs of thyme
1 teaspoon rosewater, or to taste
Pine nut praline (page 206), to serve
   (optional)

SWEET CURD
80 g (2¾ oz) soft goat's curd
50 g (1¾ oz) labne (page 244)
   or mascarpone
1 generous tablespoon honey

Preheat the oven to 180°C (350°F) fan-forced/200°C (400°F).

With a small sharp knife, make a small cross in the pointed end of each fig and gently squeeze the base so the top opens out like a flower. Arrange the figs in a small roasting tin.

Combine the sugar and orange juice in a small saucepan and heat gently, stirring occasionally, until the sugar dissolves. Bring to the boil, then lower the heat and simmer for 4–6 minutes until it forms a light honey-coloured caramel. Add the lemon juice and half the thyme sprigs, stir well and remove from the heat.

Pour the syrup over the figs and scatter on the rest of the thyme. Bake for 10 minutes.

While the figs are baking, make the curd by whisking together the goat's curd, labne and honey.

Two minutes before the end of the baking time, slip a spoonful of the curd into the centre of each fig. Sprinkle on the rosewater and return to the oven just until the cheese begins to melt. Serve the figs warm or at room temperature, sprinkled with pine nut praline, if you like.

PLUM SOUFFLÉ WITH CARDAMOM AND ORANGE

Plums are not particularly associated with the Middle East; however, we tasted some extraordinarily intense dried plum pastes and 'leathers' (see page 225) during our travels around northern Iran and Turkey, and they have an affinity with rosewater and many Middle Eastern spices, such as fennel, anise, cardamom, cinnamon and cloves. They are one of the earliest domesticated and most widespread fruits available and, given the relentlessly productive nature of most plum trees, it's a good idea to have a healthy supply of recipes for this tart, juicy fruit. This soufflé is one of our favourites.

French soufflés traditionally use variously flavoured crème pâtissières as a base for whisked egg whites. This simpler version does away with the crème pât and relies on nothing more than cornflour to provide the stabilising force to a fruity purée. It makes for a more intense soufflé and you can vary the fruit with the seasons (using the same 300 g/10½ oz weight of fruit purée). If you prepare the fruit purée well in advance – always a plus – it just leaves the egg whites to be whisked at the last minute.

Serve with very cold runny cream, or with a dollop of ice cream – plopped on top, if you like, so it sinks slowly into the hot fruity clouds. Either way, the contrast in temperatures is blissful.

SERVES 6

60 g (2 oz) melted unsalted butter,
    for brushing
50 g (1¾ oz) caster (superfine) sugar,
    plus extra for dusting
200 g (7 oz) egg whites (around 5),
    at room temperature
300 g (10½ oz) Plum purée (see below)
icing (confectioners') sugar,
    for dusting
pouring (single/light) cream or
    ice cream, to serve

PLUM PURÉE

400 g (14 oz) plums (blood plums make
    for the prettiest colour), quartered
    and pitted
seeds from 3 cardamom pods
80 g (2¾ oz) caster (superfine) sugar
zest and juice of ½ large orange
20 g (¾ oz) cornflour (cornstarch)
    or arrowroot

EQUIPMENT

1.5 litre (51 fl oz) soufflé dish,
    or six small soufflé dishes, around
    150–200 ml (5–7 fl oz)

To make the plum purée, put the plums into a saucepan. Use a mortar and pestle to grind the cardamom seeds with ½ teaspoon of the caster sugar and add to the pan along with the rest of the sugar and the orange zest and juice. Cover and bring to the boil, stirring occasionally, then lower the heat and simmer, uncovered, for 15–20 minutes or until the plums are meltingly soft. Cool briefly, then, using a food processor or hand-held blender, blitz the cooked fruit to a purée and push it through a fine-mesh sieve to remove any stubborn bits of skin. Measure out 300 g (10½ oz) of the purée (which will pretty much be all of it) and return it to the cleaned-out pan.

In a small bowl, mix the cornflour with a few tablespoons of the hot plum purée, then tip this back into the pan with the rest of the purée. Bring to the boil, then lower the heat and simmer for about a minute, stirring, until it thickens. Tip into a bowl and leave to cool completely. If making ahead of time, you can cover and refrigerate the purée for 1–2 days, but bring it to room temperature before combining with the egg whites.

When ready to bake the soufflé, preheat the oven to 180°C (350°F) fan-forced/200°C (400°F). Use a pastry brush to grease the inside of the soufflé dish(es) with melted butter. Make sure you brush upwards, from base to top, as this does help the mixture to rise evenly. Dust with a little caster sugar, shaking off any excess, then refrigerate the dish to set the butter while you finish preparing the soufflé mix.

Put the egg whites into the bowl of an electric mixer and whisk until they start to froth. Then, with the motor running, scatter on the sugar and continue whisking to medium-stiff glossy peaks.

Lightly whisk two large spoonfuls of the whisked egg whites into the plum purée to loosen it. Then use a large metal spoon to fold in the rest, making sure you cut through and lift the purée up from the base of the bowl. The aim is to incorporate the egg whites evenly, but to retain as much volume as possible.

Spoon the mixture into the soufflé dish(es) and smooth the top with a spatula. Use the tip of a knife (or your thumb) to run around the inside of the rim, creating an indent, which will also help the soufflé rise evenly. Place the dish in a small, deep roasting tin and pour in enough boiling water to come a quarter of the way up the sides. Bake for 20–25 minutes (10–15 minutes if using smaller dishes), or until the soufflés are well risen and a skewer comes out almost clean.

Remove from the oven, dust with icing sugar and serve immediately with very cold pouring cream or with ice cream.

See photo on page 24.

+ ALSO SERVE WITH
Honeyed yoghurt sorbet (page 55)
Rose jam ice cream (page 57)
Cream cheese ice cream (page 61)
Chocolate-halva ice cream (page 63)

STRAWBERRY-ROSE PAVLOVAS

As a nod to Australia, Greg often features pavlova on dessert menus – albeit with a Middle Eastern twist – and it is nearly always the most popular choice. With pavs, you can pretty much choose any fruit you fancy as a topping – and, of course, passionfruit is the Aussie classic – but this is one of Greg's favourite incarnations. As is so often the case, the best results depend on the quality of fruit you use, so make this at the height of summer when strawberries are at their intensely perfumed best.

You'll need to allow 12 hours to prepare the strawberry juice, which infuses the meringue shells with flavour and tints them the prettiest pale pink, but the dish won't suffer too much if you omit this step and just make regular pavlovas.

SERVES 6

200 g (7 oz) dried strawberries,
    to serve (optional)
pieces of honeycomb, to serve
    (optional)

STRAWBERRY JUICE
500 g (1 lb 2 oz) strawberries, hulled
50 g (1¾ oz) caster (superfine) sugar

PAVLOVAS
150 g (5½ oz) egg whites (around 4),
    at room temperature
220 g (8 oz) caster (superfine) sugar
20 g (¾ oz) cornflour (cornstarch)
2 teaspoons white vinegar
45 ml (1½ fl oz) Strawberry juice
    (see above)

BERRY SALAD
50 g (1¾ oz) caster (superfine) sugar
200 ml (7 fl oz) apple juice
juice and zest of 1 lime
40 g (1½ oz) sultanas (golden raisins)
1 cinnamon stick
1 tablespoon rosewater
500 g (1 lb 2 oz) strawberries, hulled
200 g (7 oz) blueberries
200 g (7 oz) blackberries

LABNE CREAM
250 g (9 oz) labne (page 244)
250 g (9 oz) mascarpone
2 generous tablespoons honey

EQUIPMENT
piping bag with a 1.5 cm (½ in) nozzle
    (optional)

Begin by making the strawberry juice. Combine the strawberries and sugar in a mixing bowl and tumble together gently. Cover the bowl with plastic wrap and place in the fridge for 12 hours to macerate.

Tip the berries and juice into a large saucepan. Bring the mixture to the boil over a medium–high heat, then turn the heat down and simmer gently for 30 minutes so the strawberries release more of their juice. Remove from the heat and strain through a fine-mesh sieve into a large bowl, using a spatula to press the strawberries to release as much juice as possible. Pour into a saucepan and simmer until the liquid has reduced by two-thirds to around 40–50 ml (1¼–1¾ fl oz). Set aside to cool.

Preheat the oven to 150°C (300°F) fan-forced/170°C (340°F). To make a template for the pavlovas, draw six 10 cm (4 in) circles on two pieces of baking paper and place, marked side down, on two large baking trays.

To make the pavlovas, place the egg whites into the scrupulously clean bowl of an electric mixer. Whisk at low speed until the mixture begins to foam, then increase the speed to high and whisk to smooth, soft peaks. With the motor running, sift on the sugar, a little at a time, until you have stiff, glossy peaks. Sift on the cornflour, sprinkle on the vinegar and whisk in briefly but evenly. Finally, use a large metal spoon to fold in the strawberry juice briefly, so the meringue is streaky and marbled, rather than thoroughly amalgamated.

Spoon the meringue into the piping bag and pipe in concentric circles to fill each of the marked outlines. Alternatively, dollop on spoonfuls of meringue and smooth into shape with a small spatula.

As you put the pavlovas into the oven, reduce the temperature to 100°C (210°F) fan-forced/120°C (250°F). Bake for 80 minutes, then turn the oven off and leave them to cool completely inside. Resist the temptation to open the oven door and accept that this is likely going to take 3–4 hours – or you could leave them overnight. Remove from the oven and lift them carefully onto a wire rack to decorate.

For the berry salad, combine the sugar, apple juice, lime juice and zest in a small saucepan and heat gently to dissolve the sugar. Add the sultanas and cinnamon stick and bring to the boil. Lower the heat and simmer for a few minutes, then remove from the heat and leave to cool to room temperature. Stir in the rosewater and refrigerate.

When ready to serve, strain the syrup. Mix the strawberries, blueberries and blackberries together with enough syrup to moisten them.

For the labne cream, fold together the labne, mascarpone and honey.

Pipe or spoon the labne cream onto the pavlovas then pile the strawberry salad on top. If using dried strawberries, pound half of them to a powder and sprinkle onto the labne cream. Decorate with the remaining dried strawberries and tiny blobs of honeycomb, if using, then drizzle with extra syrup.

See photo on page 25.

+ ALSO MAKE WITH
Middle Eastern clotted cream (page 32)
Blackberry-nectarine compote (page 48)
Citrus-scented blueberries (page 128)

DATES IN CARDAMOM COFFEE

Dates' fudge sweetness marries brilliantly with coffee, and the addition of cardamom, as here, is very typical of the Arabian Gulf. The macerated dates are lovely just on their own as a sort of sweetmeat – maybe to accompany a strong morning coffee – but we think they merit being made even more of. Below we offer the option of using them in a sort of Middle Eastern–inspired tiramisu, but you could also serve them with ice cream, custard or whipped cream.

SERVES 8–10

500 ml (17 fl oz) freshly made espresso coffee
1 teaspoon caster (superfine) sugar
20 cardamom pods, crushed
½ cinnamon stick
400 g (14 oz) medjool dates (around 20), pitted

Combine the coffee, sugar, cardamom pods and cinnamon stick in a small saucepan and bring just to the boil. Remove from the heat.

Put the dates into a small container or glass jar so they fit snugly. Pour on the coffee, ensuring the dates are submerged. Store for at least 12 hours, inverting every now and then, so the dates absorb the coffee. They will keep in a sealed container for up to 4 days.

+ ALSO SERVE WITH
Berber 1000-hole pancakes (page 181)

DATE TIRAMISU, MIDDLE EASTERN STYLE

SERVES 4–6

1 × Dates in cardamom coffee (see above)
1 tablespoon marsala (or brandy)
1 tablespoon orange blossom water
20 Perfumed ladyfingers (page 90), ready-made savoiardi or even amaretti cookies
500 ml (17 fl oz) Chantilly-yoghurt cream (page 48), Middle Eastern clotted cream (page 32) or whipped cream
1 tablespoon cocoa powder
½ teaspoon grated nutmeg
very finely chopped pistachio nuts, to serve

Strain off around half the coffee syrup from the dates into a shallow dish and stir in the marsala and orange blossom water. Dip the ladyfingers into the syrup, one at a time, turning them around briskly so they don't become soggy.

Pile the soaked ladyfingers into the bottom of an attractive glass dish and arrange the dates on top. Mound on your choice of cream and smooth it out roughly. Mix the cocoa powder and nutmeg together and sieve over the cream. Finish with some chopped pistachios.

POMEGRANATE-LIME JELLY

There are few things simpler – or more popular – than homemade jelly. This version is tangy and refreshing, perfect for when you want a sharper, brighter dessert. The meringues make a pretty accompaniment, adding sweetness and crunch, but let's be honest: sometimes all you want with jelly is a dribble of runny cream or a scoop of ice cream.

SERVES 6

700 ml (23½ fl oz) good-quality
    fresh pomegranate juice
100 ml (3½ fl oz) lime juice
1 tablespoon rosewater, or to taste
30 g (1 oz) caster (superfine) sugar
10 small gelatine leaves (see Cook's
    notes, page 243)
Mini meringue kisses (page 194),
    to serve (optional)
whipped cream, pouring (single/light)
    cream or ice cream, to serve
    (optional)

EQUIPMENT

6 × 180 ml (6 fl oz) small moulds or
    1 × 1 litre (34 fl oz) jelly mould

In a measuring jug, combine 400 ml (13½ fl oz) of the pomegranate juice with the lime juice and rosewater.

Put the remaining 300 ml (10 fl oz) of pomegranate juice into a small saucepan along with the sugar and heat gently to dissolve. Bring to a simmer, then remove from the heat.

Soak the gelatine in cold water for a few minutes until softened. Squeeze out the excess liquid and add the gelatine to the hot juice, stirring to dissolve completely.

Combine the hot juice with the cold juice and pour through a fine-mesh sieve into the jelly mould(s). Leave at room temperature to cool, then refrigerate for 4–6 hours, or until set.

To turn out the jellies, dip the base of the mould(s) in a dish of hot water for 5–10 seconds, then invert onto a serving plate and shake gently to release. Serve topped with mini meringue kisses sandwiched together with softly whipped cream, if you like, or with runny cream or ice cream.

+ ALSO SERVE WITH
    Cream cheese ice cream (page 61)

DAIRY

It might seem counterintuitive given the strong tradition of olive and olive oil production in the Middle East, but there's a healthy dairy tradition in the region, too. Archaeological records suggest that the earliest domestication of cows, eleven thousand years ago, took place in the Middle East. And it's thought that it was those early farmers who learned how to ferment dairy products into yoghurt and cheese.

To the present day, dairy consumption is surprisingly high in Middle Eastern countries. While it predominantly consists of yoghurt and fresh cheeses, milk, and, to a lesser extent, cream, are the cornerstone of a whole range of puddings – perhaps most famously in Turkey, where there are even dedicated milk pudding shops. These sell thick rolls of *kaymak* (Turkish clotted cream), as well as milky desserts thickened with rice, cornflour and even burghul (bulgur wheat), and flavoured with dried fruit and nuts, spices, citrus and flower waters.

We love dairy in all its forms, and, with its range of flavour profiles (from fresh or tangy to rich and creamy) and textures (from delicate and milky, to creamy, to spoon-standingly thick and unctuous), we consider it to be a brilliant foundation for all sorts of desserts and baked goods. We mainly use cow's milk and cream, but we'll often choose goat's (and sheep's) yoghurt and soft cheeses over cow varieties, because we enjoy their more pronounced, tangy flavour. (See our Cook's notes on pages 242 and 245 for more detailed information about these ingredients.)

Many of the desserts in this chapter are interpretations of Middle Eastern classics, such as *ashta* clotted cream, *muhallabeya* or rice pudding. We also love to use yoghurt and other sour creams (such as crème fraîche, mascarpone and goat's cheese) in European-style desserts, such as mousses, possets and other set creams. If dairy is your thing, then we'd also recommend looking through the recipes in the following chapter for some of our favourite ice creams.

Dairy desserts are intrinsically simple – in terms of ingredients and technique – by comparison with more complicated confectionery, cakes and pastries, and they require almost no special equipment, other than a range of different sized ramekin and timbale moulds for setting them. That said, our crème brûlée will be easier to caramelise if you have a kitchen blowtorch, but this is strictly optional!

MIDDLE EASTERN CLOTTED CREAM

Known as *kaymak* in Turkey and Iran, and *ashta* in Lebanon, Syria and Arab countries, Middle Eastern clotted creams are sublimely rich and luxurious – and are often thick enough to be cut with a knife. Ashta can be served at breakfast or with desserts, and is indispensable as a topping, accompaniment or filling for various sweet pastries.

In the Middle East, many versions of ashta are made with buffalo's or sheep's milk, which makes for the most luxurious result. Domestic recipes often use semolina or cornflour as a shortcut to achieve the desired thickness, but we prefer the approach offered below, using a mixture of milk and cream, which results in a purer, richer flavour. The process does take 1–2 days, but requires absolutely no attention – and the result is superlative.

For a super-thick, luscious (and rather more stable) result, we sometimes add three small gelatine leaves to the cream along with the rosewater, but this is purely optional.

MAKES AROUND 700 ML (23½ FL OZ)

1.2 litres (41 fl oz) full-cream (whole) milk
400 ml (13½ fl oz) thick (double/heavy) cream (minimum 40% fat content)
1 teaspoon rosewater
3 small gelatine leaves (see Cook's notes, page 243) (optional)

Combine the milk and cream in a wide, shallow pan. You want the largest surface area possible, rather than depth, to obtain the greatest quantity of thickly clotted cream. Bring to the boil, then lower the heat to the lowest simmer you can achieve – the surface should shimmer, rather than bubble. Leave, uncovered, for 7 hours. Turn off the heat, stir in the rosewater (and softened gelatine, if using), then cover the pan and leave it alone for a further 6 hours without disturbing.

Refrigerate for 6 hours or overnight. The surface layer will be thickly clotted and almost buttery, the cream below will be slightly looser, but still unctuous.

Keep in the fridge for up to 5 days. To serve, cut or scoop into portions.

+ SERVE WITH
Strawberry-rose pavlovas (page 26)
Date tiramisu, Middle Eastern style (page 28)
Bitter walnut cake (page 106)
Clementine-cardamom cake (page 109)
Blood orange steamed puddings (page 121)
Caramelised apple and blackberry Eve's pudding (page 122)
Free-style peach pie (page 158)
Persian cream puffs (page 164)
Baby babas (page 174)
Berber 1000-hole pancakes (page 181)
Turkish fresh and dried fruit salad (page 212)

APRICOT-AMARETTO FOOL

Here, we combine a tangy, perfumed apricot purée with chantilly-yoghurt cream to make a sublimely simple fruit fool. Fools are traditionally made with whipped cream or custard, but this mousse holds its shape better if you're preparing it ahead of time. If you don't like the almond flavour of amaretto – or don't drink alcohol – replace it with orange blossom- or rosewater for an equally pleasing result.

SERVES 8

600 g (1 lb 5 oz) apricots, halved
  and pitted
100 ml (3½ fl oz) fresh orange juice
  or water
100 g (3½ oz) golden caster
  (superfine) sugar
juice of ½ lime
1 tablespoon amaretto, or to taste
1 × Chantilly-yoghurt cream (page 48)
Perfumed ladyfingers (page 90)
  or your favourite wafers, to serve

Preheat the oven to 170°C (340°F) fan-forced/190°C (375°F).

Arrange the apricot halves, skin sides down, in a single layer in a large roasting tin. Pour on the orange juice, then sprinkle with the sugar. Roast for 40–45 minutes, or until the apricots are collapsing and the liquid has reduced to a sticky syrup.

Leave the apricots to cool a little, then transfer to a food processor and whiz to a purée. The skins should virtually disappear in the processing, but if you want a very smooth finish, push the mix through a sieve. Stir in the lime juice and amaretto to taste. Chill until required.

Spoon the yoghurt cream into an attractive glass serving bowl. Add the purée and swirl it through prettily. Serve straight away with perfumed ladyfingers, or refrigerate for up to 5 hours until ready to serve.

ORANGE BLOSSOM POSSETS WITH POMEGRANATE–BLOOD ORANGE JELLY

Jelly and cream, Middle Eastern style. What more needs to be said?

MAKES 8

ORANGE BLOSSOM POSSET
grated zest and juice of 1½ blood
  oranges (100 ml/3½ fl oz)
125 g (4½ oz) caster (superfine) sugar
450 ml (15 fl oz) pure (double or heavy)
  cream, no less than 40% fat
½ teaspoon ground ginger
1 tablespoon orange blossom water

JELLY
350 ml (12 fl oz) good-quality fresh
  pomegranate juice
20 g (¾ oz) caster (superfine) sugar
5 small gelatine leaves (see Cook's
  notes, page 243)
50 ml (1¾ fl oz) fresh blood
  orange juice
1 tablespoon orange blossom water,
  or to taste

To make the possets, combine the blood orange zest and juice and the sugar in a small saucepan and heat gently until the sugar dissolves. Bring to the boil, then remove from the heat.

Pour the cream into a different saucepan and add the ground ginger. Heat gently until it comes to the boil. Pour in the hot syrup and return to a simmer, whisking all the time. Simmer for 20 seconds then remove from the heat. Cool slightly then strain through a sieve into a jug. Stir in the orange blossom water, then pour into small glasses and refrigerate.

For the jelly, put half the pomegranate juice into a small saucepan along with the sugar and heat gently to dissolve. Bring to a simmer, then remove from the heat.

Soak the gelatine in cold water for a few minutes until softened. Squeeze out excess liquid and add it to the hot juice, stirring to dissolve completely. Stir in the remaining fruit juices and the orange blossom water, then tip through a fine-mesh sieve into a jug. Once cool, pour a 1 cm (½ in) layer of jelly on top of the possets and refrigerate overnight, or until set.

NECTARINE-CARAMEL MUHALLABEYA

No Middle Eastern dessert book would be complete without a recipe for *muhallabeya* – the classic milk pudding that is a stalwart of Lebanese restaurants. Because it's so easy to make, muhallabeya is also a very popular home dessert. At its simplest, it's served very cold and drizzled with a rose-flavoured syrup, which adds the requisite sweet counterpoint to the pudding's own delicate creaminess. Our favourite twist is to enrich the pudding mix with a little labne, which adds a welcome tang. Here, we liven things up even more by serving it with an intense nectarine caramel. (See page 246 for our note about fruit caramels.)

Mastic grains come from the resinous gum of the mastic tree. Traditionally used in milk puddings to add a subtle pine flavour, they are available online and from Middle Eastern grocers.

SERVES 8

4 small mastic grains
120 g (4½ oz) caster (superfine) sugar
40 g (1½ oz) cornflour (cornstarch)
1 litre (34 fl oz) full-cream
   (whole) milk
long strip of peel from ½ lemon
long strip of peel from ½ orange
30 ml (1 fl oz) orange blossom water
200 g (7 oz) labne (page 244)
edible flowers, to garnish (optional)
Orange wafers (page 91) or Chocolate
   arabesque wafers (page 92), to serve

NECTARINE CARAMEL

4 nectarines, skin on
100 g (3½ oz) caster (superfine) sugar
80 ml (2½ fl oz) water
juice of 1 orange

To make the nectarine caramel, first blanch the nectarines in a saucepan of boiling water for 2 minutes. Refresh in cold water and, when cool enough to handle, use a very sharp knife to peel away the skins. Cut them in half, remove the pits and chop the flesh roughly.

Combine the sugar and water in a saucepan and heat gently, stirring from time to time, until the sugar has dissolved. Once the liquid is clear, bring to the boil, then lower the heat and simmer briskly for about 8 minutes to make a deep chestnut caramel. Take the pan off the heat and add the chopped nectarines to the caramel, taking care in case it sputters, then return to the heat and bring to a simmer. Add the orange juice and bring just to the boil, then remove from the heat and leave to cool a little before transferring to a food processor and whizzing to a purée. If you want a very smooth finish, push the mix through a sieve. Chill until required.

Grind the mastic with ½ teaspoon of the sugar in a mortar, then mix with the cornflour and remaining sugar in a small bowl. Stir in a few tablespoons of the milk to make a paste.

Put the rest of the milk in a large heavy-based saucepan set over a low heat. Whisk in the mastic paste until smooth, then add the citrus peels and bring to the boil, whisking all the time. As it comes to the boil, the mixture will thicken. Lower the heat and simmer for 4–5 minutes to cook out the cornflour, still whisking continuously to make sure it doesn't catch and burn.

Remove the pan from the heat, then strain the mixture into a bowl and cool in a sink of iced water, whisking so that it becomes light and fluffy. Once it has cooled to blood temperature, stir in the orange blossom water, then fold in the labne.

Spoon the muhallabeya into eight pretty serving glasses. Carefully spoon on a layer of chilled nectarine caramel, then refrigerate until chilled. Garnish with edible flowers, if you like, and serve with orange wafers.

+ ALSO SERVE WITH
   Burnt orange sauce (page 36)
   Blackberry-nectarine compote (page 48)
   Pear caramel (page 65)

RICE PUDDING WITH BURNT ORANGE SAUCE

Chilled rice puddings arc takcaway favourites from specialist pudding shops all around the Middle East and Eastern Mediterranean. They tend to be more sophisticated than the school dinner–style rice puddings of the West and are often flavoured with mastic or flower waters, tinted with saffron, decorated with dried fruits and nuts and even grilled (broiled) for a dark 'burnt' surface layer.

We've featured several different versions of rice pudding in our previous books, but this is a new favourite, combining the milky richness of the pudding with an intense orange caramel sauce. You might not want to make this for a midweek meal, but it's definitely dinner-party worthy.

The orange sauce might seem overly complicated and blanching the fruit so many times might seem like overkill, but it's necessary to remove any bitterness, and the effort is well rewarded. It's nothing less than sublime and, better still, it keeps well in the fridge, just waiting to be spooned onto ice cream, Greek-style yoghurt, or even your morning porridge. Blood oranges make for a gorgeous colouring, and have their own uniquely tart flavour, but ordinary sweet oranges are equally fine.

SERVES 6–8

150 g (5½ oz) short-grain rice
375 ml (12½ fl oz) full-cream (whole) milk
190 ml (6½ fl oz) thick (double/heavy) cream
½ vanilla bean, split lengthways and seeds scraped
½ cinnamon stick
50 g (1¾ oz) unsalted butter
110 g (4 oz) caster (superfine) sugar
finely grated zest of 2 oranges
3 egg yolks
Pistachio dust (page 73) (optional)

BURNT ORANGE SAUCE

2 oranges (sweet or blood oranges)
200 g (7 oz) caster (superfine) sugar
200 ml (7 fl oz) water
30 ml (1 fl oz) sherry vinegar
350 ml (12 fl oz) orange juice or blood orange juice

For the sauce, start by making 4–5 deep vertical slashes in the oranges. Put them in a small saucepan and cover with boiling water. Bring to a rolling boil for 30 seconds, then lift into a bowl of cold water using tongs or a slotted spoon. Repeat this blanching and refreshing five more times. Next, add fresh water, bring to the boil, then simmer for 30 minutes until very soft. Drain and set aside.

Combine half the sugar and half the water in a saucepan and heat gently, stirring from time to time, until the sugar has dissolved. Once the liquid is clear, bring to the boil, then lower the heat and simmer briskly for 6–8 minutes until a deep golden caramel forms. Add the oranges to the pan. Cook, stirring every now and then, until the oranges have collapsed and broken down. Stir in the vinegar and boil briskly for 2 minutes. Add the orange juice and simmer for 6–8 minutes, or until reduced by two-thirds. Remove from the heat and leave to cool, then tip into the bowl of a food processor and blitz to a super-smooth purée.

Put the remaining sugar and water in a saucepan and heat gently, stirring from time to time, until the sugar has dissolved. Once the liquid is clear, bring to the boil, then simmer briskly for 6–8 minutes until a deep golden caramel forms. Stir in the orange purée. Blitz in the food processor a second time, then push through a sieve to remove any lingering bits. The sauce should be the consistency of thick custard – if it's very thick, loosen it with a little orange juice. Chill until required.

For the rice pudding, first rinse the rice well under cold running water, working your fingers through it to loosen the starch. Drain and repeat twice more. Cover with cold water and leave to soak for 10 minutes, then drain the rice and rinse a final time.

Put the rice in a heavy-based saucepan with the milk, cream, vanilla and cinnamon. Bring to the boil, then lower the heat and simmer gently for

15–18 minutes, or until the mixture becomes thick and creamy and the rice is tender. Stir occasionally to prevent it catching and burning on the bottom of the pan, especially towards the end of the cooking time. Remove from the heat and set aside.

Put the butter, sugar and orange zest into the bowl of an electric mixer and beat with the paddle attachment on high speed for around 3 minutes, or until thick and pale. Lower the speed to medium and add the egg yolks, one at a time, beating in well after each addition.

With the speed on low, pour the hot rice onto the egg mixture and continue beating for 2–3 minutes. Allow to cool, then fish out the cinnamon stick and vanilla bean (save the latter to perfume your sugar canister). Spoon into small serving bowls and refrigerate until chilled.

Just before serving, sprinkle the surface of the puddings with pistachio dust, if using, and serve with the burnt orange sauce. It's lovely to play around with the temperatures: warm rice pudding with cold sauce ... chilled rice pudding with hot sauce ... all combinations are delicious.

See photo on pages 38–39.

+ ALSO SERVE WITH
   Candied almonds (page 206)
   Nectarine caramel (page 35)

TURKISH COFFEE PETITS POTS WITH CHOCOLATE MARSHMALLOWS

Most Middle Eastern milk puddings are thickened with ground nuts, rice, semolina or – at their simplest – cornflour (see Nectarine-caramel muhallabeya, page 35). They tend to be a little lighter than European custards, which are thickened and set by large numbers of egg yolks. Every now and then, though, you just crave something that feels super-luxurious, and here a classic French chocolate pot is flavoured with cardamom-scented Turkish coffee for a rich, creamy and distinctly Oriental result. Serve with little chocolate marshmallows, which look very pretty, and set a jug of cold runny cream on the table, for each diner to puddle into their own personal pot.

You can buy Turkish coffee powder from Turkish or Middle Eastern grocers. Start a day ahead of time to infuse the milk.

SERVES 8

600 ml (20½ fl oz) full-cream (whole) milk
40 g (1½ oz) Turkish coffee powder
10 cardamom pods, roughly crushed
1 vanilla bean, split lengthways and seeds scraped
300 ml (10 fl oz) thick (double/heavy) cream
180 g (6½ oz) caster (superfine) sugar
40 ml (1¼ fl oz) water
100 g (3½ oz) good-quality dark chocolate (60–70% cocoa solids), chopped
1 egg
120 g (4½ oz) egg yolks (about 6)
Chocolate marshmallows (page 193), to serve
pouring (single/light) cream or ice cream, to serve

EQUIPMENT

eight small (approx. 140 ml/4½ fl oz) custard pots or ramekin dishes

Pour half the milk into a saucepan and add the Turkish coffee powder, cardamom pods and vanilla bean and seeds. Heat to just below boiling. Remove from the heat and leave at room temperature to infuse overnight.

The next day, preheat the oven to 160°C (320°F) fan-forced/180°C (350°F). Sit eight small custard pots or ramekin dishes in a small, deep baking tin.

Strain the infused milk into a saucepan through a sieve lined with a double layer of muslin (cheesecloth). Pick out the vanilla bean and save it to perfume your sugar canister. Stir in the remaining milk and the cream and heat to just below boiling. Remove from the heat.

Combine half the sugar with the water in a saucepan and heat gently, stirring from time to time, until the sugar has dissolved. Once the liquid is clear, bring to the boil, then lower the heat and simmer briskly for 5 minutes to form a honey-coloured caramel.

Pour the caramel into the infused cream (be careful in case it sputters) and whisk to combine. Add the chopped chocolate and whisk very gently until everything is smooth. Set aside.

Put the egg, egg yolks and remaining sugar into the bowl of an electric mixer and beat with the paddle attachment on high speed for around 3 minutes, or until thick and pale. Lower the speed and gradually dribble in the hot chocolate cream until it has all been incorporated.

Strain the mixture into a jug and pour into the pots or ramekins. Pour hot water (from the tap) into the roasting tin to come halfway up the sides. Bake for 45 minutes until the creams are just set and a fine skewer inserted into the centre comes out clean. Refrigerate for 4–6 hours until firm.

Serve the chilled pots with chocolate marshmallows and with a jug of runny cream for pouring.

+ ALSO SERVE WITH
Chocolate arabesque wafers (page 92)
Mini meringue kisses (page 194)
Candied walnuts (page 206)
Pine nut praline (page 206)

LIQUORICE PANNA COTTA WITH ROASTED STAR ANISE PLUMS

Liquorice root grows abundantly in the Middle East and is widely used in drinks and infusions. We are huge fans of this dark and ancient spice: in earlier books, we've offered recipes for liquorice ice cream and had long wanted to make a liquorice panna cotta. In our experiments, melting down liquorice confectionery proved to be unsatisfactory (not to mention unspeakably tedious) as the gelatine content interfered with the set of the panna cottas. Thankfully, liquorice powders and syrups have become available online (the Danish brand Lakrids is our favourite) and both have become indispensable staples in our respective larders. The panna cotta dream has become a reality.

Liquorice's aniseed flavour works brilliantly with plums. Their sweetness depends on ripeness – and variety – so you may want to add a bit more star anise sugar if yours are especially tart. We think that mirabelle or greengage plums make for a particularly pretty dessert: all soft wobble and gorgeous golden hues. This is unquestionably one of our favourite recipes in this book.

You won't need all of the star anise sugar for the panna cottas – use leftovers with poached or baked fruit, sprinkle it onto our Dried apple wafers (page 224) or use it in our Apple-mint tea (page 236). It also works beautifully with Chocolate prune truffles (page 192) or Spiced plum tarte tatin (page 151).

SERVES 8

360 ml (12 fl oz) thickened (whipping) cream, plus extra to serve

450 ml (15 fl oz) full-cream (whole) milk

35 g (1¼ oz) Star anise sugar (see below)

40 g (1½ oz) caster (superfine) sugar

1½–2 tablespoons liquorice powder or 3 tablespoons sweet liquorice syrup (we use Lakrids)

4 small gelatine leaves (see Cook's notes, page 243)

160 g (5½ oz) Greek-style yoghurt

STAR ANISE SUGAR

5 star anise

100 g (3½ oz) raw (demerara) sugar

ROASTED STAR ANISE PLUMS

16 plums, halved

80 ml (2½ fl oz) Pedro Ximénez sherry

juice of 1 orange

2–3 tablespoons Star anise sugar (see above)

EQUIPMENT

eight 130 ml (4½ fl oz) plastic timbale moulds, very lightly oiled

Start by making the star anise sugar. Preheat the oven to 180°C (350°F) fan-forced/200°C (400°F). Put the star anise on a small baking tray and bake for 5 minutes until lightly roasted. Pound them coarsely in a mortar or spice grinder. Add a tablespoon of the sugar and grind as finely as you can. Pass through a sieve and re-grind any stubborn woody bits. Sieve once more, then stir into the rest of the sugar. You'll need roughly half the full amount for this recipe, but the rest will keep well in an airtight jar.

To make the panna cotta, combine the cream, milk and both of the sugars in a heavy-based saucepan and heat gently, stirring to dissolve the sugar. Bring to the boil then remove from the heat.

Add 100 ml (3½ fl oz) of the hot liquid to the liquorice powder or syrup in a small bowl and whisk until dissolved and smooth. Tip back into the hot milk and stir until well combined.

Soak the gelatine in cold water for a few minutes until softened. Squeeze out the excess liquid and add the gelatine to the hot cream, stirring to dissolve completely. Cool briefly, then pour through a fine-mesh sieve into a bowl set over ice. Leave to cool completely.

When cold, lightly whisk in the yoghurt. Pour into the eight timbale moulds. Leave to set in the fridge for 4–6 hours.

To roast the plums, preheat the oven to 180°C (350°F) fan-forced/200°C (400°F). Arrange the plum halves, skin sides down, in a single layer in a large roasting tin. Pour in the sherry and orange juice and sprinkle liberally with star anise sugar. Bake for 15–20 minutes, or until the plums are tender and lightly caramelised on top and the liquid has reduced to a sticky syrup. Once the plums are cool enough to handle, remove the stones.

Serve the warm plums and their syrup with the chilled panna cottas for a delicious temperature contrast – although this dish is equally lovely when both elements are cold. Serve with extra runny cream if you're feeling especially sinful.

See photo on pages 44–45.

+ ALSO SERVE WITH
The roasted plums go nicely with the Cinnamon brioche (page 16)

SAFFRON–BLOOD ORANGE BRÛLÉE

Saffron and blood orange might not seem like an obvious partnership, and, in truth, this particular dessert came about as the result of confusion in the pastry section one afternoon. Aside from the glorious golden colour, it turned out that these two flavours work very well together: both have a slightly acrid sharpness, which is mellowed by the cream and rounded out by the sweetness of the juice.

These custards will be soft and wobbly after baking and need to be chilled for a minimum of 6–8 hours (or preferably overnight) to set firm.

SERVES 8

500 ml (17 fl oz) thick (double/heavy) cream
280 ml (9½ fl oz) blood orange juice
25 saffron threads (we use Iranian)
juice of ½ lime
finely grated zest of 1 orange
160 g (5½ oz) egg yolks (roughly 8–9)
65 g (2¼ oz) caster (superfine) sugar, plus extra to brûlée
Orange and ginger nougatine (page 85) or Orange-cardamom wafers (page 91), to serve

EQUIPMENT

eight 140 ml (4½ fl oz) ramekin dishes
kitchen blowtorch (optional)

Preheat the oven to 140°C (275°F) fan-forced/160°C (320°F). Set one of the oven shelves in the centre of the oven. Arrange the ramekin dishes in a deep roasting tin. Fill a small ovenproof dish with cold water.

Combine the cream, orange juice, saffron, lime juice and orange zest in a saucepan and bring to just below the boil. Remove from the heat.

Put the egg yolks and sugar in a large heatproof bowl and sit it over a saucepan of simmering water. Make sure the water itself doesn't touch the bowl. Whisk for around 5 minutes, or until the sugar has dissolved and the mixture is thick, pale and creamy.

Sit the bowl on a folded tea towel (dish towel) on your work surface (to stop it slipping) and pour a third of the hot orange cream onto the eggs, whisking all the time. Whisk in the remaining cream, then return the bowl to its position above the pan and cook over a low heat for around 8 minutes, stirring all the time, until the mixture thickens. Check by running a finger through the custard on the back of a spoon; if it leaves a clean line, it is done. Strain into a jug.

Put the prepared roasting tin on the centrally positioned oven shelf and pull it out slightly for ease of access. Pour the custard into the ramekin dishes to fill them to just below the rims and carefully pour hot water (from the tap) into the roasting tin, to come halfway up the sides.

Place the small dish of cold water in the bottom of the oven – this creates extra moisture in the oven and makes for a more delicate heat – and cook for around 50 minutes, or until the custards have set around the edges but still have a slight wobble in the middle (they will firm up as they chill). Remove the tin from the oven and leave the ramekins in the water bath for a couple of minutes, then lift them out onto a wire rack and cool to room temperature. Chill in the fridge for 6–8 hours, or overnight.

Just before serving, dust the surface of each custard with a thin, even layer of caster sugar. Use a kitchen blowtorch to caramelise the sugar. If you like a thicker toffee layer, return the custards to the fridge for 5 minutes, then dust with another layer of sugar and torch again. If you don't have a blowtorch, sit the custards under a very hot grill (broiler) until the sugar is brown and bubbling. Serve with nougatine, wafers or another delicate biscuit.

CHANTILLY-YOGHURT CREAM WITH BLACKBERRY-NECTARINE COMPOTE

Yoghurt is one of the staples of the Middle Eastern kitchen and we are always looking for ways to incorporate it into recipes. This lovely, hard-working moussey cream goes with just about anything. It has a slight lactic tang, which works especially well with fruit purées and compotes. A summery combination of blackberries and nectarines achieves just the right tart–sweet balance.

SERVES 8

200 g (7 oz) Greek-style yoghurt, chilled
200 g (7 oz) crème fraîche, chilled
20 g (¾ oz) icing (confectioners') sugar
½ teaspoon vanilla extract
30 g (1 oz) caster (superfine) sugar
80 ml (2½ fl oz) water
2 small gelatine leaves (see Cook's notes, page 243)
dried raspberry powder, to decorate (optional)
Perfumed ladyfingers (page 90), to serve

BLACKBERRY-NECTARINE COMPOTE
3 nectarines
150 g (5½ oz) blackberries
60 g (2 oz) caster (superfine) sugar
1 tablespoon leatherwood honey (or heather honey)
125 ml (4 fl oz) water
splash of rosewater, or to taste

Combine the yoghurt, crème fraîche, icing sugar and vanilla extract in the bowl of an electric mixer and whisk to soft peaks. Set aside.

Combine the caster sugar and half of the water in a saucepan and heat gently, stirring from time to time, until the sugar has dissolved. Once the liquid is clear, bring to the boil, then lower the heat and simmer briskly for 4 minutes to form a light syrup. Remove from the heat and stir in the rest of the water to stop it cooking.

Soak the gelatine in cold water for a few minutes until softened. Squeeze out the excess liquid and add the gelatine to the syrup, stirring to dissolve completely. Leave for around 2 minutes, until cooled to room temperature, but not for too long, or the gelatine will begin to set and become unworkable.

With the mixer on low speed, drizzle the gelatine syrup into the whipped yoghurt mixture, then increase the speed and continue whisking until it thickens and holds medium peaks. Scrape into a bowl and refrigerate for 3–4 hours until set.

For the compote, bring a saucepan of water to the boil. Add the nectarines and blanch for 2 minutes. Transfer to a bowl of iced water and, when they are cool enough to handle, use a very sharp knife to peel away the skins. Cut them in half, remove the pits and cut the flesh into 2 cm (¾ in) dice.

Put the nectarine flesh into a saucepan along with the blackberries, sugar, honey and water and simmer gently for 5–8 minutes, or until the fruit has softened and the liquid is slightly reduced and syrupy. Allow to cool, then add a splash of rosewater and refrigerate.

Make quenelles of mousse with two spoons and arrange on dessert plates. Sprinkle on a little dried raspberry powder, if using, then spoon the chilled compote alongside. Serve with perfumed ladyfingers.

+ ALSO SERVE WITH
Slow-roasted quinces (page 17)
Date tiramisu, Middle Eastern style (page 28)
Apricot-amaretto fool (page 33)
Scheherazade ice cream–meringue cakes (page 68)
your favourite wafer (pages 91–92)
Persian cream puffs (page 164)
Turkish fresh and dried fruit salad (page 212)

HONEY MOUSSE WITH PINE NUT PRALINE AND SPICED PEARS

A delicate, airy mousse with a honeyed sweetness and lovely nutty crunch. It just works brilliantly with all sorts of things: think of cakes and puddings, fresh fruit, poached fruits and fruit compotes. Here we suggest cinnamon-spiced poached pears with just a hint of saffron. Any leftovers of these are delicious on your breakfast cereal or served with a drizzle of runny cream.

Serve the mousse in small glasses or – our preference – spoon out soft quenelle curls from an attractive large serving bowl at the table.

SERVES 8

90 g (3 oz) mild-flavoured honey

3 small gelatine leaves (see Cook's notes, page 243)

400 ml (13½ fl oz) thick (double/ heavy) cream, whipped to soft peaks

1 tablespoon Cointreau

100 g (3½ oz) Pine nut praline (page 206)

4 egg whites, whisked to soft peaks

Orange and ginger nougatine (page 85) or Orange wafers (page 91), to serve

CINNAMON-SPICED PEARS

200 ml (7 fl oz) white wine

220 g (8 oz) golden caster (superfine) sugar

300 ml (10 fl oz) water

juice and strips of peel from 1 lemon

2 cinnamon sticks

3–4 cloves

15 saffron threads (we use Iranian saffron)

4 small honey pears, peeled, quartered and cored

For the pears, combine the white wine, sugar and water in a medium saucepan and heat gently, stirring from time to time, until the sugar has dissolved. Once the liquid is clear, bring to the boil, then add the lemon juice and peel, cinnamon sticks and cloves.

Meanwhile, lightly toast the saffron threads in a dry frying pan over a medium heat for about 30 seconds. They must be crisp and dry, but be careful not to let them burn. Cool slightly before crushing to a powder.

Lower the syrup temperature to a simmer and add the saffron. Simmer for 2–3 minutes, then slip the pears into the syrup. Cover with a circle of baking paper (to keep them submerged in the poaching syrup), then cover the pan and simmer gently for 15–20 minutes, or until the pears are tender. Leave them to cool in the syrup, then refrigerate for up to a week.

To make the mousse, heat the honey in a small saucepan to just below a simmer, then remove from the heat.

Soak the gelatine in cold water for a few minutes until softened. Squeeze out the excess liquid and add the gelatine to the honey, stirring to dissolve completely. Leave to cool to room temperature, but not for too long, or the gelatine will begin to set and become unworkable.

Fold into the whipped cream, together with the Cointreau and pine nut praline. Add a spoonful of egg whites to the cream and mix it in lightly to slacken. Fold in the remaining egg whites, then tip it into your chosen serving bowl and refrigerate for 2–3 hours until set.

To serve, make quenelles of mousse with two spoons and arrange on dessert plates. Serve with the chilled pears, plenty of extra syrup and your choice of accompanying crunchy biscuit.

+ ALSO SERVE WITH

Arabic five-spice pineapple (page 18)

Berry salad (page 26)

Blackberry-nectarine compote (page 48)

Little lemon-ginger syrup cakes (page 97)

Clementine-cardamom cake (page 109)

Blood orange steamed puddings (page 121)

FROZEN

Some of our best memories from travels in the Middle East involve ice cream. There's sahlab-stretchy bouza from Damascus's legendary Bakdach ice cream parlour, or our first taste of pungent saffron ice cream in the northern Iranian city of Mashhad. On one baking afternoon in Anatolia, we discovered blocks of snow-white mastic-flavoured *dondurma*, suspended by hooks from a street vendor's truck, and wondered at its unyielding, unmelting staunchness as he hacked at it with a cruel knife. Then there's the veritable rainbow of sorbets we've tasted over the years, made from cherry, grape, mango, mulberry, pomegranate, peach, prickly pear, quince and watermelon, to name just a few – each one, irresistible.

It's not until you've experienced the stifling heat of a Middle Eastern summer that you understand true ice cream joy. It's easy to see just why the early inhabitants of these lands – the Persians, Romans and Egyptians, and the Sumerians and Babylonians before them – would have seen the value in arduous treks into the mountains to bring back ice and snow for storing in ice-houses for summertime relief.

The earliest iced concoctions were little more than shaved ice mixed with wine, juices or distillations made from blossoms, herbs or spices. Modern-day granitas are much the same – they require no equipment other than a freezer and a fork, and couldn't be simpler to make.

The word 'sorbet' comes from the old Persian *sharbat*, and these dairy-free delights can be made with just about any fresh fruit purée and syrup you like. Sorbets should be silky-smooth, not icy, and the ideal consistency depends on using the correct ratio of sugar to other ingredients (and adding alcohol changes things again), so please don't be tempted to alter the quantities. Our top tip is to add a little liquid glucose to the mix; it really does make a difference to the outcome. (If you live in the US, then corn syrup may be more readily available.)

If there's one real secret to ice cream and sorbet success, it's to use an ice cream maker. These incorporate air as they churn, without which ice creams can be very dense, however frequently you stir them. We'd encourage you to invest in the best one you can afford. For a bit of fun, you might like to consider setting your ices in silicone moulds (see page 63). We'd also recommend a sugar thermometer and lidded plastic containers for storing your ices in the freezer.

CLEMENTINE-NEGRONI GRANITA

An icy version of Greg's favourite cocktail, this very grown-up granita makes a lovely end – or even a beginning – to a meal on a hot summer's day. The addition of gelatine might seem a little strange (and if you are vegetarian, feel free to omit it) but it means you can let the whole thing set solid in the freezer, without the frequent beating with a fork that granitas usually require to break up the ice crystals. Instead, you simply use a fork to scrape it into small chilled glasses as you serve.

We use good-quality fresh fruit juice from the supermarket for this recipe, which makes it a breeze to prepare.

MAKES AROUND 600 ML (20½ FL OZ)

400 ml (13½ fl oz) clementine juice
100 ml (3½ fl oz) blood orange juice
150 g (5½ oz) caster (superfine) sugar
1 small gelatine leaf (see Cook's notes, page 243)
40 ml (1¼ fl oz) Campari
40 ml (1¼ fl oz) sweet vermouth
1 tablespoon gin

Combine the fruit juices and sugar in a saucepan and heat gently, stirring from time to time, until the sugar has dissolved. Once the liquid is clear, bring to the boil, then lower the heat and simmer briskly for 1 minute. Take off the heat and leave to cool slightly.

Soak the gelatine in cold water for a few minutes until softened. Squeeze out the excess liquid and add the gelatine to the hot juice, stirring to dissolve completely. Pour through a fine-mesh sieve and leave to cool.

When cold, stir in the alcohol. Pour the mixture into a shallow container and allow to freeze into a solid block.

To serve, scrape the surface with a fork to create a smooth icy slush and pile into small chilled glasses.

HONEYED YOGHURT SORBET

A terrific use for that Middle Eastern essential, yoghurt, which combines here with lime juice to temper the sweetness of honey. One of Greg's favourite sorbets and a great all-rounder.

MAKES AROUND 1 LITRE (34 FL OZ)

250 g (9 oz) Greek-style yoghurt
80 g (2¾ oz) crème fraîche
60 ml (2 fl oz) thick (double/heavy) cream
225 g (8 oz) caster (superfine) sugar
350 ml (12 fl oz) water
1 tablespoon liquid glucose
2 tablespoons honey
juice of 1 lime

EQUIPMENT
ice cream maker

Whisk together the yoghurt, crème fraîche and cream. Transfer to the fridge and leave to chill.

Combine the sugar, water and liquid glucose in a saucepan and heat gently, stirring from time to time, until the sugar has dissolved. Once the liquid is clear, bring to the boil, then simmer briskly for 3 minutes. Remove from the heat and allow to cool. When cold, refrigerate until chilled.

Stir the honey and lime juice into the cold syrup, then stir this into the chilled yoghurt mixture.

Pour into an ice cream maker and churn according to the manufacturer's instructions. Spoon into an airtight container and freeze for at least an hour before serving.

See photo on pages 58–59.

+SERVE WITH
Roasted apricots with cinnamon brioche (page 16)
Slow-roasted quinces (page 17)
Plum soufflé with cardamom and orange (page 22)

BLACKBERRY-ROSE SORBET

This is a sorbet to make when you have access to an abundance of blackberries. Which probably means picking them yourself. Lucky you if you live near a self-pick fruit farm – or in an area where brambles grow wild. The added benefit of using foraged blackberries is that they are tarter than the sweet cultivated kind, which makes for a more intense sorbet.

MAKES AROUND 1 LITRE (34 FL OZ)

600 g (1 lb 5 oz) blackberries
125 g (4½ oz) caster (superfine) sugar
1 tablespoon liquid glucose
60 ml (2 fl oz) water
juice of 1 lemon
splash of rosewater

EQUIPMENT
ice cream maker

Put the berries into a food processor or blender and blitz to a very smooth purée. Push through a fine-mesh sieve to remove the seeds. Weigh the purée to yield 500 g (1 lb 2 oz).

Combine half of the purée with the sugar, glucose and water in a heavy-based saucepan. Bring to the boil, stirring regularly to ensure the sugar dissolves. Remove from the heat and leave to cool, then stir into the remaining purée together with the lemon juice and rosewater.

Pour into an ice cream maker and churn according to the manufacturer's instructions. Spoon into an airtight container and freeze for at least an hour before serving.

See photo on pages 58–59.

MINT SORBET

We created this fantastic and slightly unusual sorbet as a way of using an overabundance of mint in Lucy's garden. It proved to be addictive. Different varieties of mint will impart subtly different flavours to your sorbet, so do experiment.

MAKES AROUND 1 LITRE (34 FL OZ)

120 g (4½ oz) mint (roughly 1 very big bunch of mint)
100 ml (3½ fl oz) water
150 g (5½ oz) caster (superfine) sugar
1 tablespoon liquid glucose
700 g (1 lb 9 oz) Greek-style yoghurt

EQUIPMENT
ice cream maker

Wash the mint and pick off the leaves. Weigh them to ensure you have 100 g (3½ oz).

Put the mint leaves into a food processor or blender with the water, sugar and liquid glucose and blitz to as smooth a purée as you can achieve. Transfer the minty slush to a saucepan and bring to the boil slowly, stirring regularly to ensure the sugar dissolves. Remove from the heat and leave to cool.

Once cold, stir in the yoghurt. Push through a fine-mesh sieve into an ice cream maker and churn according to the manufacturer's instructions. Spoon into an airtight container and freeze for at least an hour before serving.

See photo on pages 58–59.

ROSE JAM ICE CREAM

An effective and easy way to add a perfumed touch of the Middle East to your dessert table. This ice cream makes a pleasing accompaniment to summer berries and goes surprisingly well with chocolatey things.

Without the addition of the rose jam and rosewater, this is our very useful, go-to vanilla ice cream recipe, so if you don't feel up to making your own ice cream, just buy a tub of the best vanilla you can find and stir them in. Middle Eastern jams and flower waters are available from Middle Eastern grocers and, increasingly, from major supermarkets.

MAKES AROUND 1.5 LITRES (51 FL OZ)

250 g (9 oz) caster (superfine) sugar
250 ml (8½ fl oz) water
seeds scraped from 1 vanilla bean
(save the bean to perfume your
sugar canister)
200 g (7 oz) egg yolks (about 10)
1 litre (34 fl oz) thick (double/heavy)
cream
75 g (2¾ oz) Rose petal jam (page 217)
or use good-quality ready-made jam
1½ teaspoons rosewater, or to taste

EQUIPMENT
ice cream maker

Combine the sugar, water and vanilla seeds in a medium saucepan and heat gently until the sugar dissolves. Once the liquid is clear, bring to a rolling boil.

Meanwhile, put the egg yolks into the bowl of an electric mixer and whisk for around 5 minutes, or until thick, pale and creamy. With the mixer on low, slowly pour the boiling sugar syrup onto the egg yolks. Once incorporated, increase the speed to high and whisk for around 8 minutes, or until the mixture cools completely. You will see it dramatically bulk up into a soft, fluffy mass.

Fold in the cream and chill in the fridge. Once cold, pour into an ice cream maker and churn according to the manufacturer's instructions. Towards the end of the churning time, add the rose jam and rosewater and mix in evenly. Spoon into an airtight container and freeze for at least an hour before serving.

See photo on pages 58–59.

Variation

As a lovely alternative, try making this with orange blossom jam and orange blossom water instead of the rose jam and rosewater.

+ SERVE WITH
Chilled watermelon with halva, crushed strawberries and lime syrup (page 11)
Plum soufflé with cardamom and orange (page 22)
Chocolate fondant pudding cakes with Turkish delight (page 124)
Citrus-scented blueberries (page 128)
Lebanese pikelets stuffed with crunchy walnut cheese (page 178)

SALTED BAY-BUTTERSCOTCH ICE CREAM

The bay-butterscotch caramel sauce we created in our book *New Feast* proved to be one of the most popular recipes in the whole book. We couldn't resist turning it into ice cream and the result is as wildly delicious as the sauce!

MAKES AROUND 1 LITRE (34 FL OZ)

65 g (2¼ oz) unsalted butter
200 g (7 oz) light muscovado sugar
3–4 bay leaves
250 ml (8½ fl oz) thick (double/heavy) cream
½ teaspoon salt flakes
500 ml (17 fl oz) full-cream (whole) milk
100 g (3½ oz) egg yolks (about 5)

EQUIPMENT
ice cream maker

Melt the butter in a saucepan over a low heat. Once melted, stir in the sugar and heat gently until it has dissolved, stirring to help it along. Add the bay leaves to the pan and simmer for a few minutes. Don't worry if it seems to be resolutely un-amalgamated at this stage, it will all come together when you add the cream. Pour it in (watching out for splutters) and stir briskly until it melts magically into a thick, glossy sauce. Add the salt and simmer for 2 minutes. Set aside and leave to cool completely.

Put the milk in a medium-sized saucepan and bring just to the boil, then remove from the heat.

Whisk the egg yolks in a large bowl until pale and creamy. Whisk in one-third of the hot milk then return the mixture to the pan and cook over a low heat for 10–12 minutes, stirring all the time, until the mixture thickens. Check by running a finger through the custard on the back of a spoon; if it leaves a clean line, it is done.

Remove the pan from the heat and cool immediately in a sink of iced water. Stir from time to time to help the custard cool down quickly. Refrigerate until chilled.

Stir the cooled caramel and custard together and refrigerate until completely cold. Strain through a sieve to remove the bay leaves and any rogue lumps from the custard, then pour into an ice cream maker. Churn according to the manufacturer's instructions. Spoon into an airtight container and freeze for at least an hour before serving.

See photo on page 142.

+ SERVE WITH
Bay-butterscotch baklava with caramel pears (page 142)

CREAM CHEESE ICE CREAM

An ultra-luscious, silky-smooth ice cream, this somehow feels brighter and lighter than classic vanilla – perhaps because the lemon peel adds a welcome hint of tartness. This makes a fine accompaniment for just about any dessert.

MAKES AROUND 1 LITRE (34 FL OZ)

250 ml (8½ fl oz) full-cream (whole) milk
170 g (6 oz) caster (superfine) sugar
1 vanilla bean, split lengthways and seeds scraped
5–6 cm (2–2½ in) strip of lemon peel
pinch of fine sea salt
120 g (4½ oz) egg yolks (about 6)
500 g (1 lb 2 oz) cream cheese
juice of ½ lemon

EQUIPMENT
ice cream maker

Combine the milk, sugar, vanilla bean and seeds, lemon peel and salt in a medium saucepan and heat gently until the sugar dissolves. Bring to a simmer then remove from the heat.

Whisk the egg yolks in a large bowl until pale and creamy. Whisk in one-third of the hot milk mixture then return to the pan and cook over a low heat for 10–12 minutes, stirring all the time, until the mixture thickens. Check by running a finger through the custard on the back of a spoon; if it leaves a clean line, it is done.

Remove the pan from the heat and cool immediately in a sink of iced water. Stir from time to time to help the custard cool down quickly. Refrigerate until chilled.

When ready to churn, strain the custard through a fine-mesh sieve to remove the lemon peel and vanilla bean (save the latter to perfume your sugar canister). Whisk in the cream cheese, followed by the lemon juice, then pour into an ice cream maker and churn according to the manufacturer's instructions. Spoon into an airtight container and freeze for at least an hour before serving.

See photo on pages 58–59.

+ SERVE WITH
   just about anything

CHOCOLATE-HALVA ICE CREAM

The marriage of chocolate and halva is one that Greg features regularly on dessert menus. It works very well in this delicate chocolate-flecked ice cream. There are plenty of different kinds of halva – for this recipe we like vanilla or pistachio best.

MAKES AROUND 1 LITRE (34 FL OZ)

500 ml (17 fl oz) thick (double/heavy) cream
250 ml (8½ fl oz) full-cream (whole) milk
150 g (5½ oz) caster (superfine) sugar
100 g (3½ oz) egg yolks (roughly 6–7)
150 g (5½ oz) good-quality dark chocolate (70% cocoa solids), chopped or broken into small pieces
120 g (4½ oz) halva
¼ teaspoon fine sea salt

EQUIPMENT
ice cream maker

Combine the cream, milk and sugar in a medium saucepan and heat gently until the sugar dissolves. Bring to a simmer then remove from the heat.

Whisk the egg yolks in a large bowl until pale and creamy. Whisk in one-third of the hot cream mixture then return to the pan and cook over a low heat for 10–12 minutes, stirring all the time, until the mixture thickens. Check by running a finger through the custard on the back of a spoon; if it leaves a clean line, it is done.

Remove the pan from the heat and cool immediately in a sink of iced water. Stir from time to time to help the custard cool down quickly. Refrigerate until chilled.

Once chilled, pour the custard into an ice cream maker and churn according to the manufacturer's instructions.

While the ice cream is churning, melt the chocolate in a bowl set over a saucepan of simmering water. When it has completely melted, scrape into a small jug or bowl. When the ice cream has all but finished churning, remove the lid and, with the motor still running, pour the chocolate directly into the ice cream, onto the turning blades, in a slow, steady stream. The chocolate will harden on contact and form little flakes. Add the roughly crumbled halva and the salt and continue churning for another 5–10 seconds. Spoon into an airtight container and freeze for at least an hour before serving.

Variation

Set the ice cream in silicone moulds for an attractive presentation.

+ SERVE WITH
Plum soufflé with cardamom and orange (page 22)
Ricotta fritters with chocolate, orange and candied peel (page 173)

SAFFRON ICE CREAM

We developed an addiction to saffron ice cream on our trips to Iran researching our book *Saraban*. There, the preferred stretchy consistency comes from sahlab (the ground root of a particular orchid), which can be hard to source in the West. This is our interpretation, in all its golden glory.

MAKES AROUND 1 LITRE (34 FL OZ)

40 saffron threads (we use Iranian)
500 ml (17 fl oz) thick (double/heavy) cream
250 ml (8½ fl oz) full-cream (whole) milk
½ teaspoon finely grated orange zest
100 g (3½ oz) egg yolks (about 6)
110 g (4 oz) mild honey (orange blossom or acacia are ideal)
30 g (1 oz) golden caster (superfine) sugar
¼ teaspoon fine sea salt

EQUIPMENT

ice cream maker

Toast the saffron threads in a small dry frying pan over a low heat for about 30 seconds so they slightly crisp up and release their aroma. (Be careful not to burn them though.)

Combine the cream and milk in a saucepan and add the saffron threads and orange zest. Bring to a simmer over a low heat, then take the pan off the heat and leave to infuse for around 1 hour.

Return the saffron cream to a gentle simmer.

Combine the egg yolks, honey, sugar and salt in a mixing bowl and whisk until pale and creamy. Whisk in a third of the hot cream then pour the mixture back into the pan and cook over a low heat for around 8 minutes, stirring all the time, until it thickens. Check by running a finger through the custard on the back of a spoon; if it leaves a clean line, it is done.

Remove the pan from the heat and cool immediately in a sink of iced water. Stir from time to time to help the custard cool down quickly. Refrigerate until chilled.

Once chilled, strain the custard into an ice cream maker and churn according to the manufacturer's instructions. Spoon into an airtight container and freeze for at least an hour before serving.

See photo on pages 58–59.

+ SERVE WITH
Arabic five-spice pineapple (page 18)

PISTACHIO-BARBERRY NOUGAT GLACÉ

Nougat glacé is similar to a parfait, but the consistency is a bit more gooey and chewy, just like nougat. The Arabic influence is clearly evident in the use of honey, dried fruit and nuts, and you can play around with combinations, depending on what you like. To ensure the parfait slices neatly, be sure to chop the nuts and dried fruit fairly finely.

SERVES 10

40 g (1½ oz) pistachio nut slivers
   (we use Iranian), finely chopped
20 g (¾ oz) barberries, finely chopped
70 g (2½ oz) dried pear, finely diced
40 ml (1¼ fl oz) Cointreau
25 g (1 oz) caster (superfine) sugar
1 tablespoon liquid glucose
50 g (1¾ oz) mild-flavoured honey
180 g (6½ oz) egg whites (about 4)
250 ml (8½ fl oz) thick (double/heavy)
   cream, chilled

PEAR CARAMEL
2 perfectly ripe, small pears
juice of ½ lime
100 g (3½ oz) caster (superfine) sugar
80 ml (2½ fl oz) water
40 ml (1¼ fl oz) apple juice

EQUIPMENT
1 litre (34 fl oz) terrine mould
sugar thermometer

To prepare the pear caramel, peel and core the pears and chop them finely. Toss with the lime juice and set aside. Combine the sugar and water in a small saucepan and heat gently, stirring from time to time, until the sugar has dissolved. Once the liquid is clear, bring to the boil, then lower the heat and simmer briskly for 8 minutes, to make a chestnut-coloured caramel. Throw the diced pears into the pan along with the apple juice and simmer for a further minute.

Remove from the heat, leave to cool a little, then transfer to a food processor and whiz to a purée. If you want a very smooth finish, push the mix through a sieve. Chill until required.

To make the nougat glacé, line the terrine mould with plastic wrap and place in the freezer to chill.

Combine the nuts and dried fruit in a bowl with the Cointreau and leave to macerate for 30 minutes.

Combine the sugar, glucose and honey in a small saucepan and heat gently to dissolve the sugar. Meanwhile, put the egg whites in the bowl of an electric mixer and whisk to stiff peaks.

Use a sugar thermometer to measure the temperature of the syrup. When it reaches the thread stage, at 120ºC (250ºF), pour it onto the egg whites in a slow, steady stream, whisking slowly all the time.

Once incorporated, increase the motor speed to high and whisk for around 8 minutes, or until the mixture cools completely. You will see it dramatically bulk up into a soft, fluffy mass.

Whip the chilled cream to soft peaks. Fold it gently into the ice cream base, along with the macerated fruit and nuts and any residual liquid.

Pour into the prepared terrine mould and smooth the surface with a spatula. Freeze for around 4 hours, or until firm.

To serve, dip the mould into warm water for a few seconds, then invert onto a large plate or chopping board. Remove the mould and peel away the plastic wrap. Use a sharp knife to cut the nougat glacé into thick slices and serve straight away. Serve with a slug (or elegant drizzle) of pear caramel, which is just as lovely warmed through as it is cold.

See photo on page 66.

+ ALSO SERVE WITH
   Nectarine caramel (page 35)
   Burnt orange sauce (page 36)

SCHEHERAZADE ICE CREAM–MERINGUE CAKES

With a pistachio meringue base, delicately perfumed nectarine sorbet, cloud-like yoghurt cream and a scattering of sugared rose petals, this special occasion dessert is a veritable dream of the Orient.

Although it's made of several components, none are particularly tricky and each can be made ahead of time, so all you have to do is a bit of assembly at the last minute.

SERVES 8

1 × Chantilly-yoghurt cream (page 48)
crystallised rose petals (page 226), optional (to garnish)

NECTARINE SORBET
800 g (1 lb 12 oz) nectarines (about 6)
130 ml (4½ fl oz) water
190 g (6½ oz) caster (superfine) sugar
60 ml (2 fl oz) liquid glucose
thumb-sized piece of fresh ginger, sliced
juice of 1 lime
1–1½ teaspoons orange blossom water

PISTACHIO DACQUOISE
oil, for greasing
80 g (2¾ oz) blanched pistachios
30 g (1 oz) ground almonds
125 g (4½ oz) icing (confectioners') sugar
80 g (2¾ oz) egg whites (about 2)
50 g (1¾ oz) caster (superfine) sugar
pinch of salt

EQUIPMENT
ice cream maker

To make the sorbet, first peel the nectarines and remove the stones, then weigh the flesh to yield 750 g (1 lb 11 oz), chop it roughly and set aside.

Combine the water, sugar and liquid glucose in a medium saucepan and heat gently until the sugar dissolves. Add the slices of ginger and bring to the boil. Carefully slip in the chopped nectarines and lower the heat to a simmer. Cook for 5 minutes (or up to 10 minutes, if they are firm) until tender. Remove the pan from the heat and leave to cool completely. Pick out and discard the slices of ginger, then tip the nectarines and syrup into a food processor and blitz to a very smooth purée. Stir in the lime juice and orange blossom water, then pour into an ice cream maker and churn according to the manufacturer's instructions. Spoon into a 1 litre (34 fl oz) plastic container and freeze until ready to serve.

To make the dacquoise, preheat the oven to 160ºC (320ºF) fan-forced/180ºC (350ºF). Lightly oil and line a 33 × 23 cm (13 × 9 in) shallow baking tray with baking paper.

Spread the pistachios on another small baking tray and toast for 5 minutes until lightly coloured. Remove the nuts from the oven, but keep the oven on. Cool the nuts, then tip them into a food processor. Blitz to fine, even crumbs. Add the ground almonds and icing sugar and pulse briefly so they are evenly combined.

Put the egg whites into the bowl of an electric mixer and whisk until they start to froth. Sprinkle on the caster sugar and salt and continue whisking at high speed to stiff, glossy peaks.

Add the nut mixture and use a large metal spoon to fold it in gently but evenly, taking care not to overmix.

Tip the meringue onto the prepared baking tray and use a long spatula to spread it out evenly, all the way into the corners, to a thickness of around 3–5 mm (⅛–¼ in). Bake in the centre of the oven for 8 minutes, then swivel the tray and bake for a further 8 minutes. The surface should be tinted pale gold and the meringue should feel dry to the touch.

Remove the dacquoise from the oven and let it cool in the tin for a few minutes. Invert onto a wire rack and leave to cool completely. Once cold, carefully and slowly peel away the baking paper. Use a long, sharp knife to carefully trim the edges of the dacquoise, then cut it into eight rectangles, each around 11 × 8 cm (4¼ × 3¼ in). Wrap in plastic wrap and freeze for up to 2 weeks.

When you are ready to assemble the dessert, take the sorbet out of the freezer and allow it to thaw to a workable consistency.

Take the chantilly-yoghurt cream out of the fridge, and have your crystallised rose petals at the ready.

Take the dacquoise portions out of the freezer and carefully cut each one in half, crossways, so you have a total of 16 pieces. (Do this at the last moment to stop them becoming overly chewy.)

Arrange 8 dacquoise pieces on dessert plates. Place a nice rounded scoop of nectarine sorbet on top of each, and sandwich gently with another piece of dacquoise. Top with a quenelle of chantilly-yoghurt cream, then scatter with crystallised rose petals and serve straight away.

See photo on page 67.

COOKIES

One of the great pleasures in the kitchen must be knocking out a batch of biscuits or cookies. They are nearly always a child's introduction to the joys of baking – most require little skill or precision, instead relying on enthusiastic rolling, squeezing and stamping out of shapes, which makes them rewarding for small people and supervising adults alike.

As well as resonating with childhood memories, in many Middle Eastern households biscuits and cookies hold a deeper significance. Making them is frequently a family or community activity during religious holidays. Greg remembers spending entire days crowded in at the kitchen table with his grandmothers and various aunties while they expertly turned out batches of sesame and pistachio–studded *bazarek* biscuits, nut-stuffed *ma'amoul* and ivory-hued *raybeh*. We've included versions – be they somewhat creative interpretations – of these classics (traditionalists, forgive us!), as well as other family-friendly recipes that will hopefully become firm favourites.

As you look through our selection, it might become apparent that we aren't crazy about iced cookies (and there aren't many of these in the Middle Eastern repertoire either). We find the usual icing (confectioners') sugar–based kind to be overly sweet. But we are fans of fillings! There are several jam- or ganache-filled biscuits that we're sure you'll love. Additionally, we've included delicate sponge fingers and a selection of crisp wafers, which make an ideal accompaniment to ice creams and creamy desserts as well as your afternoon cup of tea.

With some cookie doughs (our pistachio raybeh, for instance), 'hand-feel' is important, but the majority of our recipes make use of an electric mixer for speed and ease. As with cakes (see page 94), when creaming butter and sugar together remember to take your time. You'll need at least 4–5 minutes of beating until the sugar has completely dissolved. And one further tip: when baking batches using multiple trays, it's a good idea to swap them around so they bake evenly.

Most biscuits and cookies require little special equipment other than several baking trays, wire racks for cooling and airtight containers for storage. We'd also recommend investing in at least one non-stick silicone mat (rather than endless rolls of baking paper), and those tins of various-sized cutters will come in handy. A couple of recipes here involve a piping bag and nozzles, but these are usually optional.

PISTACHIO SHORTBREAD

Middle Eastern versions of shortbread – known as *raybeh* – are some of the most popular and widely available biscuits in the region. They are altogether more delicate than the Scottish style of shortbread: instead of being buttery and slightly claggy, ivory-hued raybeh are bone-dry in texture, and melt away in the mouth.

This is Greg's new definitive raybeh recipe. It's the version he remembers from his childhood as it was a speciality of his grandmother, Adèle, and her sisters, Margaret and Larisse. Although they never wrote their recipe down, Greg's uncle Alan has documented it for the family, based on many sessions spent watching and talking with his mother, Larisse, and we're very grateful to him for sharing it. Larisse's top tip was to make the biscuits in a warm kitchen, with warm hands, as this makes it easier to work the butter into the dry ingredients.

Traditional versions shape these biscuits as little rings with an almond pressed over the join, but we favour little bite-sized discs for this pistachio-dusted version.

MAKES AROUND 40

100 g (3½ oz) icing (confectioners')
    sugar, sifted
500 g (1 lb 2 oz) plain (all-purpose)
    flour, sifted
1 teaspoon baking powder
250 g (9 oz) clarified butter (page 241),
    at room temperature
1 egg white, lightly beaten

PISTACHIO DUST
30 g (1 oz) good-quality blanched
    pistachio nuts (Iranian slivers have
    the best colour)

To make the pistachio dust, blitz the pistachios to a fine powder in a food processor or spice grinder. Set aside. Line two baking trays with silicone baking mats or baking paper.

For the shortbread dough, sift the dry ingredients together into a large mixing bowl and stir them around a bit with your fingers.

Make a well in the centre and pour in the clarified butter. Use your fingertips to push all the dry ingredients into the butter and start working everything together slowly. It's important to be patient at this stage, and to rub carefully with a firm but gentle touch, until you achieve an even wet sand consistency. If you squeeze a little of the dough in the palm of your hand, it should squish together nicely.

Break off walnut-sized pieces of the dough (for consistency, we aim for 25 g/1 oz portions). Roll them between your palms into smooth, round balls and divide them between the prepared trays (you should be able to get 20 on each tray as they don't spread much as they bake). Flatten the biscuits slightly – the flat base of a glass jar or tumbler is ideal for this purpose – to 5 cm (2 in) in diameter. Rest in the fridge for 45 minutes.

When ready to bake the biscuits, preheat the oven to 140°C (275°F) fan-forced/160°C (320°F).

Bake in the centre of the oven for 20 minutes, swapping the trays around so the biscuits bake evenly (they should remain very pale). Remove from the oven and lightly brush the surface of each biscuit with beaten egg white, then sprinkle evenly with the pistachio dust and return to the oven for a final 5 minutes, watching carefully to ensure the biscuits do not brown.

Remove from the oven and leave the biscuits to cool on their trays. Once they are completely cold, store them in an airtight container for up to a week.

GINGER-SPICE BISCUITS

A great tea-time biscuit that combines the good snap and crunch of a classic English gingernut with the gentle warmth of the Spice Trail.

MAKES AROUND 16

225 g (8 oz) plain (all-purpose) flour
2 teaspoons baking powder
2 teaspoons bicarbonate of soda (baking soda)
½ teaspoon fine sea salt
2 teaspoons ground ginger
2 teaspoons ground mixed spice
1 teaspoon ground cinnamon
finely grated zest of 1 orange
finely grated zest of ½ lemon
110 g (4 oz) cold unsalted butter, chopped
50 g (1¾ oz) raw (demerara) sugar
60 g (2 oz) caster (superfine) sugar
100 g (3½ oz) golden syrup or dark corn syrup, warmed gently to liquefy

Preheat the oven to 170°C (340°F) fan-forced/190°C (375°F). Line two baking trays with silicone baking mats or baking paper. Position your oven shelves so one is in the top third and one is in the bottom third.

Sift the dry ingredients together into a large mixing bowl. Stir in the citrus zests, then rub in the butter. Alternatively, put all these items into a food processor and pulse to form fine crumbs. Mix (or pulse) in the sugars evenly. Pour in the warm golden syrup and mix briefly to a dough.

Tip the biscuit dough out onto a clean work surface and bring together with your hands. Form into balls the size of a large marble: you should get roughly 16 from the dough. Divide the biscuits between the prepared baking trays, allowing a little space between them for spreading, and flatten them out to 5 cm (2 in) rounds – we find the flat base of a glass jar or tumbler is ideal for this purpose. Don't worry if the edges are a little cracked and uneven.

Bake one tray of biscuits at a time (keep the second one refrigerated). Start the biscuits on the top shelf of the oven for 5 minutes, by which time they should be starting to brown around the edges. Move to the lower shelf and bake for a further 6 minutes, or until they are a deep toffee-gold colour.

Remove from the oven and leave to cool on the tray for 2 minutes to firm up, then transfer to a wire rack. Repeat with the second tray and allow to cool completely. The biscuits will keep for up to 1 week in an airtight container.

CHOC CHIP–TAHINI COOKIES

Tahini – the addictive Middle Eastern paste of ground sesame seeds – is often thought of in a savoury context, but we were keen to see if it could work in sweet dishes. And then, serendipitously, Lucy stumbled across this recipe for choc-chip cookies from Canadian food blogger Danielle Oron. The tahini replaces some of the butter and contributes a kind of creamy halva quality that marries brilliantly with dark chocolate. The result: insanely good.

Things to consider: do you like your cookies crisp or chewy? Everyone has their own preference and, after experimenting with varying sizes of cookie, oven temperatures and length of baking time – and even refrigerating the dough overnight, as the original version recommends – we learnt that all these factors can make slight (but sometimes barely discernible) differences. Generally speaking, for the ideal blend of crunch to chew, we found it best to use your eyes to discern when the cookies are browning at the edges, but remain somewhat pale in the centre. Browner cookies are still delicious, but will be crisper and lose some of their desirable soft chew.

MAKES AROUND 30

115 g (4 oz) unsalted butter, at room temperature

120 ml (4 fl oz) tahini, well stirred

200 g (7 oz) caster (superfine) sugar

1 large egg

1 egg yolk

1 teaspoon vanilla extract

150 g (5½ oz) plain (all-purpose) flour

½ teaspoon baking powder

½ teaspoon bicarbonate of soda (baking soda)

1 teaspoon sea salt flakes, roughly crushed, plus extra to sprinkle

250 g (9 oz) good-quality dark chocolate (60–70% cocoa solids), roughly chopped

Combine the butter, tahini and sugar in the bowl of an electric mixer and beat with the paddle attachment at medium speed for around 5 minutes, or until light and fluffy, stopping the mixer every minute or so and scraping down the sides as you go.

Add the egg, egg yolk and vanilla and continue mixing at medium speed for another 2 minutes, scraping down the sides, if necessary, to ensure the eggs are properly incorporated.

Sift together the flour, baking powder, bicarb and salt. Add to the cookie mixture and beat at low speed until just combined. Use a rubber spatula to fold in the chocolate, without overworking. The dough will be somewhat soft, rather than stiff, and needs at least 3 hours (covered) in the fridge to firm up.

To bake, preheat the oven to 160ºC (320ºF) fan-forced/180ºC (350ºF) and line two baking trays with silicone baking mats or baking paper.

Take walnut-sized pieces of the dough and roll them into balls. Arrange them on the prepared baking trays, allowing roughly 6 cm (2½ in) between them for spreading. Using the flat base of a glass jar or tumbler, flatten the cookies slightly to 5 cm (2 in) in diameter for smaller cookies, or 6 cm (2½ in) for larger ones.

Sprinkle a pinch of sea salt onto each cookie and bake for 12–15 minutes, or until they are pale gold in the centre, but turning toffee-dark at the edges. (Keep an eye on them towards the end of the cooking time to ensure they don't overbake.)

Let the cookies cool on the baking tray for a couple of minutes before lifting them onto a wire rack and leaving them to cool further. For maximum sensory pleasure (and chocolate ooze) eat while still slightly warm, accompanied by a glass of ice-cold milk.

These cookies are best eaten the same day, although they will keep for around 2 days in an airtight container. The raw cookie dough can be frozen for up to 6 months and keeps well in the fridge for up to 1 week.

LEMON CURD MA'AMOUL

These little domed shortbready beauties are another iconic Middle Eastern biscuit. They are typically filled with nuts (walnuts and pistachios are the most popular) or with date or fig paste and are shaped in special patterned moulds, or crimped by hand with small tweezers. While they're generally considered a special occasion cookie, they are wonderfully non-denominational and equally popular for both Christian and Islamic religious festivals. Greg has vivid memories of his mother, grandmothers and aunts all crowded into the kitchen preparing tray after tray of the Easter *ma'amoul* with practised ease.

We've made roll-up versions of ma'amoul in the past using a more straightforward flour-based dough, but Greg has always been slightly apprehensive about tackling the traditional semolina-based stuffed kind. It turned out to be well worth the risk. Although you need to start a day ahead of time to give the semolina time to soften – and we won't pretend there isn't an art to the stuffing – the resulting cookies are a revelation. And while the cookie dough recipe below is traditional, the lemon curd filling most definitely isn't. And yet it works deliciously well.

Mastic (an aromatic resin) and mahlab (ground cherry kernels) might seem esoteric, but they are crucial to the dough's distinctive flavour. Both can be found in Middle Eastern grocers, or purchased from specialist food stores or online suppliers.

MAKES 24

500 g (1 lb 2 oz) fine semolina
200 g (7 oz) unsalted butter, melted
100 ml (3½ fl oz) vegetable oil
½ teaspoon dried yeast
50 ml (1¾ fl oz) warm water
55 g (2 oz) caster (superfine) sugar
½ teaspoon mastic grains
160 g (5½ oz) plain (all-purpose)
    flour, sifted
½ teaspoon baking powder
¾ teaspoon anise seeds, ground
½ teaspoon ground mahlab
2 teaspoons orange blossom water
2 teaspoons rosewater
around 80 g (2¾ oz) good-quality
    ready-made lemon curd, to fill
icing (confectioners') sugar,
    for dusting

EQUIPMENT
ma'amoul mould (optional)

Put the semolina in a mixing bowl, add the melted butter and oil and rub them into the semolina until it looks like wet sand. Cover with plastic wrap and leave overnight so the grains swell and soften.

The next day, combine the yeast with the warm water and 1 teaspoon of the caster sugar in a small bowl. Stir and leave for about 10 minutes until it starts to froth.

Meanwhile, grind the mastic with ½ teaspoon of the caster sugar in a mortar. Add the mix to the bowl with the semolina along with the flour, baking powder, anise and mahlab. Mix everything together gently.

In a separate small bowl, dissolve the remaining caster sugar in the flower waters.

Tip the frothy yeast into the semolina, followed by the flower waters. Mix with your hands for 2–3 minutes, just until everything comes together. Don't overwork the dough or it will become tough. Cover and leave to rest at room temperature for 1 hour.

Preheat the oven to 200°C (400°F) fan-forced/220°C (430°F). Line two baking trays with silicone baking mats or baking paper.

To form the ma'amoul, break off pieces of the dough and roll between the palms of your hands to very smooth balls. (Because we're pedants, we like to weigh them for consistency, aiming for 40 g/1½ oz per portion.) With a ball nestling in your left hand, use your right thumb to push into the dough. Rotate and press to create a fairly deep pouch. Try to make the shell as thin as you can, and make it an even thickness all around. Add a dollop of lemon curd – don't be tempted to overfill, about two-thirds of a teaspoon should be sufficient or it will be nigh-on impossible to seal the dough successfully. The sealing is the tricky bit; you need to stretch

6" round : 29 "²   <u>the area</u>

7" round : <u><u>48</u></u> "²

8" round: 51 "²

9" round: 64 "²

10" round: 79 "²

~~48"² ÷ 64"² = .75~~

9" to 7"

48"² ÷ 64"² = (.75)

(75%)

<u>9" to 6"</u>

29"² ÷ 64"² = .453   <u>45%</u>

6" pan is 45% of an 9" pan
multiple larger ingredient
measurement by the percentage
to measurement of each ingredient of smaller ~~cake~~
the grams. (250g x .75 = 187g.)

<u>TEMP</u>

same temp. less time. Start with
10 mins, rotate cake - give another 5
mins - test with cake tester.

182. gr.
110 g.
77 .

1Phone
tax
Apple Care
هٰذا

5 eggs = 325 g.e
272 gram
cardamom
baking powder

eggs
flour
sugar
almonds

1k. 1248
7. 384
3.644

3 10 ipad (e)
3 10 pencil
220 iphone (1)
840
448 Apple
888

1 308 602-9815

and encourage the dough up and over the filling. Pinching and smearing the dough with a thumbnail helps to create a firm seal. As with all things, practice makes perfect. Place the sealed ma'amoul on a lightly floured work surface, seam side down, and rotate on the surface exerting even downward pressure (this helps to seal the bases further).

If you are using special moulds, put the ma'amoul in, seam side up, and press evenly and fairly gently. It doesn't require too much pressure for the pattern to transfer. Flatten the surface so it is flush with the sides of the mould. Again, you get a feel for this once you've done it a few times. Now the fun part: turn the mould over and whack it on your work surface to release the ma'amoul. It can take a couple of attempts, but is also a great way to release stress. Repeat with the rest of the dough and filling, transferring the completed cookies to your prepared baking trays as you go. If you don't have ma'amoul moulds, shape the cookies gently in your hands so the surface is smooth and rounded, and bake them plain and unadorned. They will still be delicious.

Bake the ma'amoul for 8–10 minutes, or until they are a warm golden colour. Swap the trays around halfway through the cooking time to ensure they bake evenly.

Remove from the oven and let the ma'amoul rest on the trays for 10 minutes. Transfer to wire racks and dust lightly with icing sugar. Leave until completely cold and dust them again. Ideally, the ma'amoul should be eaten within a day or so as the lemon curd is gradually absorbed by the pastry; however, they will keep for 2–3 days in an airtight container.

See photo on page 77.

Variation

For a more traditional filling, blitz 250 g (9 oz) walnuts or pistachios with 50 g (1¾ oz) caster (superfine) sugar in a food processor to coarse crumbs. (Be careful not to overprocess.) Stir in ½ teaspoon ground cinnamon and a big splash of orange blossom water and work it in evenly with your fingertips. Once baked, these ma'amoul will keep for up to 4 days in an airtight container.

CHOCOLATE GANACHE CRUNCH

Oats don't really feature in Middle Eastern baking, but as these are one of Lucy's favourite biscuits, they had to be included here.

MAKES AROUND 20

60 g (2 oz) rolled oats

80 g (2¾ oz) fine desiccated (shredded) coconut

150 g (5½ oz) plain (all-purpose) flour

150 g (5½ oz) unsalted butter, softened

150 g (5½ oz) golden caster (superfine) sugar

50 g (1¾ oz) golden syrup or dark corn syrup

½ teaspoon bicarbonate of soda (baking soda)

2 teaspoons boiling water

CHOCOLATE FILLING

20 g (¾ oz) unsalted butter

150 g (5½ oz) good-quality milk chocolate, chopped or broken into small pieces

Preheat the oven to 150°C (300°F) fan-forced/170°C (340°F). Line two large baking trays with silicone baking mats or baking paper.

Put the oats into a food processor and whiz to a medium-fine powder. Tip into a large mixing bowl, then add the coconut and sift in the flour. Stir everything together evenly.

Combine the butter and sugar in the bowl of an electric mixer and beat with the paddle attachment for around 4 minutes, or until very pale and fluffy.

Warm the golden syrup in a small saucepan. Mix the bicarb with the boiling water in a small cup then stir into the warmed golden syrup. Scrape into the creamed butter and mix in gently.

With the mixer on slow, add the flour-oat mixture in batches, just until evenly combined.

Divide the cookie dough in half. Use a round ½ tablespoon measuring spoon to form the dough into even 15 g (½ oz) portions and divide them between the prepared baking trays (you should be able to get 20 on each tray as they don't spread much as they bake). Flatten the cookies slightly – the flat base of a glass jar or tumbler is ideal for this purpose – to 4 cm (1½ in) in diameter.

Bake in the centre of the oven for around 15 minutes, or until medium golden brown. Swap the trays around halfway through to ensure they bake evenly.

Remove from the oven and leave the biscuits on the trays for 3 minutes to firm up before transferring to a wire rack to cool completely.

To make the filling, combine the butter and chocolate in a heatproof bowl and place over a saucepan of barely simmering water, making sure the water doesn't touch the base of the bowl. Stir occasionally until the butter and chocolate have melted. (Alternatively, put them in a microwaveable container and cook on full power in 20 second bursts until the chocolate has all but melted.) Stir to combine evenly, then leave to cool and thicken.

When the cookies are completely cold, sandwich them together with the chocolate filling – a generous teaspoon per cookie is about right. The biscuits will keep for up to 5 days in an airtight container.

TURKISH PRETTY EYE COOKIES

We were inspired by the legendary Armenian food writer Arto der Haroutunian to make these irresistibly named modern Turkish cookies. While they are similar in concept to English Jammie Dodgers, in execution they are a world away from those claggy and oversweet supermarket offerings.

These crisp, buttery cookies are best filled with sour cherry jam (although another tangy preserve would also do). While it's not entirely necessary (or part of the original recipe), we like to add a zesty lime buttercream to the filling, too.

MAKES AROUND 16

150 g (5½ oz) unsalted butter, softened
85 g (3 oz) golden caster (superfine) sugar
finely grated zest of 1 lemon
150 g (5½ oz) plain (all-purpose) flour, sifted, plus extra for dusting
25 g (1 oz) cornflour (cornstarch), sifted
50 g (1¾ oz) ground almonds
1 medium egg yolk
125 g (4½ oz) good-quality sour cherry jam

LIME BUTTERCREAM

55 g (2 oz) unsalted butter
115 g (4 oz) icing (confectioners') sugar, plus extra if necessary
finely grated zest and juice of ½ lime

EQUIPMENT

6 cm (2½ in) pastry cutter
5 mm (¼ in) pastry cutter (optional)
piping bag fitted with a 5 mm (¼ in) nozzle

Line two baking trays with silicone baking mats or baking paper.

Combine the butter and sugar in the bowl of an electric mixer and beat with the paddle attachment for around 4 minutes, or until very pale and fluffy.

Beat in the lemon zest, then lower the speed and gradually beat in the flour and cornflour, followed by the ground almonds and egg yolk. Mix just until everything is evenly combined.

Tip the dough out onto a floured work surface and use your hands to bring it together briskly into a rough flattish disc. Wrap in plastic wrap and refrigerate for 30 minutes.

Roll the dough out between two sheets of baking paper or plastic wrap, aiming for a thickness of around 5 mm (¼ in). Use the 6 cm (2½ in) pastry cutter to cut out 30–32 cookies, re-rolling the dough as required.

Divide the cookies evenly between the prepared baking trays. One tray will be the tops, one the bottoms. For the tops of the cookies, use the 5 mm (¼ in) pastry cutter or piping nozzle to stamp out three holes, discarding the little offcuts. (We also find the end of a biro is perfect for this.) Refrigerate both trays for another 30 minutes.

Preheat the oven to 160°C (320°F) fan-forced/180°C (350°F).

Bake the cookies for 10–12 minutes, or until they are an even pale gold, swapping the trays around halfway through to ensure they bake evenly.

Remove from the oven and leave the cookies to cool on the baking trays for 5 minutes. Transfer to wire racks and leave to cool completely.

To make the buttercream, combine the butter and icing sugar in a mixing bowl and cream together with a fork. Once evenly mixed, add the lime juice and zest and beat in vigorously until it fluffs up a little. You are aiming for a smooth, pliable piping consistency. If it seems very runny, add a little more icing sugar. Spoon into the piping bag and chill in the fridge.

Once cold, pipe a thin border of buttercream just within the outer edge of the cookie bases. Dollop a spoonful of jam in the middle and sandwich with the cookie tops. Squish together gently so the jam just oozes from the little holes. The cookies will keep for 2–3 days in an airtight container. They soften slightly with time, but are none the worse for it.

SESAME BISCUITS WITH PISTACHIOS AND SOUR CHERRIES

While versions of these favourite Lebanese biscuits, known as *bazarek*, have appeared in our earlier books, we make no excuses for including them again here as they are such a traditional favourite and are very addictive. The strictly non-traditional addition of chopped sour cherries might lead some to accuse us of attempting to gild the lily here, but we think it works brilliantly.

MAKES 25–30

40 g (1½ oz) soft brown sugar

45 g (1½ oz) icing (confectioners') sugar

150 g (5½ oz) unsalted butter, softened

1 egg

1 teaspoon vanilla extract

200 g (7 oz) self-raising flour, sifted

40 g (1½ oz) sour cherries or barberries (sour cherries should be fairly finely chopped)

50 g (1¾ oz) pistachio slivers (we use Iranian)

60 g (2 oz) sesame seeds, lightly toasted

Combine the sugars and butter in the bowl of an electric mixer and beat with the paddle attachment for around 5 minutes, or until light and fluffy. Scrape down the sides and beat in the egg and vanilla extract, then add the flour and beat at low speed until just combined. Remove the bowl from the mixer and use a rubber spatula to fold in the chopped cherries, without overworking. Cover in plastic wrap and chill for at least 30 minutes.

Preheat the oven to 140°C (275°F) fan-forced/160°C (320°F). Line two baking trays with silicone baking mats or baking paper.

Take little pieces of dough and roll them between the palms of your hands into large marble-sized balls. Flatten gently to form little discs around 5 mm (¼ in) thick.

Line up two dishes on your work surface, one with the pistachio slivers and one with the sesame seeds. Press one side of the biscuits into the pistachios then press the other side into the sesame seeds. Carefully brush off any excess seeds and nuts and place the biscuits, sesame side up, on the prepared baking trays, allowing about 5 cm (2 in) between them for spreading.

Bake the biscuits for 10–12 minutes, or until golden brown, swapping the trays around halfway through to ensure they bake evenly.

Remove from the oven and leave the biscuits to cool on the baking trays for 5 minutes. Transfer to wire racks and leave to cool completely. They will keep for around 1 week in an airtight container.

See photo on page 86.

ORANGE AND GINGER NOUGATINE

Nougat and nougatine, its crunchier cousin, are thought to have been born in Baghdad (or thereabouts) in the tenth century. What's more certain is that versions of the popular European confection of beaten egg white and honey studded with roasted almonds (and sometimes candied fruit) was introduced by Arab traders. Nougatine is simpler to make than nougat as it's less of a confectionery and more of a biscuit. Think of it as a sort of naked Florentine (we've included an optional glaze for chocoholics).

The toasty almond-toffee flavours make nougatine a lovely accompaniment to all sorts of ice creams and creamy desserts. And it's pretty good to snack on with your afternoon cuppa, too!

MAKES AROUND 30, DEPENDING ON SIZE AND SHAPE

175 g (6 oz) golden caster (superfine) sugar

160 ml (5½ fl oz) thick (double/heavy) cream

80 g (2¾ oz) unsalted butter, roughly chopped

210 g (7½ oz) flaked almonds

50 g (1¾ oz) plain (all-purpose) flour, sifted

pinch of fine sea salt

1 teaspoon ground ginger

80 g (2¾ oz) crystallised ginger, finely chopped

finely grated zest of 2 oranges

250 g (9 oz) good-quality dark chocolate (50–60% cocoa solids), chopped or broken into small pieces (optional)

EQUIPMENT

sugar thermometer

+ SERVE WITH

Nectarine-caramel muhallabeya (page 35)

Saffron–blood orange brûlée (page 47)

Honey mousse with pine nut praline and spiced pears (page 50)

your favourite ice cream or sorbet (pages 55–64)

Preheat the oven to 150ºC (300ºF) fan-forced/170ºC (340ºF). Line two baking trays with silicone baking mats or baking paper.

Combine the sugar, cream and butter in a small saucepan and heat gently to dissolve, stirring to help it along. Increase the heat and bring to the boil, then simmer vigorously for around 5 minutes.

Meanwhile, combine the flaked almonds, flour, salt, ground and crystallised ginger and orange zest in a mixing bowl and mix very well.

Pour the hot cream onto the almond mixture and stir to combine thoroughly. Divide the mixture evenly between the two prepared baking trays and use a firm spatula to spread it out as evenly and thinly as you can. Bake for 15 minutes, then remove from the oven and let sit for a minute. Cover the surface with a sheet of baking paper and use a rolling pin to roll it out even more thinly.

Return the nougatine to the oven for a further 5–8 minutes, or until it colours a rich golden brown.

While still warm, use a very sharp long knife to trim the edges neatly so you have an even rectangle. Cut in half lengthways, then cut into two rows of triangles. Alternatively use a small cookie cutter to cut out neat circles, although you will get more wastage with this second option.

Leave the nougatine to cool completely, then transfer to a wire rack.

For a glossy chocolate coating you'll need to temper the chocolate by first heating, then cooling it. Put three-quarters of the chocolate in a heatproof bowl and place over a saucepan of barely simmering water, making sure the water doesn't touch the base of the bowl, and stir occasionally until it has completely melted. It should reach 45ºC (115ºF) on a sugar thermometer. Remove the bowl from the heat and add the reserved chocolate. Use a silicone spatula to work it in gently. Once the temperature drops to 31ºC (88ºF), it is ready to use. Use a pastry brush to paint it onto the flat (under) side of the nougatines, then use a fork to create the traditional wavy pattern. Hey presto – you have Florentines!

Once cold, store either version of biscuit in an airtight container, with baking paper between the layers. They will keep for up to 5 days. (Alternatively, you can freeze them for up to 2 months.)

See photo on page 87.

SWEET ANISE–OLIVE OIL TORTAS

Lucy fell in love with *tortas de aceite* during recent holidays in Spain, where they are a popular breakfast snack. While their history is unclear, the combination of almonds, sugar, sesame and anise seeds hints strongly at an Arab origin. The best-known version is made by Ines Rosales (you can find them in pricey delis worldwide) and each torta comes individually, and expensively, wrapped in attractive wax paper. They are reputedly made by the loving hands of local Seville women – which might also account for the cost.

Lucy was determined to attempt a homemade version as the combination of flaky crunch, salt, anise spices and just a hint of sweetness is addictive. We are pretty confident that this recipe comes close to the original.

They are good for breakfast, it's true, but for us, their appeal is much broader. They also make a brilliant addition to a cheese board and are particularly good with soft goat's cheese – especially when paired with quince paste. A drizzle of honey is delicious, too.

MAKES 16

2 teaspoons aniseeds or fennel seeds
130 ml (4½ fl oz) warm water
120 ml (4 fl oz) extra-virgin olive oil
2 teaspoons dried yeast
zest of 1 orange
230 g (8 oz) plain (all-purpose)
    flour, sifted
½ teaspoon fine sea salt
2 teaspoons sesame seeds
1 egg white, beaten
2 teaspoons caster (superfine) sugar

Preheat the oven to 180°C (350°F) fan-forced/200°C (400°F). Line two large baking trays with silicone baking mats or baking paper.

Put the aniseeds on a small baking tray and bake in the oven for 5 minutes, or until lightly roasted. Be careful not to burn them. Let them cool for a few minutes, then crush them roughly with a pestle.

Combine the warm water, olive oil, yeast and orange zest in the bowl of an electric mixer fitted with a dough hook. Add the flour and salt. Knead for 5 minutes, or until the dough is becoming supple and shiny. Add the crushed aniseeds to the dough together with the sesame seeds and knead for another minute to incorporate evenly.

Cover the bowl loosely with a clean tea towel (dish towel) and leave the dough to rise in a warm place for around 45 minutes. It should double in size.

Divide the dough into quarters, then divide each quarter into four golf-ball sized portions.

Dust your work surface and rolling pin lightly with flour, then roll each ball out to 8–10 cm (3¼–4 in) circles. Use a broad spatula to transfer the tortas to the prepared baking trays and brush the surface of each with a little egg white. Sprinkle lightly and evenly with sugar and bake for 7–8 minutes, then lower the oven temperature to 160°C (320°F) fan-forced/180°C (350°F) and bake for a further 3–4 minutes, or until the tortas are golden and crisp. They may puff up slightly.

Leave the tortas to cool on the baking trays for 1–2 minutes. Transfer to wire racks and leave to cool completely. The tortas will keep for 2–3 days in an airtight container.

PERFUMED LADYFINGERS

Our version of these delicate sponge fingers – also known as boudoir biscuits or savoiardi biscuits – are lightly perfumed with orange blossom water, in a subtle nod to the Middle East. They are possibly best known for the part they play in desserts such as trifles, tiramisu or old-fashioned Charlottes, but they also make a lovely light accompaniment to a cup of tea or coffee. They are at their freshest and best on the same day as baking, but will keep for 2–3 days in an airtight container. They will slightly dry out over time, which makes them ideal for making the aforementioned desserts. You can freeze them for up to a month. Ladyfingers are best made with low protein sponge or cake flour, but if you can't find this, then plain (all-purpose) flour will do.

MAKES AROUND 36

75 g (2¾ oz) egg yolks (about 4)
100 g (3½ oz) caster (superfine) sugar
1 tablespoon orange blossom water
½ teaspoon vanilla extract
zest of 1 orange
120 g (4½ oz) egg whites (about 2½)
½ teaspoon cream of tartar
100 g (3½ oz) sponge flour, sifted
75 g (2¾ oz) icing (confectioners') sugar, sifted

EQUIPMENT
large pastry bag fitted with 2.5 cm (1 in) nozzle

Preheat the oven to 180°C (350°F) fan-forced/200°C (400°F). Line two baking trays with silicone baking mats or baking paper.

Put the egg yolks and 70 g (2½ oz) of the sugar in the bowl of an electric mixer and whisk on high speed for 5 minutes, or until the mixture becomes very thick and pale and falls in ribbons from the whisk.

Reduce the speed and whisk in the flower water, vanilla and orange zest. Increase the speed to high and beat for 30 seconds or until it thickens again. Scrape into a large bowl.

Clean out the bowl and the whisk.

Whisk the egg whites on medium–slow speed until they start to froth. Add the cream of tartar and whisk on medium–high to soft peaks. Gradually whisk in the remaining 30 g (1 oz) of sugar to stiff, glossy peaks.

Sift the flour onto the egg yolk mixture. Add a large spoonful of meringue and mix in to slacken. Add the rest of the meringue and use a large metal spoon to fold it in gently but evenly, taking care not to lose volume.

Working quickly so the mixture doesn't slacken too much, spoon into the pastry bag. Pipe onto the prepared trays in 8 cm (3¼ in) fingers, leaving a small gap between them. For the traditional 'pearled' finish, sprinkle on the icing sugar in two even layers. Bake for 8–10 minutes, or until the biscuits are pale gold and springy to the touch.

Use a small spatula to remove the biscuits from the baking trays promptly, or they can stick. Leave to cool on wire racks. The ladyfingers will keep for 2–3 days in an airtight container.

+ SERVE WITH
Dates tiramisu, Middle eastern style (page 28)
Apricot-amaretoo fool (page 33)
Chantilly-yoghurt cream with blackberry-nectarine compote (page 48)

ORANGE WAFERS

It's always lovely to have homemade wafers on hand for serving with ice cream or creamy desserts, and they also make the perfect accompaniment to your afternoon cuppa. This is our wafer gold standard: the recipe is foolproof and you can incorporate different flavours, to slightly different effect. We've included three useful variations, using cardamom, cinnamon or sesame seeds.

For his restaurant desserts, Greg enjoys playing with different-shaped wafers, which is a simple but effective way of delighting your guests: camels, palm trees and minarets have all proven popular. You can buy plastic template mats from specialist baking and confectionery retailers. Or to make your own more inventive personalised wafers, draw (or download from the internet) your choice of image, trace it onto a thin plastic container lid and use a Stanley knife to cut out the shape.

MAKES AROUND 30

75 g (2¾ oz) unsalted butter
60 g (2 oz) plain (all-purpose) flour
60 g (2 oz) caster (superfine) sugar
finely grated zest of 1½ oranges
90 g (3 oz) egg whites (around 2),
    lightly beaten
1 teaspoon orange blossom water
milk, for spreading

EQUIPMENT
stencil mats, various shapes and
    sizes (optional)

✚ SERVE WITH
Arabic five-spice pineapple with
    saffron ice cream (page 18)
Apricot-amaretto fool (page 33)
Nectarine-caramel muhallabeya
    (page 37)
Saffron–blood orange brûlée (page 47)
Honey mousse with pine nut praline
    and spiced pears (page 50)
your favourite ice cream (pages 57–64)
    or dessert

Preheat the oven to 130ºC (265ºF) fan-forced/150ºC (300ºF). Line two baking trays with silicone baking mats or baking paper.

Melt the butter then leave it to cool to room temperature.

Combine the flour, sugar and grated orange zest in a large mixing bowl, then add the egg whites and mix to a smooth paste. Add the cooled butter, followed by the orange blossom water, and stir until smoothly combined. The batter will be quite loose and sloppy.

Spoon small, well-spaced teaspoons of the batter on the prepared baking tray, aiming for 5–6 per tray. Wet your finger in a little milk and carefully flatten and smear the batter out into rounds as thinly as possible. They should be around 9 cm (3½ in) in diameter.

If using stencil templates, then spread batter over the template spaces and scrape off any excess to create a smooth, neat surface. Lift the template away carefully, to maintain the perfect shape. Chill in the fridge for 10 minutes.

Bake in the centre of the oven for 7–9 minutes, or until the wafers are golden. Remove from the oven and cool for 2 minutes. Lift the wafers onto a wire rack with a spatula and when they are completely cold, store them in an airtight container for up to 1 week.

See photo on page 93.

Variations

For orange-cardamom wafers, add ¼ teaspoon finely ground cardamom seeds along with the orange zest.

For cinnamon wafers, replace the orange zest with ¼ teaspoon ground cinnamon.

For sesame wafers, before chilling, sprinkle liberally with sesame seeds, tipping off any excess.

CHOCOLATE ARABESQUE WAFERS

Many people find it hard to resist chocolatey things, and these delicate lace wafers, with their slightly bitter edge, make a sophisticated accompaniment to ice creams, custards and fruity desserts. Best of all, they make virtue of their fragility as you simply break the entire sheet up into random-sized shards.

MAKES 2 TRAYS

100 g (3½ oz) unsalted butter, softened

100 ml (3½ fl oz) fresh orange juice

150 g (5½ oz) icing (confectioners') sugar

80 g (2¾ oz) plain (all-purpose) flour, sifted

25 g (1 oz) unsweetened (Dutch) cocoa powder

1 tablespoon dried rose petals (optional)

Preheat the oven to 130°C (265°F) fan-forced/150°C (300°F). Line two baking trays with silicone baking mats or baking paper.

Put the butter into a saucepan and heat gently to melt. Add the orange juice and the icing sugar, stir gently until evenly combined, then remove from the heat.

Sift the flour and cocoa into a mixing bowl and make a well in the centre. Pour in the hot butter mixture and stir until smooth and well combined. Chill in the fridge for 30 minutes.

Spread the batter out on the prepared baking trays, as thinly and evenly as you can (this is the time to use a step spatula, if you have one). Bake for 8–10 minutes, or until the batter is beginning to bubble and darken. Towards the end of baking, sprinkle with dried rose petals, if using.

Remove from the oven and leave on the tray for 2–3 minutes, then transfer to a wire rack to cool completely. Break into random-sized shards and store in an airtight container for up to 1 week.

If the wafers soften, you can flash them for 2 minutes in a 140°C (275°F) fan-forced/160°C (320°F) oven. They'll crisp up again as they cool.

+ SERVE WITH

Stone fruit 'fattouche' with sweet lemon dressing (page 13)

Apricot-amaretto fool (page 33)

Nectarine-caramel muhallabeya (page 35)

Turkish coffee petits pots (page 40)

your favourite ice cream (pages 55–64)

CAKES AND PUDDINGS

There isn't the same broad tradition of home baking in the Middle East as there is in the West, and what there is comprises a somewhat limited repertoire of syrup-soaked sponge cakes. In countries where there has been any kind of French influence, versions of fancy, cream-filled gateaux can be found in smart patisseries, and, in truth, most Middle Easterners would generally buy one of these as a treat for a special occasion, rather than baking themselves.

But we feel this just gives us licence to let our imaginations run wild, and, as we've included recipes for the more traditional cakes in our previous books, here we've been a bit more freewheeling. Nearly all the following recipes incorporate some kind of Middle Eastern influence – be it ingredients or technique – and we think we've come up with a selection that will suit all kinds of occasions.

There are a few tips we'd like to share to help you achieve full baking success. First, preheat your oven for at least 20 minutes and prepare your equipment by buttering the sides and base of your cake tin. Next, weigh all your ingredients carefully before you start mixing (see Measuring, page 249). Ingredients should all be at room temperature and butter and eggs should come out of the fridge at least 1–2 hours before you start your preparation. We can't stress enough how important this is: cold ingredients will not mix together easily and you risk ending up with a curdled batter. Butter and sugar need to be energetically beaten for at least 4–5 minutes so that the sugar dissolves completely and you have a pale, fluffy mix. Scrape down the sides of the bowl several times with a spatula, too.

For maximum rise, cakes should go into the oven as soon as the batter is finished as the raising agent starts work the moment it is added. When testing for doneness, a skewer will tell part of the story, but also assess colour and see how the surface springs back when lightly pressed. Generally, we let cakes rest on a rack for 5–10 minutes before unmoulding. And lastly, cool completely before icing.

There are endless shapes and sizes of cake tins. We've tried not to go overboard: the majority of recipes require a 23 cm (9 in) loose-bottom or springform tin, although we do love our Raspberry-yoghurt bundt cake! You'll also need a selection of smaller tins (muffin, madeleine, mini-loaf, dariole moulds) and a couple of rectangular baking tins. While wire cooling racks are essential, a piping bag is useful and a blowtorch optional.

PISTACHIO FRIANDS WITH SUMMER BERRIES

These moist little cakes are traditionally made with ground almonds, but the flavour of pistachios works really well too, especially with tart-sweet summer berries. They are simplicity itself to make.

MAKES 12

100 g (3½ oz) pistachio nuts
70 g (2½ oz) plain (all-purpose) flour, sifted, plus extra for dusting
160 g (5½ oz) icing (confectioners') sugar, sifted, plus extra for dusting
pinch of salt
260 g (9 oz) egg whites (about 6), lightly beaten with a fork
115 g (4 oz) unsalted butter, melted, plus extra for greasing
200 g (7 oz) mixed berries (your choice of raspberries, blackberries, blueberries, etc.)

EQUIPMENT
non-stick 12-hole friand or muffin tin

Preheat the oven to 150°C (300°F) fan-forced/170°C (340°F). Grease and flour the friand or muffin tin.

Finely grind the pistachios in a food processor, then transfer to a mixing bowl. Add the flour, sugar and salt and stir to combine.

Put the egg whites in the bowl of an electric mixer and whisk until light and foamy. Tip into the bowl of dry ingredients and stir until just combined. Stir in the melted butter. Fold in the berries evenly with a rubber spatula.

Spoon the batter into the prepared tin and bake for 30–35 minutes. The friands should spring back when touched and be starting to come away from the sides of the tin.

Remove from the oven and leave the friands in the tin for 5 minutes before turning out and cooling on a wire rack. Dust with a little icing sugar and serve while still warm.

LITTLE LEMON-GINGER SYRUP CAKES

Many Middle Eastern cakes use the syrup-soaking technique, which we fondly imagine to be the origin of the ubiquitous lemon drizzle cake. This is our nod to that English tea-time favourite.

MAKES 12–18

250 g (9 oz) unsalted butter, softened, plus extra for greasing
200 g (7 oz) caster (superfine) sugar
2 teaspoons lemon zest (1–2 lemons)
260 g (9 oz) eggs (around 4)
50 g (1¾ oz) plain (all-purpose) flour
2 teaspoons baking powder
2 teaspoons ground ginger
¼ teaspoon fine sea salt
200 g (7 oz) fine semolina
200 g (7 oz) ground almonds
5 pieces stem ginger, finely diced, plus 3 to garnish
60 ml (2 fl oz) lemon juice (about 1–2 lemons)
50 g (1¾ oz) Greek-style yoghurt

LEMON-BRANDY SYRUP
100 g (3½ oz) caster (superfine) sugar
100 ml (3½ fl oz) lemon juice (2–3 lemons)
2 teaspoons brandy

EQUIPMENT
twelve 13 × 6.5 cm (5 × 2½ in) rectangular mini-loaf tins or three standard six-hole muffin tins

Preheat the oven to 180ºC (350ºF) fan-forced/200ºC (400ºF). Grease the mini-loaf or muffin tins.

Combine the butter, sugar and lemon zest in the bowl of an electric mixer and beat with the paddle attachment for around 4 minutes, or until pale and fluffy. Beat in the eggs little by little, ensuring that each amount is incorporated thoroughly before you add more.

Sift on the flour and baking powder, then add the ground ginger, sea salt, semolina and almonds and fold everything in. Finally, mix in the stem ginger, lemon juice and yoghurt, gently but evenly.

Spoon the batter into the prepared tins, aiming for roughly two-thirds full. Slice the extra stem ginger very thinly and set a slice on top of each little cake. Bake for 20–30 minutes, or until the cakes are golden brown and feel firm to the touch.

While the cakes are baking, prepare the syrup. Combine the sugar, lemon juice and brandy in a small saucepan and heat gently, stirring from time to time, until the sugar has dissolved. Once the liquid is clear, bring to the boil, then lower the heat and simmer briskly for 5 minutes.

Remove the cakes from the oven and pierce them all over with a fine skewer. Carefully pour the hot syrup over each cake – they will drink it up. Repeat until all the syrup is used up and leave to soak in as the cakes cool. Once completely cold, turn the cakes out. They will keep for 2–3 days in an airtight container.

HONEY-CITRUS MADELEINES

Made famous by Proust, these little buttery cakes, with their distinctive humps and pretty scalloped bottoms, are indeed perfect with a cup of tea. One slightly controversial explanation for their scalloped shape links madeleines to the famous Compostela pilgrimage. And when you consider that early recipes for madeleines include ground almonds and orange flower water, it's quite easy to accept a Moorish-Spanish origin.

If (like us) you only have one madeleine tin, allow it to cool, then fill with the remaining batter and place in the freezer for 20 minutes before baking.

MAKES 24

90 g (3 oz) unsalted butter, plus extra
   for greasing
2 teaspoons honey
2 eggs
75 g (2¾ oz) caster (superfine) sugar
15 g (½ oz) soft brown sugar
pinch of fine sea salt
finely grated zest of 1 orange
2 teaspoons orange blossom water
   (optional)
90 g (3 oz) plain (all-purpose) flour
1 teaspoon baking powder

ORANGE GLAZE (OPTIONAL)
juice of ½ orange (about 40 ml/
   1¼ fl oz)
60 g (2 oz) icing (confectioners')
   sugar, sifted

EQUIPMENT
two 12-hole madeleine tins

Melt the butter together with the honey in a small saucepan, then remove from the heat and allow to cool to room temperature.

Combine the eggs with both the sugars, the salt and the orange zest in the bowl of an electric mixer and whisk for 2–3 minutes until pale and increased in volume. Whisk in the cooled butter mixture together with the orange blossom water, if using.

Sift the flour and baking powder onto the batter and fold it in gently. Cover with plastic wrap and rest in the fridge for a minimum of 1 hour, or up to 12 hours.

Towards the end of the resting time, liberally grease the madeleine tins and dust lightly with flour, shaking off the excess. (You don't need to do this if using non-stick tins.) Place in the fridge to chill.

When ready to bake, preheat the oven to 180°C (350°F) fan-forced/ 200°C (400°F). Position an oven shelf in the top third of your oven.

Dollop spoonfuls of batter into the prepared madeleine moulds, without smoothing the batter out. Aim for roughly two-thirds full. Place in the freezer for 15–20 minutes while the oven is heating.

Bake the madeleines for 8–9 minutes, keeping a watchful eye on them towards the end of the baking time. When they are honey-gold and feel just set, remove from the oven and cool for a moment. Slide the madeleines out onto a wire rack.

When all the madeleines are cool, combine the glaze ingredients in a small bowl and mix together until smooth.

Dip the scalloped sides of the madeleines in the glaze, then return them to the wire rack, glazed side up, and leave until cold. Alternatively, dust with icing or caster sugar just before serving. Madeleines are at their best eaten on the day they are made, but will keep well for 2–3 days in an airtight container.

Variation
For a lovely alternative, replace the orange zest and orange blossom water with lime zest and rosewater and make a glaze using lime juice.

PERSIAN PARADISE SLICE

The word paradise derives from the ancient Persian *paradaeza*, and this was all we needed to know when it came to naming our version of this delectable tray bake. The inspiration for it came from the brilliant Fatto a Mano bakery in Lucy's old neighbourhood in Melbourne. Our tweaks replace raisins with sour cherries and raspberry jam with sour cherry jam. These tangier, more exotic elements combine with a shortbready base and light coconut sponge topping to make a true slice of heaven.

MAKES 12

SHORTBREAD BASE
175 g (6 oz) unsalted butter
75 g (2¾ oz) golden caster (superfine) sugar
150 g (5½ oz) plain (all-purpose) flour, sifted
100 g (3½ oz) ground almonds
finely grated zest of 1 orange

FILLING
150 g (5½ oz) good-quality sour cherry jam

SPONGE TOPPING
110 g (4 oz) dried sour cherries
juice of 1 orange
110 g (4 oz) unsalted butter, diced
150 g (5½ oz) golden caster (superfine) sugar
260 g (9 oz) eggs (around 4)
150 g (5½ oz) desiccated (shredded) coconut
75 g (2¾ oz) ground almonds
1 teaspoon baking powder
icing (confectioners') sugar, for dusting

EQUIPMENT
30 × 23 × 4 cm (12 × 9 × 1½ in) non-stick baking tin

Combine all the shortbread ingredients in a food processor and pulse to crumbs. Continue pulsing for a few more seconds, just until everything comes together as a ball. It will be very soft and sticky.

Push into the base of the baking tin and use the flat base of a glass jar or tumbler to press the surface out evenly. Cover with plastic wrap and refrigerate for at least 1 hour.

While the shortbread is chilling, roughly chop the dried sour cherries for the sponge topping and mix them with the orange juice in a small bowl. Leave to macerate until required.

Preheat the oven to 140°C (275°F) fan-forced/160°C (320°F). Prick the shortbread all over with a fork and bake for 25–30 minutes until just starting to colour. Remove from the oven and set aside.

Increase the oven temperature to 170°C (340°F) fan-forced/190°C (375°F).

Warm the jam briefly in the microwave or in a small saucepan over a low heat to make it workable, then spread it evenly over the shortbread base.

For the sponge topping, combine the butter and sugar in the bowl of an electric mixer and beat with the paddle attachment for around 4 minutes, or until very pale and fluffy. Add the eggs, little by little, ensuring that each amount is incorporated thoroughly before you add more. Fold in the coconut, almonds, baking powder and cherries, including any remaining soaking liquid, with a rubber spatula. Spoon onto the base and spread it out evenly.

Return to the oven and bake for 25–35 minutes, or until the sponge is springy to the touch and is golden on top. If you think it is darkening too quickly, cover with aluminium foil.

Remove from the oven, run a knife around the edge to loosen, then leave it to cool completely in the tin. Cut into squares and dust with icing sugar to serve.

PLUM TRAY BAKE WITH CARDAMOM-CLOVE CRUMBLE

A delectably moist tray bake that showcases plum's affinity with cardamom. There is a generous quantity of crumble in the recipe below because, frankly, who doesn't love crumble? This is a useful recipe to have on hand to make fruit crumble puddings; either freeze it in its raw state and use from frozen as a topping for par-cooked fruit, or bake it for 15 minutes or so and store the crunchy crumbs in an airtight container to use as a handy garnish for all sorts of stewed fruits, ice creams or creamy desserts.

MAKES 12 PIECES

180 g (6½ oz) plain (all-purpose) flour
1¼ teaspoons baking powder
¼ teaspoon bicarbonate of soda (baking soda)
¼ teaspoon salt
240 g (8½ oz) sour cream or Greek-style yoghurt
1½ teaspoons vanilla extract
140 g (5 oz) unsalted butter, softened, plus extra for greasing
200 g (7 oz) golden caster (superfine) sugar
2 large eggs
8 plums, quartered and pitted

CARDAMOM-CLOVE CRUMBLE

80 g (2¾ oz) plain (all-purpose) flour
80 g (2¾ oz) ground almonds
80 g (2¾ oz) soft brown sugar
16 cloves, ground to a powder (or ½ teaspoon ground cloves)
seeds from 20 cardamom pods, ground (or ½ teaspoon ground cardamom)
¼ teaspoon sea salt flakes
80 g (2¾ oz) chilled unsalted butter, diced small

EQUIPMENT

20 × 30 cm (8 × 12 in) baking tin

To make the cardamom-clove crumble, combine all the dry ingredients in the bowl of a food processor and pulse a few times to combine. Add the butter and pulse until it forms clumpy crumbs. Place in the freezer for at least 30 minutes (or seal in a zip-lock bag for future use).

Preheat the oven to 170°C (340°F) fan-forced/190°C (375°F) and lightly grease the baking tin.

For the cake, first sift the flour, baking powder, bicarb and salt into a mixing bowl.

Whisk the sour cream and vanilla together in a small bowl.

Combine the butter and sugar in the bowl of an electric mixer and beat with the paddle attachment on medium speed for 4–5 minutes, or until very pale and fluffy. Beat in the eggs, little by little, ensuring that each amount is incorporated thoroughly before you add more.

Lower the speed and add the flour in three batches, alternating with the sour cream. When the batter is very smooth, tip it into the prepared baking tin and smooth the surface. Arrange the plum pieces on top and bake for 25 minutes.

Sprinkle the crumble evenly over the cake's surface and return to the oven for 20–25 minutes, or until a skewer inserted into the cake comes out clean. Set the tin on a wire rack and leave to cool completely.

Cut into squares and serve from the tin with tea or coffee, or as dessert with whipped cream.

See photo on page 104.

RASPBERRY-YOGHURT BUNDT WITH MAPLE GLAZE

Many Eastern Mediterranean and Middle Eastern cakes include yoghurt, both for flavour and moistness, although we've also made this delectable cake with sour cream, which works just as well. We like to chop the raspberries, rather than leave them whole, which creates flashes of sharp sweetness that speckle the lovely tender crumb. It's easier to do this with frozen fruit, so if you're using fresh raspberries, stick them in the freezer for 30 minutes before getting started.

You could substitute a ring pan or a regular circular tin for the bundt tin; however, when made in a regular tin the cake will need a few minutes longer in the oven.

SERVES 8–10

300 g (10½ oz) plain (all-purpose) flour
1½ teaspoons baking powder
½ teaspoon bicarbonate of soda (baking soda)
½ teaspoon fine sea salt
240 g (8½ oz) Greek-style yoghurt or sour cream
1½ teaspoons vanilla extract
250 g (9 oz) unsalted butter, softened, plus extra for greasing
300 g (10½ oz) caster (superfine) sugar
195 g (7 oz) eggs (roughly 3), lightly whisked
150 g (5½ oz) frozen or fresh raspberries, roughly chopped
fresh raspberries or blueberries, to decorate (optional)
edible flowers, to decorate (optional)

MAPLE GLAZE

25 g (1 oz) unsalted butter
50 ml (1¾ fl oz) maple syrup
60 g (2 oz) icing (confectioners') sugar, sifted
1 tablespoon Greek-style yoghurt or thick cream

EQUIPMENT

23 cm (9 in) ring (bundt) tin

Preheat the oven to 170°C (340°F) fan-forced/190°C (375°F) and grease the bundt tin. (We do this even with non-stick tins, and if your tin is not non-stick be especially liberal and thorough, so that the cake turns out easily and you don't spoil the shape.)

Set aside a teaspoon of the flour, then sift the rest together with the baking powder, bicarbonate of soda and salt. Mix together the yoghurt and vanilla extract.

Combine the butter and sugar in the bowl of an electric mixer and beat with the paddle attachment for around 4 minutes, or until very pale and fluffy. Beat in the eggs, little by little, scraping down the sides and ensuring each amount is incorporated thoroughly before you add more.

Lower the speed and add the flour in three lots, interspersed with the vanilla yoghurt. After each addition, increase the speed and mix in well for 10–20 seconds.

Toss the chopped frozen raspberries with the reserved teaspoon of flour, then fold into the cake batter gently, but so they are distributed evenly.

Spoon the cake batter into the prepared tin and smooth the top evenly. Bake for 1–1¼ hours, or until the cake is coming away from the sides of the tin pan and an inserted skewer comes out clean. The surface of the cake should be golden brown and spring back when gently pressed.

Allow the cake to rest in the tin for 10–15 minutes, then invert onto a wire rack and cool completely before transferring to a serving plate.

For the glaze, combine the butter and maple syrup in a small saucepan and heat until the butter has melted. Remove from the heat, stir in the icing sugar and mix until smooth. Allow to cool and thicken a little, then stir in the yoghurt. Drizzle the glaze over the cake, garnish with berries and edible flowers, if desired, and serve at room temperature.

See photo on page 105.

BITTER WALNUT CAKE

Walnuts are hugely popular in Middle Eastern desserts – although they are more likely to feature in syrupy stuffed pastries than in this more Western-style cake. But they are one of our favourite nuts – for both sweet and savoury dishes – and we are always looking for ways to celebrate them.

All too often, dishes that star walnuts call for their papery skins to be rubbed away after a brisk toasting in the oven. But it is in the skins that their tantalising bitterness lies, and what a joy it is to offer up a recipe that celebrates that quality, rather than attempting to disguise or remove it altogether. The resulting flavour is rich and nutty and, fear not, the bitterness is discernible only as a pleasing top note. All in all, this is one of our very favourite cakes: moist, dense and not too sweet. Eat it warm, if you like, with a dribble of cream, or accentuate that bitterness further and serve it, more austerely, alongside a strong, tannic cup of tea. Perfect for a cold autumn afternoon.

SERVES 8–10

160 g (5½ oz) walnut halves

2 slices good-quality white bread (not the sliced supermarket variety)

seeds from 22 cardamom pods, ground (or a generous ½ teaspoon ground cardamom)

pinch of fine sea salt

finely grated zest of 1 orange

150 g (5½ oz) unsalted butter, diced, plus extra for greasing

130 g (4½ oz) caster (superfine) sugar

260 g (9 oz) eggs (roughly 4–5), separated

pinch of cream of tartar

unsweetened (Dutch) cocoa powder, for dusting

softly whipped cream, to serve (optional)

EQUIPMENT

23 cm (9 in) springform or loose-based cake tin

Preheat the oven to 160°C (320°F) fan-forced/180°C (350°F). Grease the springform or loose-based cake tin and line the base of the tin with baking paper.

Spread the walnuts and bread slices out on a baking tray, keeping them separate, and toast for 8–10 minutes, or until the bread is dry and the nuts are darkening. Remove from the oven and lower the oven temperature to 140°C (275°F) fan-forced/160°C (320°F).

Cool the nuts and the toasted bread completely, then blitz them separately in a food processor until evenly and finely ground. Take particular care with the walnuts; it is all too easy to over-process them, which will turn them to nut butter!

Mix the bread and nut crumbs with the cardamom, salt and orange zest and set aside.

Put the butter into the bowl of an electric mixer with two-thirds of the sugar and beat with the paddle attachment for 3–4 minutes, or until very pale and fluffy. Add the egg yolks, little by little, ensuring that each amount is incorporated thoroughly before you add more. Stir in the nut-breadcrumb mixture.

Put the egg whites into the bowl of an electric mixer and whisk until they start to froth. Add the cream of tartar and whisk to soft peaks. Then, with the motor running, scatter on the rest of the sugar and continue whisking to stiff, glossy peaks.

Add a large spoonful of meringue to the cake batter and mix in to slacken, then add the rest of the meringue and fold in gently but evenly with a large metal spoon, taking care not to lose volume.

Tip the batter into the prepared cake tin and smooth the surface evenly. Bake for 50 minutes, or until the cake is a deep golden brown and a skewer comes out clean. It will rise in the oven and then fall, so don't panic. Cool the cake in the tin for 5 minutes, then turn it out onto a wire rack and leave to cool completely.

Dust with cocoa just before serving on its own, or with whipped cream.

CLEMENTINE-CARDAMOM CAKE

Sephardic in origin and justifiably made famous by Claudia Roden, the boiled citrus-almond cake is a signature dish of the Middle Eastern sweet table. It keeps well for a couple of days – in fact it's better the day after baking. This is our riff on the more familiar orange version.

SERVES 8–10

4–5 medium clementines
butter, for greasing
390 g (14 oz) eggs (around 6)
200 g (7 oz) caster (superfine) sugar
250 g (9 oz) ground almonds
seeds from 30 cardamom pods, ground
   (or 1 teaspoon ground cardamom)
1 teaspoon baking powder
Candied citrus zest (page 220),
   to decorate (optional)

SCENTED ORANGE CREAM

125 ml (4 fl oz) thick (double/heavy)
   cream
80 g (2¾ oz) mascarpone
finely grated zest of 1 orange
1 tablespoon orange marmalade
1 teaspoon orange blossom water

EQUIPMENT

23 cm (9 in) springform or loose-based
   cake tin

Put the clementines in a saucepan with enough cold water to barely cover them. Bring to the boil, then lower the heat and simmer, covered, for 1½–2 hours, or until completely tender. Drain the clementines and leave them to cool. When they are cold, cut them in half and remove any pips. Put them into a food processor and blitz to a very smooth purée. Weigh out 375 g (13 oz) of purée and set aside.

Preheat the oven to 160°C (320°F) fan-forced/180°C (350°F). Grease the springform or loose-based cake tin and line the base of the tin with baking paper.

Put the eggs into a large mixing bowl and beat them well. Add the clementine purée together with the remaining ingredients and mix everything together well.

Pour the batter into the prepared cake tin and bake for about 1 hour. You can test for doneness with a skewer if you like, although this is a wet cake and some of the batter will inevitably stick. Really, though, it's hard to go wrong. What we would suggest, though, is checking on it after 40 minutes or so and cover with foil if the top looks as if it's browning too fast.

While the cake is baking, prepare the orange cream. Combine the cream and mascarpone in a mixing bowl and whisk very gently to soft peaks. Fold in the orange zest, marmalade and orange blossom water with a large metal spoon and chill until required.

Once the cake is cooked, remove it from the oven and leave it in the tin on a wire rack to cool. Turn out when cold.

Serve the cake with the scented orange cream on the side, or dollop it on top to make a sort of impromptu icing. Garnish with candied citrus zest, if using.

LUCY'S CHOCOLATE WEDDING CAKE

This is one of our go-to special occasion cakes and over the years we have made different versions using different nuts. With its smooth rounded chocolate dome, it is glossily elegant. Within, the cake itself is moist, nutty and deeply chocolatey, the perfect foil to a perfumed honey cream. Lucy loves this particular hazelnut version so much that she requested it as dessert at her wedding dinner.

The key thing to bear in mind is that when you come to assemble the cake, the icing should be at the same temperature as the cream, or it will melt it. Don't leave it too long, though, or it will thicken up too much to pour freely.

Orange blossom water is widely available nowadays, but do try to track down orange blossom jam, if you can – it makes all the difference to the honey cream. It should be available from Middle Eastern food stores.

SERVES 10–12

200 g (7 oz) blanched hazelnuts

200 g (7 oz) golden caster (superfine) sugar, plus 1 tablespoon extra

200 g (7 oz) good-quality dark chocolate (60–70% cocoa solids), chopped or broken into small pieces

200 g (7 oz) softened unsalted butter, plus extra for greasing

6 eggs, separated

45 ml (1½ fl oz) amaretto (or use fresh orange juice)

pinch of salt

fresh summer berries, to serve (optional)

edible flowers, to garnish (optional)

CHOCOLATE GLAZE

200 g (7 oz) good-quality dark chocolate (60–70% cocoa solids), chopped or broken into small pieces

2 tablespoons mild-flavoured honey

80 g (2¾ oz) unsalted butter

HONEY CREAM

300 ml (10 fl oz) thick (double/heavy) cream

1 tablespoon honey

splash of orange blossom water or 1 heaped tablespoon orange blossom jam

EQUIPMENT

23 cm (9 in) springform or loose-based cake tin

Preheat the oven to 180°C (350°F) fan-forced/200°C (400°F). Grease and line the base of the springform or loose-based cake tin.

Put the hazelnuts on a baking tray and roast them in the oven for 10 minutes, shaking them around every so often so they brown evenly. Set aside to cool. Once cool, tip into a food processor with the extra tablespoon of sugar and blitz to fairly fine crumbs. Be careful not to over-process; you don't want a paste.

Put the chocolate and butter in a heatproof bowl and place over a saucepan of barely simmering water, making sure the water doesn't touch the base of the bowl. Stir occasionally until both have melted. (Alternatively, put them in a microwaveable container and cook on full power in 20 second bursts until the chocolate has all but melted.) Stir to combine evenly, then leave to cool to room temperature.

Put the egg yolks into the bowl of an electric mixer along with 150 g (5½ oz) of caster sugar and beat with the paddle attachment on high speed for around 5 minutes, or until thick and pale. Stir in the chocolate mixture, followed by the ground hazelnuts. Then stir in the amaretto.

Put the egg whites and salt into the bowl of an electric mixer and whisk until they start to froth. Then, with the motor running, scatter on the remaining 50 g (1¾ g) sugar and continue whisking to stiff, glossy peaks.

Add a large spoonful of meringue to the cake batter and mix in to slacken, then add the rest of the meringue and fold in gently but evenly, taking care not to lose volume.

Pour into the prepared cake tin and bake for 20 minutes, then turn the oven down to 160°C (320°F) fan-forced/180°C (350°F) and cook for a further 20–30 minutes. The cake will be ready when it starts to come away from the sides of the tin. Allow to cool in the tin before carefully turning out onto a wire rack set over a baking tray. The cake should be completely cold before icing.

To make the chocolate glaze, combine the chocolate, honey and butter in a small saucepan and heat gently, stirring from time to time, until the chocolate has completely melted. Remove from the heat and leave to cool to room temperature.

While the glaze cools, make the honey cream by whipping the cream together with the honey and orange blossom water to form stiff peaks. Mound the cream on top of the cake and use a small spatula to smooth it into a high rounded dome.

When you are happy that the glaze is the same temperature as the honey cream, pour it on very slowly and evenly, so it entirely covers the cream dome and the sides of the cake. Don't be tempted to rush this – or to use a spatula – or you won't achieve a smooth, glossy finish. Leave the cake for 1–2 hours to set the icing. Serve at room temperature, garnished with edible flowers, if using, and fresh berries, if you like.

See photo on pages 112–113.

CHOCOLATE SOUR CHERRY–SHERRY CAKE

A riff on a traditional French prune and Armagnac cake, this is rich, elegant and deceptively simple. It makes a lovely dessert, served warm or cold, on its own or with soft dollops of sherry-spiced cream.

For maximum flavour and plumptious texture, soak the dried cherries overnight, although a few hours will do.

SERVES 8–10

130 g (4½ oz) dried sour cherries
150 ml (5 fl oz) Pedro Ximénez sherry
250 g (9 oz) unsalted butter, cut
    into cubes, plus extra for greasing
250 g (9 oz) good-quality dark
    chocolate (60–70% cocoa solids),
    chopped or broken into small pieces
260 g (9 oz) eggs (around 4), separated
100 g (3½ oz) caster (superfine) sugar
100 g (3½ oz) light muscovado sugar
50 g (1¾ oz) plain (all-purpose)
    flour, sifted
50 g (1¾ oz) finely ground almonds
icing (confectioners') sugar,
    for dusting

SHERRY CREAM
reserved cherry-soaking liquid
    (see method)
300 ml (10 fl oz) thick (double/heavy)
    cream or crème fraîche
1 teaspoon icing (confectioners') sugar,
    or to taste

EQUIPMENT
23 cm (9 in) springform or loose-based
    cake tin

Soak the cherries in the sherry overnight. The following day, drain the cherries, reserving the sherry, and gently pat them dry on paper towel.

Preheat the oven to 150°C (300°F) fan-forced/170°C (340°F). Grease the springform or loose-based cake tin and line the base with baking paper. Grease the paper too.

Put the butter and chocolate in a bowl and place over a saucepan of barely simmering water, making sure the water doesn't touch the base of the bowl. Stir occasionally until the butter and chocolate have melted, then leave to cool slightly.

Put the egg yolks and sugars into the bowl of an electric mixer and beat with the paddle attachment on high speed for around 3 minutes, or until thick and pale. Scrape in the melted chocolate mixture and mix to combine evenly.

Sift on the flour, then add the almonds. Fold everything together evenly with a spoon or spatula.

Put the egg whites into the bowl of an electric mixer and whisk until they hold firm peaks.

Add a large spoonful of meringue to the cake batter and mix in to slacken, then add the rest of the meringue and fold in gently but evenly, taking care not to lose volume.

Pour half the cake batter into the prepared tin. Arrange the cherries over the surface, then spoon in the rest of the cake batter and smooth the surface lightly.

Bake for about 30 minutes, until the cake is only just set – it should still wobble slightly in the centre – then remove from the oven and leave to cool for about 15 minutes before unmoulding. Transfer to a wire rack and leave to cool completely. Dust with icing sugar just before serving.

For the sherry cream, simmer the reserved cherry-soaking liquid in a small saucepan until reduced by half, then allow to cool completely. Whip the cream to floppy peaks, then add icing sugar to taste. Swirl the reduced soaking liquid through the cream and serve alongside the cake.

LEBANESE LOVE CAKE

In recent years, Persian love cakes have had a big moment in the sun and Greg was amused by the idea of creating his very own Lebanese love cake. He wanted it to showcase some of the defining flavours of his childhood – cardamom, rose and, naturally, his favourite, lemon – and he wanted to pull out all the stops on the glamour front.

The cake itself is a moist lemon-scented white chocolate sponge and was inspired by a recipe from American baker Rose Levy Beranbaum. It's pretty straightforward to make, which is pleasing, given there are several other component parts to achieve as well. There's a lemon mousseline icing and Italian meringue for decorating. We add Mini meringue kisses (page 194) as an additional decoration, but you could buy or omit these if it's a step too far.

We're not going to pretend this cake isn't a bit of a labour of love, as well as a love song to Lebanon, but we think the results speak for themselves. It's visually stunning and, crucially, tastes divine. Lucy's husband, George, rates it as a 'more-than-two-slicer', which is praise indeed.

SERVES 10–12

WHITE CHOCOLATE–LEMON CAKE

170 g (6 oz) good-quality white chocolate, chopped or broken into small pieces

110 g (4 oz) egg yolks (around 5–6)

240 ml (8 fl oz) full-cream (whole) milk

finely grated zest of 1 large lemon

240 g (8½ oz) caster (superfine) sugar

300 g (10½ oz) plain (all-purpose) flour, sifted

4 teaspoons baking powder

¾ teaspoon fine sea salt

seeds from 25 cardamom pods, ground (or around ¾ teaspoon ground cardamom)

130 g (4½ oz) unsalted butter, softened, plus extra for greasing

120 g (4½ oz) good-quality ready-made rose-petal jam, for filling (or use sour cherry, or raspberry at a pinch)

1 teaspoon rosewater

Preheat the oven to 150°C (300°F) fan-forced/170°C (340°F). Grease and line the loose-based or springform cake tins, then grease the paper too.

Put the chocolate in a heatproof bowl and place over a saucepan of barely simmering water, making sure the water doesn't touch the base of the bowl. Stir occasionally until the chocolate has melted. (Alternatively, put it in a microwaveable container and cook on full power in 20 second bursts until the chocolate has all but melted.) Stir to combine evenly, then leave to cool to room temperature.

Use a fork or balloon whisk to mix the egg yolks with a third of the milk.

Rub the lemon zest into the sugar, to release the citrus oils and to stop the zest clumping. Put into the bowl of an electric mixer along with the flour, baking powder, salt and ground cardamom. Beat on low speed with the paddle attachment for 20 seconds. Add the butter and beat for another 20 seconds, then add the remaining milk and beat until it has been mostly absorbed by the dry ingredients. Increase the speed to medium and beat for a good minute. Scrape down the sides of the bowl.

Add the egg mixture in three batches, beating in well after each addition. Scrape down the sides of the bowl and add the melted white chocolate. Beat in evenly.

Divide the cake batter between the prepared cake tins. Use scales if you are pedantic, around 550 g (1 lb 3 oz) per tin. Bake in the lower third of the oven for 20–25 minutes. Once a skewer comes out clean and the cake springs back to the touch, remove from the oven and rest in the tins on a wire rack for 10 minutes. Run a spatula around the edge of the pans to loosen the cakes, then unmould them onto the wire rack, top-sides up, and leave to cool completely. Peel away the baking paper very carefully.

For the lemon mousseline, first combine the sugar and lemon zest in a small heatproof bowl and rub them together. Whisk in the eggs, then the lemon juice.

LEMON MOUSSELINE

125 g (4½ oz) caster (superfine) sugar
finely grated zest of 2 large lemons
115 g (4 oz) eggs (2 large)
90 ml (3 fl oz) lemon juice (1½ lemons)
220 g (8 oz) unsalted butter, softened
   and roughly chopped

ITALIAN MERINGUE TOPPING

100 g (3½ oz) caster (superfine) sugar
100 ml (3½ fl oz) water
90 g (3 oz) egg whites (around 2)

Decorate with your choice of
Mini meringue kisses (page 194)
fresh flower petals
dried raspberry powder
baby thyme leaves
blueberries or raspberries

EQUIPMENT

two 23 cm (9 in) loose-based or
   springform cake tins
sugar thermometer
piping bag with a 1.5 cm (½ in) nozzle
kitchen blowtorch

Set the bowl over a saucepan of barely simmering water, making sure the water doesn't touch the base of the bowl, and whisk until it reaches 83ºC (180ºF) on a sugar thermometer. Push through a fine-mesh sieve and cool to 60ºC (140ºF).

Measure 100 g (3½ oz) of the butter and drop it into the lemon emulsion in small pieces, mixing with a hand-held blender. Continue blending for 10 minutes to form a very smooth, pale lemon curd. Set aside at room temperature.

Put the remaining 120 g (4½ oz) butter in the bowl of an electric mixer. Whisk for 8 minutes, until very thick, pale and fluffy. Add a quarter of the lemon curd to the butter. Whisk in slowly, but thoroughly. Repeat in three more batches until all the curd is incorporated into the butter. Set aside.

It's easiest to ice and decorate this cake on a stand. First, warm the jam briefly to make it workable, then mix in the rosewater. If it is very stiff, you might need to add a squeeze of lime juice (or a splash of warm water) too. With a long serrated knife, carefully slice away the tops of each cake to even them, if need be, then slice each cake in half, crossways. Spread a generous layer of the jam onto the two bottom cake layers, then sandwich each with its top.

Carefully lift one cake onto the cake stand. (A large dinner plate or clean board can help with this.) Spread the surface with a thick layer of lemon mousseline, almost to the edges, then carefully lift the second cake on top and squeeze gently. Use a small spatula to ice the surface and sides of the cake thickly and evenly with the remaining mousseline. Refrigerate for 45 minutes for the mousseline to firm up.

Meanwhile, make the Italian meringue. Combine the sugar and water in a small saucepan. Heat gently to dissolve the sugar. Put the egg whites in the bowl of an electric mixer and whisk to stiff peaks. Use a sugar thermometer to measure the temperature of the syrup. When it reaches thread stage, at 120ºC (250ºF), pour it onto the egg whites in a slow, steady stream, whisking slowly all the time. Once incorporated, increase the motor speed to high. Whisk for around 8 minutes, or until the mixture cools completely. You will see it dramatically bulk up into a soft, fluffy mass. Spoon into the piping bag. Set aside.

Now comes the time to unleash your inner artist: you can exercise restraint, and limit your decoration to the top of the cake, or go wild and cover the sides, too. Pipe on little drops of meringue, holding the piping bag vertically above the baking tray. As you pipe, lift the nozzle straight up to form tiny peaks. Aim to pipe a range of sizes, ranging from 2–3.5 cm (¾–1½ in) in diameter.

Use a kitchen blowtorch to lightly brown the tops of the meringues, working quickly so you don't melt the mousseline icing. Complete the decoration by adding meringue kisses, fresh flowers, raspberry powder, thyme and some artfully arranged berries. Be sure to serve at room temperature so the sponge cake softens to optimum moist tenderness.

See photo on page 119.

BLOOD ORANGE STEAMED PUDDINGS

The blood orange season is all too short, but very welcome, coming as it does in the dreary depths of winter. Their lovely blush-red hue and more intensely sour and complex flavour works a treat in these mini steamed puddings, but of course you can use regular sweet oranges too.

MAKES 8

2 blood oranges
200 g (7 oz) orange marmalade
180 g (6½ oz) golden syrup or honey
    or light treacle
150 g (5½ oz) self-raising flour
75 g (2¾ oz) ground almonds
75 g (2¾ oz) golden caster
    (superfine) sugar
1 teaspoon bicarbonate of soda
    (baking soda)
seeds from 22 cardamom pods, ground
    (or a generous ½ teaspoon
    ground cardamom)
195 g (7 oz) eggs (around 3),
    lightly beaten
200 g (7 oz) Greek-style yoghurt
150 g (5½ oz) unsalted butter, melted,
    plus extra for greasing
75 g (2¾ oz) mild honey
chilled cream or custard, to serve

EQUIPMENT

eight 180 ml (6 fl oz) metal or
    heatproof plastic dariole moulds
    or small pudding basins

Preheat the oven to 160ºC (320ºF) fan-forced/180ºC (350ºF). Liberally butter the dariole moulds or small pudding basins.

Finely zest the blood oranges and mix the zest together with 2 tablespoons of the marmalade. Set aside.

With a sharp serrated knife, remove the remaining skin and all traces of pith from the oranges. Cut the oranges into fairly thick slices, crossways. Select eight that will fit snugly into the base of the moulds. Put 1 tablespoon each of the marmalade and golden syrup into the prepared dariole moulds and arrange the blood orange slices on top.

In a large mixing bowl, combine the flour, ground almonds, sugar, bicarb and cardamom. Mix together evenly.

Add the eggs, yoghurt, butter, honey and reserved marmalade and beat until evenly incorporated. Spoon the batter into the pudding basins to about three-quarters full, then sit them in a deep roasting tin.

Pour hot water (from the tap) into the tin, to come halfway up the sides of the moulds. Bake for 20–25 minutes. To test for doneness, insert a fine skewer and if it comes out clean, they are ready. If your moulds are ceramic, rather than metal, you may find they take longer, in which case return them to the oven and test again at 10 minute intervals. Once cooked through, remove the puddings from the oven and leave them in the water bath for 5 minutes to settle. Turn them out onto dessert plates and serve with chilled cream or custard.

+ ALSO SERVE WITH
    Middle Eastern clotted cream (page 32)
    Cream cheese ice cream (page 61)

CARAMELISED APPLE AND BLACKBERRY EVE'S PUDDING

Eve's pudding is an English classic that Lucy remembers well from her childhood. Now she lives in Kent – the garden of England – where she is surrounded by fruit orchards and the hedgerows are dense with wild blackberries, and this pudding just begs to be made. Our version is darker and more intensely caramelised than is traditional, but makes the very best of an English autumn.

SERVES 6

50 g (1¾ oz) unsalted butter, plus extra
    for greasing
50 g (1¾ oz) soft brown sugar
juice of 1 orange
1.25 kg (2 lb 12 oz) tart apples, peeled,
    cored and chopped into chunks
½ teaspoon ground cinnamon
200 g (7 oz) ripe blackberries
icing (confectioners') sugar,
    for dusting
pouring (single/light) cream,
    to serve

BROWN BUTTER SPONGE TOPPING

100 g (3½ oz) unsalted butter
80 ml (2½ fl oz) buttermilk
1 large egg
150 g (5½ oz) sponge or plain
    (all-purpose) flour
2 teaspoons baking powder
100 g (3½ oz) caster (superfine) sugar
1 teaspoon vanilla extract
zest of 1 orange
1 teaspoon cornflour (cornstarch)
80 g (2¾ oz) soft brown sugar
250 ml (8½ fl oz) boiling water

EQUIPMENT

2 litre (68 fl oz) baking dish

Preheat the oven to 160°C (320°F) fan-forced/180°C (350°F) and liberally butter the baking dish.

Make a start with the brown butter sponge topping. Add the butter to a large frying pan and cook over a medium heat for around 2 minutes until nut brown. Tip out of the pan and leave to cool.

Now move on to preparing the fruit. Add the 50 g (1¾ oz) butter to the frying pan and cook over a medium–high heat until sizzling. Add the sugar and cook for around 5 minutes, stirring, until it turns to a medium-dark caramel, then add the orange juice and simmer for 2 minutes. Add the apple chunks and cinnamon and turn them around in the caramel. Simmer for 6–8 minutes, or until the apple pieces are caramelised and tender. (The exact time will depend on your apples, with cooking apples softening faster than a hard eater, such as a granny smith – you want the fruit to be starting to break down, but not become mushy.)

Pile the apples and caramel sauce into the prepared baking dish and stud with the blackberries. Set aside.

To complete the topping, combine the reserved brown butter with the buttermilk and egg in a large mixing bowl and whisk together. Sift the flour and baking powder together in a separate bowl and mix in the sugar. Whisk this into the egg mixture, together with the vanilla and orange zest, to form a smooth batter.

Spoon the topping onto the apple-blackberry mixture and spread it out evenly. Sift on the cornflour evenly. Dissolve the brown sugar in the boiling water and pour it carefully over the topping.

Bake for 45–55 minutes, or until the pudding is darkly golden and slightly puffed. Remove from the oven and dust with icing sugar. Serve straight away with runny cream.

+ ALSO SERVE WITH
    Middle Eastern clotted cream (page 32)
    Cream cheese ice cream (page 61)

CHOCOLATE FONDANT PUDDING CAKES WITH TURKISH DELIGHT

Hot chocolate puddings are hard to resist and this recipe, with a hidden cache of softly melting Turkish delight jewels, is one of the first to vanish whenever Greg includes it on the menu.

There's no avoiding the fact that, for molten perfection, you need to use the correct kind of mould (metal, for even heat distribution) and you need to be extremely well acquainted with your oven. We recommend baking a sacrificial test pudding – or even baking a whole batch as a trial run – to check temperature and timings. But once you've cracked it, you'll have a speedy and impressive dessert recipe on hand to wow dinner guests. You can prepare the batter up to six hours ahead of time: fill the moulds, cover with plastic wrap and refrigerate, then bake them straight from the fridge, adding another minute to the cooking time.

We like to serve these puds with crème fraîche or Cream cheese ice cream (page 61), as the slight sourness offsets the richness.

MAKES 8

150 g (5½ oz) unsalted butter, plus
    extra for greasing
130 g (4½ oz) good-quality dark
    chocolate (50–60% cocoa solids),
    chopped or broken into small pieces
250 g (9 oz) eggs (around 5)
160 g (5½ oz) caster (superfine) sugar
2 teaspoons vanilla extract
65 g (2¼ oz) sponge or plain
    (all-purpose) flour
ice cream, chilled crème fraîche or
    whipped cream, to serve

TURKISH DELIGHT 'JEWELS'

1 tablespoon icing (confectioners'
    sugar)
1 tablespoon cornflour (cornstarch)
100 g (3½ oz) orange blossom or
    pistachio Turkish delight

EQUIPMENT

eight 6.9 × 6 cm (2¾ × 2½ in) metal
    timbale or dariole moulds

For the Turkish delight 'jewels', combine the icing sugar and cornflour in a bowl. Cut each piece of Turkish delight in half. Roll it out on your work surface into a long skinny snake, around 5 mm (¼ in) thick. Cut into little coins, dust lightly with the icing sugar mixture, then set aside.

Preheat the oven to 160°C (320°F) fan-forced/180°C (350°F). Liberally grease the metal timbale or dariole moulds.

Put the butter and chocolate in a heatproof bowl and place over a saucepan of barely simmering water, making sure the water doesn't touch the base of the bowl. Stir occasionally until the butter and chocolate have melted. (Alternatively, put them in a microwaveable container and cook on full power in 20 second bursts until the chocolate has all but melted.) Stir to combine evenly, then leave to cool slightly.

Combine the eggs, sugar and vanilla extract in the bowl of an electric mixer and beat with the paddle attachment until very pale and fluffy, about 5 minutes.

Sift on the flour and fold it in gently by hand. Now add the cooled chocolate mixture and fold in gently and evenly. Finally, fold in 90 g (3 oz) of the Turkish delight jewels, reserving the rest for later.

Spoon the batter into the prepared moulds to about three-quarters full, then sit them on a large baking tray.

Bake for 7½ minutes, or until they are puffed, and the surface springs back when lightly pressed. Remove from the oven and leave to rest for 1½ minutes. Use a small knife to run around the sides, then turn the puddings out onto dessert plates, decorate with extra jewels of Turkish delight and serve straight away with ice cream, chilled crème fraîche or whipped cream.

+ ALSO SERVE WITH
    Rose jam ice cream (page 57)
    Cream cheese ice cream (page 61)

LABNE CHEESECAKE WITH CITRUS-SCENTED BLUEBERRIES

A light, lemony cheesecake that's set with gelatine rather than baked. This gives it a soft, silky texture, rather than the damp, mouth-sticking creaminess of the baked kind. It makes a lovely summertime dessert, especially when topped with a tumble of citrusy blueberries.

SERVES 8–10

BASE
150 g (5½ oz) ginger nut biscuits
   (ginger snaps)
80 g (2¾ oz) wheaten (digestive)
   biscuits
110 g (4 oz) unsalted butter, melted,
   plus extra for greasing

LABNE FILLING
110 g (4 oz) unsalted butter, softened
220 g (8 oz) caster (superfine) sugar
3 eggs, separated
250 g (9 oz) cream cheese, beaten
   with a fork until very smooth
350 g (12½ oz) labne (page 244)
finely grated zest and juice of 2 lemons
250 ml (8½ fl oz) thick (double/heavy)
   cream
8 small gelatine leaves (see Cook's
   notes, page 243)

CITRUS-SCENTED BLUEBERRIES
350 g (12½ oz) blueberries
75 g (2¾ oz) icing (confectioners')
   sugar
finely grated zest of 1 orange and juice
   of ½ orange
finely grated zest and juice of 1 lime

EQUIPMENT
23 cm (9 in) springform or loose-based
   cake tin

Grease the springform or loose-based cake tin and line the base of the tin with baking paper.

To make the base, put the ginger biscuits in the bowl of a food processor and blitz to medium-fine crumbs. Tip out into a mixing bowl and blitz the digestive biscuits to medium-fine crumbs. (Alternatively, put the biscuits into a plastic bag and whack them with a rolling pin.) Stir the melted butter into the crushed biscuits. Tip into the prepared tin and press in firmly and evenly.

To make the filling, combine the butter and sugar in the bowl of an electric mixer and beat with the paddle attachment for around 4 minutes, or until very pale and fluffy. Add the egg yolks, one at a time, incorporating each one thoroughly before you add the next. Add spoonfuls of cream cheese, beating it in well, then beat in the labne, followed by the lemon zest and juice. Set aside.

Pour 100 ml (3½ fl oz) of the cream into a small saucepan and bring to a simmer.

Soak the gelatine in cold water for a few minutes until softened. Squeeze out the excess liquid and add the gelatine to the hot cream, stirring to dissolve completely. Leave to cool to room temperature, but not for too long, or the gelatine will begin to set and become unworkable.

Meanwhile, whisk the rest of the cream to medium-stiff peaks. Whisk the egg whites to stiff peaks in a separate bowl.

When the gelatine mixture has cooled a little, stir it into the filling mixture. Using a large metal spoon, fold in the cream followed by the egg whites. Pour the filling into the tin and bang it on the work surface a few times to allow the air bubbles to rise to the surface and burst. Refrigerate for around 4 hours, until set.

For the citrus-scented blueberries, combine all the ingredients in a mixing bowl and tumble together well. Spoon on top of the cheesecake just before serving.

See photo on pages 126–127.

BAKED MAPLE-APPLE CHEESECAKE

Apples make a surprising, and very successful, appearance in this delectable cheesecake. The autumn flavours are further enhanced by the golden maple topping and by the use of ginger, which makes a double appearance, both in the biscuit base and in the apple filling.

SERVES 10–12

Dried apple wafers (page 224) or
　Sesame brittle (page 207) to serve
　(optional)
pouring (single/light) cream, to serve

BASE
150 g (5½ oz) ginger nut biscuits
　(ginger snaps)
50 g (1¾ oz) unsalted butter, melted,
　plus extra for greasing

APPLE FILLING
4 small granny smith apples, peeled,
　cored and thinly sliced
40 g (1½ oz) caster (superfine) sugar
zest of 1 lime and juice of ½ lime
5 eggs, lightly whisked
140 g (5 oz) caster (superfine) sugar
100 g (3½ oz) mild-flavoured honey
3 knobs stem ginger or crystallised
　ginger
30 ml (1 fl oz) Calvados (optional)
600 g (1 lb 5 oz) cream cheese
200 g (7 oz) mascarpone

MAPLE TOPPING
200 g (7 oz) sour cream
60 ml (2 fl oz) maple syrup

EQUIPMENT
23 cm (9 in) springform or loose-based
　cake tin

Preheat the oven to 160°C (320°F) fan-forced/180°C (350°F). Grease the springform or loose-based cake tin and line the base with baking paper.

To make the base, put the ginger biscuits in the bowl of a food processor and blitz to medium-fine crumbs. (Alternatively, put the biscuits into a plastic bag and whack them with a rolling pin.) Add the melted butter slowly to combine. Tip into the prepared tin and press it in firmly and evenly. Put in the oven for 15 minutes to par-bake while you make the filling. When you take the base out of the oven, lower the oven temperature to 140°C (275°F) fan-forced/160°C (320°F).

For the filling, heat a large frying pan over a medium–high heat. Toss the apples together with the sugar, lime zest and juice in a bowl, then tip into the pan and cook for around 5 minutes, shaking frequently, until the apples are beginning to soften and turn translucent. Tip onto a plate and set aside.

Combine the eggs and sugar in the bowl of an electric mixer and whisk together for 3–4 minutes until pale and smooth. Add the honey, stem ginger and Calvados, if using, and whisk in gently to combine.

Put the cream cheese and mascarpone into a large mixing bowl and beat them together with a wooden spoon until smooth and creamy. Add a large spoonful of the whisked egg mixture and mix it in to slacken. Add the rest of the egg mixture and use a large balloon whisk to whisk everything together gently, but evenly.

Arrange the apple slices evenly over the cheesecake base. Pour in the filling and shake the tin gently to pop any bubbles. Lift onto a baking tray and bake for 1 hour 20 minutes, or until set, but still a little soft and wobbly in the centre.

Whisk together the maple topping ingredients and pour carefully over the cheesecake. Smooth the surface gently, then cook for a further 10 minutes. Turn off the oven and prop the door slightly ajar with the handle of a wooden spoon. Leave well alone until the cheesecake has cooled completely.

Once cold, remove the cheesecake from the oven and refrigerate in the tin until ready to serve. Bring to room temperature for 20 minutes before unmoulding. Garnish with the apple wafers or sesame brittle (or both!) and serve with a dribble of runny cream.

CANDIED PUMPKIN CHEESECAKE

Pumpkin (squash) is generally considered a vegetable, but its high level of natural sugars means it lends itself well to desserts, too. The Americans understand this very well, as evidenced by the ubiquitous pumpkin pie at Thanksgiving dinners – albeit that many recipes use an overly heavy hand with the spice jar.

Well, Middle Easterners love pumpkin too! It is often served as a dessert or as a sweetmeat, candied in sugar syrup until it is gorgeously translucent. We worked with that idea to develop this wonderfully subtle and ethereally light-textured cheesecake, and we reckon it might convert even the most devoted pumpkin pie lover!

SERVES 8

butter, for greasing
Candied walnuts (page 206),
   to decorate (optional)

FILLING

1 butternut pumpkin (squash), peeled,
   seeds and stringy bits removed
50 g (1¾ oz) unsalted butter
50 g (1¾ oz) light soft brown sugar
200 g (7 oz) mascarpone
125 g (4½ oz) crème fraîche
70 g (2½ oz) mild feta, crumbled
2 large eggs, separated
1½ tablespoons honey

BASE

50 g (1¾ oz) walnut halves
150 g (5½ oz) ginger nut biscuits
   (ginger snaps)
80 g (2¾ oz) unsalted butter, melted

CINNAMON SUGAR

1 tablespoon icing (confectioners')
   sugar
½ teaspoon ground cinnamon

EQUIPMENT

23 cm (9 in) springform or
   loose-based cake tin

Preheat the oven to 160°C (320°F) fan-forced/180°C (350°F). Butter the springform or loose-based cake tin and line it with baking paper.

For the filling, weigh out 700 g (1 lb 9 oz) of peeled butternut pumpkin and cut it into large chunks. Reserve the rest for another recipe.

Melt the butter and half of the sugar in a medium roasting tin. Add the pumpkin to the pan and toss to coat. Bake for 30–40 minutes, or until the pumpkin is very tender. Toss every now and then to ensure even cooking, and if it looks as if it's browning, lower the oven temperature; you want it to be soft and translucent, not crisp and brown.

Cool the pumpkin briefly then tip into a food processor, together with any remaining juices from the roasting tin, and blitz to a very smooth purée. Scrape into a sieve set over a sink or bowl and leave to drain and cool completely. Refrigerate until needed. (You can prepare the pumpkin a day ahead of time, which has the benefit of concentrating the flavour – discard any liquid that separates out from the flesh before using.)

To make the cheesecake base, spread the walnuts out on a small baking tray and toast in the oven at 160°C (320°F) fan-forced/180°C (350°F) for 8–10 minutes, or until they are darkening. Let them cool, then tip into a food processor and blitz to coarse, rather chunky crumbs. Take care not to over-process them. Tip into a mixing bowl.

Put the ginger biscuits into the food processor and blitz to medium-fine crumbs. (Alternatively, put the biscuits into a plastic bag and whack them with a rolling pin.) Add them to the walnuts, then stir in the melted butter evenly. Tip into the prepared tin and press it in firmly and evenly. Put in the oven for 15 minutes to par-bake.

While the base is par-baking, finish the filling. Combine the mascarpone, crème fraîche, feta, egg yolks and honey in a food processor and blitz together until evenly blended. Mix in the pumpkin purée, just until evenly combined.

Put the egg whites into the bowl of an electric mixer and whisk until they start to froth. Then, with the motor running, scatter over the rest of the sugar and continue whisking to medium-stiff, glossy peaks.

Add a large spoonful of meringue to the pumpkin filling and mix in to slacken. Add the rest of the meringue and fold in gently but evenly with a large metal spoon, taking care not to lose volume.

Remove the base from the oven and lower the oven temperature to 140°C (275°F) fan-forced/160°C (320°F). Pour the filling into the tin and bake for around 40 minutes, or until the cheesecake is set, but still a little soft and wobbly in the centre. Turn off the oven and prop the door slightly ajar with the handle of a wooden spoon. Leave well alone until the cheesecake has cooled completely. This should help to prevent the surface cracking, but it is not the end of the world if this does happen.

Once the cheesecake is completely cold, carefully remove it from the tin. Refrigerate until ready to serve, bringing to room temperature 20 minutes before eating.

For the cinnamon sugar, mix together the icing sugar and cinnamon and sift over the cheesecake just before serving. Finish with candied walnut halves, if using.

See photo on pages 132–133.

PASTRIES AND TARTS

If you ask the average Westerner to name a Middle Eastern dessert, there's a strong chance the reply will be baklava. Which is ironic, considering the baklava family of sweet pastries is never actually eaten as dessert. In truth, these syrupy, nut-stuffed flaky delights are considered more as a treat. They're saved for special occasions – often religious festivals – and for entertaining. It would be unthinkable not to bring an exquisitely wrapped box of pastries as a gift when visiting, and likewise, no household would invite guests without offering these delicacies alongside strong cardamom-scented coffee.

Middle Eastern pastries are predominantly made from layers of translucent filo with fillings made from ground nuts (almonds, pistachios and walnuts are all popular) and are drenched in a floral-scented syrup. Some pastries use kadaifi, a shredded version of filo. The virtue of both of these is that you won't have to make them yourself. Nonetheless, quality is all-important and, depending on where you live, you may only have access to a supermarket variety (which may well be frozen, rather than fresh). This is your bad luck, as mass-manufactured filo will not provide the same results as the finer, fresher small-batch filo that you find in Middle Eastern grocers. Unhelpfully, filo comes in different sizes, too. The ones we have used for our recipes are around 48 × 25 cm (19 × 10 in). If yours are different, you may need to adapt by trimming to size.

In this chapter you'll find a selection of Middle Eastern pastries, many with an unusual twist. We've also included some tarts and pies using our other favourite pastries: puff, sweet shortcrust and choux. While we recommend buying a good-quality butter puff, our shortcrust recipes are all utterly simple to knock up in a food processor.

Each recipe has specific instructions, but here are our top tips for making pastry: use chilled butter and pulse it into the dry ingredients in short bursts, just until things clump together. Rest and chill the pastry each time it's handled, once after making and then again after rolling out and lining the tin. To account for shrinkage, leave an overhang of pastry and don't trim the edges until after blind baking (see page 246). To keep your base crisp, brush it with a little egg white after blind baking, then return it to the oven for a few minutes to seal.

As well as a range of different sized tart tins (ideally with removable bases), you'll need a rolling pin, a pastry brush and baking beans.

ZNOUD EL SIT

Znoud el sit translates, rather evocatively, to 'ladies' upper arms'. They are delightfully plump little fried pastry rolls, with a crunchy outer layer and a thick clotted-cream stuffing, and come drenched in orange blossom syrup. They are a popular treat at Iftar (the post-sunset meal) during the month of Ramadan and it's easy to imagine how dangerously addictive they might be after a day of fasting. The addition of orange juice to the cream filling is a Greg variation, and it adds pleasing colour and an extra flavour dimension – but if you want to be a purist, replace the juice with milk. Znoud are best eaten hot from the fryer.

Znoud el sit come in varying sizes, but we tend to prefer smaller versions – perhaps because you don't feel so greedy eating more than one. Filo pastry sheets also come in various dimensions and for our znoud, we used 48 × 25 cm (19 × 10 in) sheets, cut to 13 × 8 cm (5 × 3¼ in) pastry strips. Depending on the size of your filo sheets, you may need to adapt our instructions to achieve similar-sized strips.

MAKES 24

4 sheets filo pastry (see our note on
  page 135)
sunflower or vegetable oil,
  for deep-frying
orange blossom jam or Candied orange
  zest (page 220), to serve (optional)
pistachio slivers (we use Iranian),
  to serve (optional)

BLOOD ORANGE CREAM
250 ml (8½ fl oz) blood orange juice
250 ml (8½ fl oz) thickened
  (whipping) cream
30 g (1 oz) cornflour (cornstarch)
100 g (3½ oz) caster (superfine) sugar
1 teaspoon rosewater
1 teaspoon orange blossom water

FLOWER WATER SYRUP
275 g (9½ oz) caster (superfine) sugar
185 ml (6 fl oz) water
1 teaspoon lemon juice
1½ teaspoons orange blossom water
1 teaspoon rosewater

EQUIPMENT
piping bag fitted with a 1 cm (½ in)
  nozzle

To make the blood orange cream, combine all the ingredients, except for the flower waters, in a saucepan and whisk well to dissolve the cornflour. Turn on the heat to low and cook, whisking all the time, for about 8 minutes, until the cream thickens to a custard consistency. Cool to room temperature, then add the flower waters. Chill for at least 1 hour, or up to a day ahead of time. It will set firm in the fridge.

To make the syrup, combine the sugar, water and lemon juice in a small saucepan and heat gently, stirring from time to time, until the sugar has dissolved. Once the liquid is clear, bring to the boil, then lower the heat and simmer briskly for 10 minutes. Remove from the heat and allow to cool, then stir in the flower waters and set aside. The syrup will keep in a sealed container in the fridge for up to 1 month.

To prepare the pastry strips, lay the filo sheets on top of each other on a very lightly floured work surface. Cut this stack in half lengthways and then place one stack on top of the other. Now cut the whole stack into six even portions. You should end up with a total of 48 pastry strips, each about 13 × 8 cm (5 × 3¼ in) in size. Keep them covered with a damp cloth.

To assemble the znoud, work with two strips of pastry at a time. Lay one strip vertically in front of you on the work surface and place the second across it horizontally, forming a fat little cross. Aim to get them crossing as neatly and evenly as you can. Now use a spoon – or preferably a piping bag – to place a sausage-shaped portion of blood orange cream in the centre, where the pastry intersects. It should stretch horizontally from edge to edge of the pastry strip. Fold in the exposed side sections of the pastry cross neatly, just so they cover the ends of the cream. Use a wet finger to moisten both ends of the two remaining exposed pastry sections. Fold in the one that is closest to you, then keep on rolling up and over the filling, away from you, to create a plump pastry roll. Use a little more water to seal the seams. Repeat with the remaining pastry strips and cream to make a total of 24 znoud. Keep them covered with a damp cloth.

When ready to fry the znoud, pour oil into a heavy-based saucepan or deep-fryer to a depth of around 10 cm (4 in) and heat to 160°C (320°F). If you don't have a thermometer, the oil will have reached temperature when it is shimmering and when a small cube of bread sizzles up to the surface in 20–30 seconds. At the same time, bring the flower water syrup to a slow simmer.

Fry the znoud in batches of six, for 3–4 minutes, or until golden, rolling them around in the oil so they colour evenly. Lift out with a slotted spoon onto paper towel. Remove the flower water syrup from the heat, then transfer the znoud to the hot syrup for a few minutes. Don't allow the syrup to cool.

Serve the znoud piping hot, garnished with orange blossom jam, or candied orange and pistachios if you feel fancy.

See photo on page 138.

GREG'S SCRUNCHY CIGARS

Baklava is a many-splendoured thing: every country from the Maghreb to the Middle East has its own version of these nutty, syrupy pastries. They are variously shaped as lozenges, rolls, nests or cigars (to name but a few). Some favour ground pistachios as a filling, others ground almonds or walnuts. Sometimes a touch of cinnamon is included with the nuts, or honey is added to the syrup. There are endless small variations, but these scrunchy cigar baklava are one of Greg's favourites. And yes, we know it's a lot of syrup, but they drink it up!

MAKES 32

150 g (5½ oz) whole blanched
    almonds, very roughly chopped
150 g (5½ oz) pistachio nuts
½ teaspoon ground cinnamon
½ teaspoon ground ginger
butter, for greasing
8 sheets filo pastry (the dimensions
    are not critical here, but see our note
    on page 135)
100 g (3½ oz) clarified butter
    (page 241)
2 tablespoons finely ground pistachio
    nuts, to decorate

ORANGE BLOSSOM SYRUP

500 g (1 lb 2 oz) caster
    (superfine) sugar
350 ml (12 fl oz) water
1 cinnamon stick
1 vanilla bean, split lengthways
    and seeds scraped
2 teaspoons orange blossom water

EQUIPMENT

long metal skewers

To make the syrup, combine the sugar and water in a small saucepan and heat gently, stirring from time to time, until the sugar has dissolved. Once the liquid is clear, bring to the boil, then add the cinnamon and vanilla bean and seeds and simmer briskly for 10 minutes. Remove from the heat and allow to cool, then stir in the orange blossom water. The syrup will keep in a sealed container in the fridge for up to 1 month.

For the baklava, first put all the nuts and spices in a food processor and pulse to the texture of coarse wet sand. Be careful not to over-process.

Preheat the oven to 140°C (275°F) fan-forced/160°C (320°F). Lightly grease a large heavy-based baking tray.

Stack four sheets of filo pastry on a very lightly floured work surface, long sides in front of you, brushing each liberally with clarified butter as you go. Keep the remaining four sheets covered with a damp cloth. Cut the stack crossways into eight strips, each around 6 cm (2½ in) wide and brush with more butter. Sprinkle a line of the nut mixture along the length of each strip.

Working with one strip at a time, place a metal skewer along its length and roll the pastry around it tightly. Push the ends together to create a scrunched effect. Carefully pull out the skewer and place the cigar on the prepared baking tray. Repeat with the remaining strips to make a total of 8 long cigars. Try to get them all the same length, around 18 cm (7 in). Then repeat the process with the reserved four filo sheets to make another 8 cigars, for a grand total of 16.

Brush all the cigars with more clarified butter and bake for around 30 minutes. Increase the oven temperature to 155°C (310°F) fan-forced/175°C (345°F) and cook the cigars for a further 10 minutes, or until crisp and golden brown.

While the cigars are baking, fish the cinnamon stick and vanilla bean out of the syrup (keep the vanilla bean to perfume your sugar canister) and gently reheat it. Increase the heat to a vigorous bubble just before the cigars come out of the oven.

Remove the tray of pastries from the oven and place over a medium heat on your stove top. Heat for 10 seconds then pour on the boiling syrup until all the cigars are drenched.

Remove from the heat and allow to cool to room temperature (do not refrigerate). To serve, trim the ends neatly with a serrated knife, cut the cigars in half to make 32 pieces and sprinkle with crushed pistachio nuts.

BAY-BUTTERSCOTCH BAKLAVA WITH CARAMEL PEARS

Over the years, ice cream baklavas have become a bit of signature dish for Greg. They make a hugely appealing and attractive dessert – essentially a kind of filo pastry ice cream sandwich – and are infinitely versatile as you can vary their shape and the flavour of ice cream depending on your whim. This incarnation uses our current favourite, salted bay-butterscotch, with pear caramel as a harmonious accompaniment.

There are three things to note. First, the total number of filo sheets required will depend on how fine it is; some varieties are noticeably thicker than others. Better-quality filo is usually finer and more delicate and you will therefore need more sheets to create sufficiently robust outer layers for sandwiching.

Second, you can make your baklava in any shape you like. We have made triangles here, but diamonds or rectangles are equally attractive – and probably more straightforward to cut. You'll need to do some basic geometry to work out how many portions you can cut from your filo sheets. We used a stack of 48 × 25 cm (19 × 10 in) sheets from which we cut sixteen triangles, each around 10 cm (4 in).

And finally, once you know the size of your individual portions, you can calculate the size of the container to set your ice cream in. We used a shallow dish roughly half the dimensions of the filo (24 × 20 cm/9½ × 8 in) so we could cut out eight ice cream triangles.

SERVES 8 (OR MORE)

1 × Salted bay-butterscotch ice cream (page 60)
7–12 sheets filo pastry, depending on thickness (see our note on page 135)
60 g (2 oz) clarified butter (page 241)
Pistachio dust (page 73) (optional)

HONEY-CINNAMON SYRUP

200 g (7 oz) caster (superfine) sugar
80 g (2¾ oz) honey
125 ml (4 fl oz) water
2 cinnamon sticks
strip of peel from ½ lemon
1 teaspoon rosewater

CARAMEL PEARS

2 perfectly ripe, small pears
juice of ½ lime
100 g (3½ oz) caster (superfine) sugar
80 ml (2½ fl oz) water
40 ml (1¼ fl oz) apple juice

EQUIPMENT

shallow dish (see introduction for dimensions)
water spray bottle

First, make the ice cream. Line the shallow dish with plastic wrap and set the ice cream in it. Once the ice cream has set hard, tip it out of the dish, wrap tightly with extra plastic wrap and return to the freezer.

To make the syrup, combine the sugar, honey and water in a small saucepan and heat gently, stirring from time to time, until the sugar has dissolved. Once the liquid is clear, bring to the boil, then lower the heat, add the cinnamon sticks and lemon peel and simmer briskly for 3 minutes. Remove from the heat and allow to cool, then stir in the rosewater. The syrup will keep in a sealed container in the fridge for up to 1 month.

When ready to make the filo pastry layers, preheat the oven to 160°C (320°F) fan-forced/180°C (350°F). Line two large baking trays with silicone baking mats or baking paper.

Start stacking the filo sheets neatly on a very lightly floured work surface, brushing with clarified butter as you go. Use a very sharp knife to trim around 5 cm (2 in) from one long edge of the pastry stack. Now cut the pastry stack lengthwise, creating two long strips, each around 48 × 10 cm (19 × 4 in). Cut each strip into eight nearly-equilateral triangles, giving a total of sixteen.

Carefully transfer the pastry triangles to the prepared baking trays – eight per tray – and spray lightly with water. Pop the trays into the centre of the oven. Bake for 30 minutes. The pastry should turn golden brown and puff up a bit.

Just before the end of the baking time, strain the syrup and gently reheat it, increasing the heat to a vigorous bubble just before the pastry comes out of the oven.

Pour a generous slug of boiling syrup over each tray of pastry as it comes hot from the oven. Leave the pastry to cool down completely.

To prepare the caramel pears, peel, core and cut them into 2 cm (¾ in) wedges or dice. Toss with the lime juice and set aside. Combine the sugar and water in a small saucepan and heat gently, stirring from time to time, until the sugar has dissolved. Once the liquid is clear, bring to the boil, then lower the heat and simmer briskly for 4–5 minutes to a honey-coloured caramel. Throw the pears into the pan along with the apple juice and keep warm.

To assemble, remove the block of ice cream from the freezer and sit it on a clean chopping board. Remove the plastic wrap. Arrange eight of the pastry triangles on the surface of the ice cream and use a very sharp knife to cut the ice cream to shape. Dip the knife in a jug of boiling water as you work to make the job easier.

Invert the ice cream and pastry triangles onto dessert plates and place another pastry triangle on top of each to complete the sandwich. Serve straight away (standing the sandwiches up on the plate is an impressive way to present the dish) with the caramel pears alongside. Sprinkle with pistachio dust, if using.

See photo on page 144.

MOROCCAN GIANT SNAKE

This almond-filled Moroccan pastry is known as *m'hannsah* – or giant snake – for obvious reasons. It makes a wonderful pull-apart pastry for afternoon tea – ideally you'd want that to be fresh mint tea. We also like to serve it as a dessert, maybe accompanied by a fruit compote or some summer berries.

The dimensions of your filo sheets are not critical here, but see our note on page 135 about quality.

The rolling up is easier if you have a helper standing by, as it's tricky to get it even if you're on your own. Another useful tip is to bake the pastry in a cake tin, which provides support and helps maintain the coiled shape in the oven. But if you find it easier, bake it free-form on a baking tray.

SERVES 8–10

butter, for greasing
8 sheets filo pastry, plus 1 extra for
    patching
75 g (2¾ oz) clarified butter (page 241)

ROSE-LIME SYRUP
300 g (10½ oz) caster (superfine)
    sugar
150 ml (5 fl oz) water
juice of 1 lime
2 tablespoons rosewater

GROUND ALMOND FILLING
175 g (6 oz) softened unsalted butter
100 g (3½ oz) icing (confectioners')
    sugar
130 g (4½ oz) eggs (around 2)
160 g (5½ oz) ground almonds
seeds from 30 cardamom pods, ground
    (or 1 teaspoon ground cardamom)
1 teaspoon grated nutmeg
1 teaspoon ground cinnamon
1½ tablespoons plain (all-purpose)
    flour
zest of 1 lime
20 ml (¾ fl oz) rosewater

EQUIPMENT
23 cm (9 in) springform or loose-based
    cake tin

Preheat the oven to 160°C (320°F) fan-forced/180°C (350°F). Grease the springform or loose-based cake tin and lift the base out of the tin.

For the syrup, combine the sugar and water in a small saucepan and heat gently, stirring from time to time, until the sugar has dissolved. Once the liquid is clear, bring to the boil, then simmer briskly for 10 minutes. Remove from the heat and allow to cool, then stir in the lime juice and rosewater. The syrup will keep in a sealed container in the fridge for up to 1 month.

To make the ground almond filling, combine the butter and icing sugar in the bowl of an electric mixer and beat with the paddle attachment for around 5 minutes, or until very pale and smooth. Add the eggs, little by little, ensuring that each amount is incorporated thoroughly before you add more. With the mixer on low speed, mix in the ground almonds and spices, followed by the flour, lime zest and rosewater. Set aside until required.

To assemble the snake you need a large expanse of clear, clean and very lightly floured work surface. Lay out the eight sheets of filo pastry, short sides towards you, so that they overlap by about 4–5 centimetres (1½–2 inches). Brush them with clarified butter as you go, paying particular attention to the overlap.

Dollop large spoonfuls of the almond mixture along the entire length of the pastry, leaving a clear 8 cm (3¼ in) margin at the edge closest to you and a 10 cm (4 in) margin on each side. Now fold the sides in over the filling, then lift the bottom edge of pastry up and over the filling to enclose it completely. Tuck and smooth it, so it covers the filling neatly with no air pockets. This is the point where you need a helper. Working in perfect sync, roll away from you to form a long snake, keeping everything tucked in nice and tight, so that the resulting snake is neat and tidy.

Working gently, start coiling the roll from one end, using the curved palm of your hand to gently shape it into a neat spiral. It's very fragile, but don't panic if the pastry splits – you can patch it with spare bits of filo and melted butter, if need be. Once the whole thing is coiled up, ease it gently onto the loose base of your cake tin, then carefully lower it into the tin.

Sit the cake tin on a baking tray and bake for 40–50 minutes, or until the pastry colours a rich golden brown.

While the snake is baking, gently reheat the syrup, increasing the heat to a vigorous bubble just before the snake comes out of the oven.

Pour the boiling syrup over the surface of the snake. You want it to be thoroughly drenched. Return to the oven for a further 5 minutes.

Cool the snake in its tin on a wire rack. Unmould just before serving warm or at room temperature.

See photo on page 145.

+ ALSO SERVE WITH
Blackberry-nectarine compote (page 48)

KUNAFA WITH APRICOT AND SWEET CHEESE

Kunafa is the Lebanese pastry that Greg dreams about – a sublime combination of softly yielding white cheese, crisp kadaifi pastry and perfumed syrup – and it's always the first thing he hurries out to eat when he visits Beirut. Kunafa is served at any time of the day, as a snack or dessert, but Greg likes it best for breakfast with a strong cup of coffee alongside.

In the Middle East, kunafa is made with akawi cheese, a semi-hard white cheese in salty brine. It needs to be soaked for at least 6 hours – preferably overnight – with several changes of water, before being rinsed and soaked in milk for 30 minutes, so you are left with only the barest residual salt tang. Good-quality fresh mozzarella makes a reasonable substitute and doesn't need to be soaked.

This is a modern interpretation of kunafa that Greg serves as a restaurant dessert in individually baked portions. It includes a hint of apricot jam, which works superbly with the slightly savoury melty cheese, and always sells out in a flash. For individual portions you will need mini cast-iron skillets (or rösti pans), otherwise, make a larger version in a heavy, ovenproof non-stick frying pan.

SERVES 8–10

butter, for greasing
250 g (9 oz) kadaifi pastry
100 g (3½ oz) clarified butter
   (page 241)
400 g (14 oz) Easy apricot jam
   (page 217), or good-quality ready-
   made jam
½ teaspoon ground cardamom seeds
500 g (1 lb 2 oz) pre-soaked akawi or
   fresh mozzarella cheese, grated
30 g (1 oz) pistachio slivers (we use
   Iranian), to serve

ROSE-LEMON SYRUP
250 g (9 oz) caster (superfine) sugar
100 ml (3½ fl oz) water
juice of ½ lemon
30 ml (1 fl oz) rosewater

EQUIPMENT
28 cm (11 in) ovenproof non-stick
   frying pan

For the syrup, combine the sugar and water in a small saucepan and heat gently, stirring from time to time, until the sugar has dissolved. Once the liquid is clear, bring to the boil, then lower the heat and simmer briskly for 10 minutes. Remove from the heat and allow to cool, then stir in the lemon juice and rosewater. The syrup will keep in a sealed container in the fridge for up to 1 month.

To bake the pastries, preheat the oven to 160°C (320°F) fan-forced/180°C (350°F). Grease the non-stick frying pan.

Loosen the kadaifi pastry nest and separate out a handful of strands. You need enough to create a thin layer on the base of the frying pan. Drizzle with clarified butter and rub it in gently, so the pastry strands are well coated. Flatten the pastry and bake for 5–8 minutes, or until golden. Remove from the oven and leave to cool for a few minutes. Increase the oven temperature to 180°C (350°F) fan-forced/200°C (400°F).

Mix the apricot jam with the ground cardamom. If it is very thick, you might need to loosen it with a splash of water. Spread a thin layer of jam over the pastry. Don't overdo it, you just want a suggestion of its honeyed sweetness (there will be plenty more from the syrup). Sprinkle the grated cheese on top in an even layer.

Separate out another similar-sized wodge of kadaifi pastry. Loosen the strands, rubbing them with clarified butter as you go, and sit on top of the cheese to form another layer.

Now comes the slightly tricky bit: invert the contents of the pan onto a chopping board, then slide the pastry back into the pan so that the cooked layer is on top and the raw pastry is below.

Return to the oven for 8–10 minutes. The surface should have deepened to a chestnut colour. Use a small spatula to peek at the bottom layer to ensure it's cooked. At the same time, gently reheat the syrup.

Serve the kunafa hot from the oven, garnished with pistachio slivers and with a jug of hot rose syrup on the side.

SPICED PLUM TARTE TATIN WITH BAY, ANISE AND SHERRY CREAM

The spices used in this plum tart might seem slightly unusual – especially the pink peppercorns – but they all combine beautifully with the rich, slightly liquoricey bitter-caramel undertones of the plums. Pedro Ximénez, as well as being wickedly black and sweet, has its own anise qualities, making it an ideal flavouring for the accompanying chilled cream. We favour blood plums here, for their gorgeous moody colour, but use whatever variety suits you best.

SERVES 6–8

50 g (1¾ oz) unsalted butter

50 g (1¾ oz) caster (superfine) sugar

2 bay leaves

2 star anise

½ vanilla bean, split lengthways and seeds scraped

1 teaspoon pink peppercorns, lightly crushed

juice of ½ orange

12 blood plums, halved and pitted

225 g (8 oz) good-quality butter puff pastry

SHERRY CREAM

finely grated zest of 1 orange and juice of ½ orange

125 g (4½ oz) crème fraîche

80 g (2¾ oz) Greek-style yoghurt

30 ml (1 fl oz) Pedro Ximénez sherry

icing (confectioners') sugar, to taste

EQUIPMENT

25 cm (10 in) ovenproof non-stick frying pan

Start by making the sherry cream. Combine all the ingredients except the sugar together in a mixing bowl. Whisk together well, then taste and add sufficient sugar to please your own palate. Chill until required.

Preheat the oven to 190°C (375°F) fan-forced/210°C (410°F).

Combine the butter and sugar in the non-stick frying pan and cook over a low heat until the sugar dissolves. Add the bay leaves, star anise, vanilla bean and seeds, peppercorns and orange juice and cook over a high heat for 8–10 minutes until it forms a dark caramel.

Once the caramel is dark and you can smell the spices, remove the pan from the heat. Add the plums to the pan and turn them around in the caramel to coat, then arrange them neatly in concentric circles, skin side down.

Roll out the pastry to a circle roughly 26 cm (10¼ in) in diameter. Carefully lift it onto the pan and tuck it in around the edges so that it envelops and contains the fruit.

Bake for 20–25 minutes, or until the pastry is puffed and golden. Remove the pan from the oven and leave the tart to sit and settle for 15 minutes before inverting it carefully onto a serving plate. Serve with the chilled sherry cream.

+ ALSO SERVE WITH
Cream cheese ice cream (page 61)

CANDIED GINGER-PEAR 'SLIPPERS'

Sweet borek are a popular feature of the Ottoman table. Known as *sambusek* in Arabic, they are often stuffed with sugary nut combinations, in a similar way to baklava-style filo pastries, but fruit-filled versions are also popular.

Because these are simplified borek that use good-quality ready-made puff pastry instead of handmade borek pastry, it's very simple to throw them together. We've called these pastries slippers because of their resemblance to the French viennoiserie *chaussons pommes* ('chausson' being the French word for slipper).

You'll see from the ingredients list that chocolate is an optional addition and, honestly, we were conflicted about including it. On the one hand, we love the pure ginger-pear flavour of the chocolate-free version; on the other hand, who can resist soft melty chocolate in warm-from-the oven pastries? In the end, we decided to leave the decision up to you.

MAKES 6

2 sheets good-quality butter puff
    pastry
1 lightly beaten egg white, to seal
apricot jam or orange marmalade,
    to glaze

GINGER-PEAR FILLING

2 ripe pears, peeled, cored and cut into
    1 cm (½ in) dice
30 g (1 oz) dried pears, cut into 5 mm
    (¼ in) dice
25 g (1 oz) caster (superfine) sugar
½ vanilla bean, split lengthways and
    seeds scraped
juice of 1 orange
40 ml (1¼ fl oz) Poire William pear
    liqueur
30 g (1 oz) crystallised ginger, cut into
    5 mm (¼ in) dice
30 g (1 oz) good-quality dark chocolate
    (50–60% cocoa solids) (optional)

Combine all the filling ingredients, except for the chocolate, in a saucepan. Heat gently, stirring to dissolve the sugar. Bring to the boil, then lower to a simmer, cover and cook for 30–45 minutes until the fruit is tender. The dried pears will soften and almost melt into the syrup to thicken it. Remove from the heat and cool.

To bake, preheat the oven to 190°C (375°F) fan-forced/210°C (410°F). Line two large baking trays with silicone baking mats or baking paper.

Cut three 14 cm (5½ in) rounds from each sheet of pastry and lift them onto the prepared baking trays. Add a generous spoonful of filling to the centre of each round. If using chocolate, chop it roughly and sprinkle on top of the pear mixture.

Brush a little egg white around the edge of each pastry round. Fold the pastry over to make a crescent and pinch or crimp the edges together gently to seal. Use a small sharp knife to slash 4 neat parallel vents into the top of each 'slipper' and brush the surfaces with a little apricot jam. Bake for 20–30 minutes, or until puffed and golden brown.

Cool the pastries briefly on wire racks and eat while warm.

LITTLE RASPBERRY-ROSE BAKEWELLS

These individual tarts were inspired by Lucy's fond childhood memories of a popular tea-time treat. The result: a delicately perfumed twist on the English classic. And we're pleased to report that they are, indeed, exceedingly good.

MAKES 8

butter, for greasing
whipped cream, to serve (optional)

ALMOND-SESAME PASTRY

75 g (2¾ oz) blanched almonds
30 g (1 oz) sesame seeds
65 g (2¼ oz) caster (superfine) sugar
225 g (8 oz) plain (all-purpose) flour, sifted
½ teaspoon ground cinnamon
¼ teaspoon fine sea salt
zest of ½ lemon
170 g (6 oz) chilled unsalted butter, diced
1 egg

FRANGIPANE TOPPING

110 g (4 oz) unsalted butter
110 g (4 oz) caster (superfine) sugar
130 g (4½ oz) eggs (around 2)
25 g (1 oz) plain (all-purpose) flour
½ teaspoon baking powder
110 g (4 oz) ground almonds
few drops almond extract (optional)
2 teaspoons dried raspberries, ground to a powder, to dust (or use icing/confectioners' sugar)

RASPBERRY-ROSE FILLING

100 g (3½ oz) raspberries
juice of ½ lime
1 teaspoon rosewater, or to taste
100 g (3½ oz) Rose petal jam (page 217) or use good-quality ready-made jam

EQUIPMENT

eight 6 × 2 cm (2½ × ¾ in) mini non-stick fluted tart tins

Preheat the oven to 160°C (320°F) fan-forced/180°C (350°F).

Put the almonds and sesame seeds on two small baking trays and roast for 8–10 minutes, or until they are lightly browned, shaking the trays once or twice. Remove from the oven and leave to cool completely, then transfer to a food processor along with the sugar and pulse to fine crumbs. Be careful not to over-process. Add the flour, cinnamon, salt and lemon zest and pulse to combine, then add the butter and pulse to form crumbs. Add the egg and pulse until the pastry just comes together into a ball. Tip onto a lightly floured work surface and shape into a smooth disc. Wrap in plastic wrap and chill for at least an hour, or up to 2 days.

When ready to blind-bake the pastry, liberally grease the tart tins, then place in the fridge for 5–10 minutes to chill. Take the chilled pastry out of the fridge and leave at room temperature so it becomes more pliable.

Divide the pastry into eight equal portions. Roll each portion into circles. Lift onto the prepared tart tins and press into the bases and edges, leaving an overhang. Take particular care to mould into the fluted sides. Prick the pastry all over and refrigerate for at least 30 minutes before baking.

Preheat the oven to 160°C (320°F) fan-forced/180°C (350°F).

Arrange the tart shells on a large baking tray, line with baking paper and baking beans and blind bake for around 15 minutes, or until the pastry is set and golden. Remove from the oven and leave to rest for a few minutes, then remove the beans and baking paper. Use a sharp knife to shave away the pastry overhangs, leaving nice flush edges. Set aside.

For the frangipane topping, combine the butter and sugar in the bowl of an electric mixer and beat with the paddle attachment for 4 minutes, or until very light and fluffy. Beat in the eggs, little by little, ensuring that each amount is incorporated thoroughly before you add more. Stir in the flour, baking powder, ground almonds and the almond extract, if using.

To prepare the raspberry-rose filling, mash the raspberries lightly with the lime juice and rosewater. Spread a generous spoonful of rose petal jam over the base of each tart shell and dollop in the raspberries.

Divide the frangipane evenly between the eight tart shells and smooth evenly. Bake the tarts for 10–15 minutes, or until the frangipane is puffed and golden. If the edges of the pastry start to brown too much, cover lightly with a sheet of foil.

Leave the tarts to cool slightly before carefully removing them from their tins. Dust with raspberry powder (or icing sugar) and serve warm, with whipped cream, or at room temperature with a cup of tea.

See photo on page 154.

PINE NUT TOFFEE TART WITH ORANGE AND ROSEMARY

The combination of slightly resinous pine nuts, sweet citrus and savoury rosemary suspended in a thick toffee filling is intense and addictive. It's darkly rich, gooey and sweet, but somehow you can't stop at just one slice ...

SERVES 10

butter, for greasing
Scented orange cream (page 109),
    chilled crème fraîche or whipped
    cream, to serve

SWEET ALMOND PASTRY

165 g (6 oz) plain (all-purpose) flour
55 g (2 oz) caster (superfine) sugar
40 g (1½ oz) ground almonds
¼ teaspoon fine sea salt
120 g (4½ oz) cold butter, diced
1 egg, lightly whisked

PINE NUT TOFFEE FILLING

150 g (5½ oz) pine nuts
2–3 large sprigs rosemary
80 g (2¾ oz) unsalted butter
150 g (5½ oz) caster (superfine) sugar
40 g (1½ oz) mild honey
40 g (1½ oz) golden syrup or dark
    corn syrup
225 ml (7½ fl oz) thick (double/heavy)
    cream
zest of 1 orange
pinch of fine sea salt

EQUIPMENT

36 × 13 cm (14¼ × 5 in) fluted tart
    tin with a removable base
baking beans

To make the pastry, put the flour, sugar, almonds and salt into the bowl of a food processor and pulse a few times to blend. Add the butter and pulse a few more times, until the mixture looks like coarse crumbs. Don't worry if it seems a bit uneven. Drizzle in the egg, then pulse in 5 second bursts, just until the pastry starts to clump together.

Tip the pastry out onto a lightly floured work surface and use your hands to bring it together briskly into a rough flattish disc. Wrap in plastic wrap and chill for at least 2 hours.

Liberally grease the tart tin and stick it in the fridge, too.

Take the chilled pastry out of the fridge and leave it at room temperature for 5–10 minutes so it becomes more pliable. Roll the pastry out between two sheets of baking paper. Aim for a rectangle 5 cm (2 in) larger than your tart tin; it doesn't need to be too neat. Now lift the pastry onto the tin, pressing it into the base and edges and leaving an overhang. Take particular care to mould it into the fluted sides. Prick the pastry all over and return to the fridge for another 30 minutes (or longer) before blind baking.

Preheat the oven to 160°C (320°F) fan-forced/180°C (350°F).

Line the tart shell with foil and baking beans and blind bake for around 20 minutes until the edges are golden. Remove the foil and beans and return to the oven for another 5–10 minutes to set the base. Remove from the oven and leave to rest for a few minutes. Use a sharp knife to shave away the pastry overhang, leaving a nice flush edge, then set aside until you are ready to add the filling.

For the filling, scatter the pine nuts onto a small baking tray and roast for 5 minutes until just beginning to colour.

Strip one of the rosemary sprigs and finely chop the leaves – you need enough to make a generous tablespoon. Keep the other sprigs whole.

Put the butter in a heavy-based saucepan and melt over a medium heat. Add the sugar, honey and golden syrup and stir over a low heat until the sugar is completely dissolved. Bring to the boil, then lower the heat and simmer for around 12 minutes until it caramelises to a deep amber colour. Swirl the pan every now and then.

Take the pan off the heat and pour in the cream, taking care in case it splutters. Swirl to combine and return to a low heat. Stir in the pine nuts, rosemary sprigs, chopped rosemary, orange zest and salt and remove from the heat. Set aside for 20 minutes so the flavours infuse.

Remove the rosemary sprigs, then tip the infused pine nut mixture into the tart shell. Sit the tart tin on a large baking tray and bake for 30 minutes. You may need to cover the edges of the pastry with strips of foil to stop them browning too much. Once the filling has coloured a lovely deep chestnut brown, remove the tart from the oven. Transfer to a wire rack and leave to cool completely before unmoulding and serving. This tart is gooey at room temperature and thickens up to a firmer toffee in the fridge; delicious both ways.

Serve with orange-scented cream, or with chilled crème fraîche or whipped cream.

See photo on page 155.

FREE-STYLE PEACH PIE

This wonderfully rustic midsummer pie is perfect for those precious weeks when there is a glut of stone fruit. In truth, it works equally well with nectarines, plums or apricots – or even cherries – as all combine well with the rich, buttery pastry and the flavours of rum and hazelnuts.

The pastry is of the reassuringly simple, blitz-in-a-food-processor variety, because who wants to be rubbing in butter on a hot summer's day? There is enough to make one medium pie, or to line a 25 cm (10 in) tart tin for a more formal tart.

SERVES 8

4 ripe peaches, pitted and sliced
30 g (1 oz) caster (superfine) sugar
2 tablespoons dark rum
30 g (1 oz) ground hazelnuts
pouring (single/light) cream,
    for brushing and serving
golden caster (superfine) sugar or raw
    (demerara) sugar, for sprinkling
splash of orange blossom water, for
    sprinkling

SWEET ORANGE SHORTCRUST
200 g (7 oz) plain (all-purpose) flour,
    plus extra for dusting
40 g (1½ oz) caster (superfine) sugar
zest of 1 orange
¼ teaspoon fine sea salt
120 g (4½ oz) chilled unsalted
    butter, diced
60 ml (2 fl oz) ice-cold water

To make the pastry, put the flour, sugar, orange zest and salt into the bowl of a food processor and pulse a few times to blend. Add the butter and pulse a few more times until the mixture looks like coarse crumbs. Don't worry if it seems a bit uneven. Add the ice-cold water in three goes, pulsing after each addition. Then continue pulsing, just until the pastry starts to clump together.

Tip the pastry out onto a lightly floured work surface and use your hands to bring it together briskly into a rough flattish disc. Roll the pastry out between two sheets of baking paper into a rough 30 cm (12 in) circle; it doesn't need to be too neat. Now lift the whole thing onto a baking tray and refrigerate for at least 2 hours.

Take the chilled pastry out of the fridge and lift it off the baking tray. Dust the tray lightly with flour. Peel away the baking paper from both sides of the pastry, return it to the baking tray, then leave at room temperature for 5 minutes or so to make it more pliable.

Toss the sliced peaches with the caster sugar and rum.

Scatter the ground hazelnuts onto the pastry, leaving a rough 8 cm (3¼ in) border around the edges. Pile on the peach slices – or mound them in neat concentric circles, if that is more your style. If the fruit is very wet, try to leave most of the syrup aside for the time being. Carefully fold in the edges of the pastry, pleating roughly as you go and leaving the central part exposed. If the pastry is still very stiff you may find it cracks a little at the base and you run the risk of the juices leaking as it bakes, but it's easy enough to pinch off little bits of pastry from the edges and use them to seal any gaps. Return the pie to the fridge to chill for 20 minutes.

Meanwhile, arrange a second baking tray in the top third of the oven and preheat to 160°C (320°F) fan-forced/180°C (350°F).

Remove the pie from the fridge and drizzle any reserved syrup onto the fruit. Brush the pastry with cream and sprinkle with golden caster sugar. Place on top of the preheated baking tray. Bake for 30–35 minutes, or until the pastry is golden and the fruit is bubbling. Check after 20 minutes to ensure the pastry isn't browning too fast. If it is, cover lightly with foil or baking paper.

Allow the pie to cool on the baking tray for at least 10 minutes before carefully transferring it to a serving platter. Just before serving, sprinkle with orange blossom water and serve with extra cream.

DATE CUSTARD TART

Velvety smooth date custard in a buttery crisp tart shell: this dessert needs nothing more than pouring cream, or possibly a scoop of ice cream, to accompany it. You can prepare the filling and blind-bake the tart shell a day ahead of time.

SERVES 8–10

butter, for greasing
pouring (single/light) cream or
    vanilla ice cream, to serve (optional)

SWEET SHORTCRUST PASTRY

200 g (7 oz) flour
60 g (2 oz) icing (confectioners') sugar
¼ teaspoon fine sea salt
130 g (4½ oz) chilled unsalted
    butter, diced
1 egg yolk, lightly whisked

DATE-SHERRY FILLING

200 g (7 oz) medjool dates
60 ml (2 fl oz) Pedro Ximénez sherry
400 ml (13½ fl oz) full-cream
    (whole) milk
200 ml (7 fl oz) thick (double/heavy)
    cream
strips of peel from 1 lemon
½ vanilla bean, split lengthways and
    seeds scraped
60 g (2 oz) caster (superfine) sugar
130 g (4½ oz) eggs (about 2)
40 g (1½ oz) egg yolks (about 2)

EQUIPMENT

23 cm (9 in) loose-based fluted tart tin
baking beans

To make the pastry, put the flour, sugar and salt into the bowl of a food processor and pulse a few times to blend. Add the butter and pulse a few more times, until the mixture looks like coarse crumbs. Don't worry if it seems a bit uneven. Drizzle in the egg yolk, then pulse in 5 second bursts, just until the pastry starts to clump together.

Tip the pastry out onto a lightly floured work surface and use your hands to bring it together briskly into a rough flattish disc. Roll the pastry out thinly between two sheets of baking paper. Aim for a circle, roughly 5 cm (2 in) larger than your tart tin; it doesn't need to be too neat. Now lift the whole thing onto a large baking tray and freeze for 1 hour.

Liberally grease the tart tin.

Take the chilled pastry out of the freezer and leave it at room temperature for 5 minutes or so to make it more pliable. Peel away the baking paper then lift the pastry onto your prepared tart tin, pressing it into the base and edges and leaving an overhang. Take particular care to mould it into the fluted sides. Prick the pastry all over and return to the freezer for another 30 minutes (or longer) before blind baking.

Preheat the oven to 160°C (320°F) fan-forced/180°C (350°F).

Line the tart shell with foil and baking beans and blind bake for around 20 minutes until the edges are golden. Remove the foil and beans and return to the oven for another 5–10 minutes to set the base. Remove from the oven and leave to rest for a few minutes. Use a sharp knife to shave away the pastry overhang, leaving a nice flush edge, then set aside until you are ready to add the filling.

For the filling, first prepare the dates. Bring a small saucepan of water to the boil. Carefully drop in the dates and simmer briskly for 1 minute. Drain and leave them to cool for a couple of minutes. Use a small sharp knife to peel away the skins and remove the pits, then chop the dates roughly and put them into a small bowl with the sherry. Set aside for 30 minutes to infuse.

Meanwhile, combine the milk, cream, lemon peel and vanilla bean and seeds in another saucepan. Bring just to boiling point, then remove the pan from the heat. Stir in the sugar to dissolve and set aside for 20 minutes to infuse.

Combine the eggs and yolks in a mixing bowl and whisk them together.

Strain the milk mixture and discard the solids (keep the vanilla bean to perfume your sugar canister). Return the liquid to the cleaned out pan and bring to the boil, then slowly whisk the hot liquid into the eggs.

Put the dates and sherry into a food processor and blitz to a purée. With the motor running, slowly pour in the hot custard mixture, blitzing until it is evenly blended and very smooth. Strain the mixture through a fine-mesh sieve, then use straight away or refrigerate for up to 24 hours. (If making ahead of time, heat the custard to blood temperature before filling your tart shell.)

When you are ready to bake the filling, set the oven temperature to 150°C (300°F) fan-forced/170°C (340°F).

Sit the tart tin on a large baking tray and bake for 5 minutes. Carefully pour in the date custard and bake for 45–55 minutes. You may need to cover the edges of the pastry with strips of foil to stop them browning too much. The filling should be set around the edges and still wobble slightly in the centre.

Cool the tart in its tin on a wire rack for at least 30 minutes before serving. Unmould the tart carefully and serve at room temperature with a drizzle of runny cream or a scoop of your favourite vanilla ice cream.

See photo on page 162.

PERSIAN CREAM PUFFS

Known as *nân-e khâmeh-i*, we saw the Persian version of French choux puffs in cake shops all around Iran. They are usually a little smaller than French profiteroles and typically come filled with thick rosewater-scented cream and dredged in cardamom icing sugar.

Whether Persian or French, choux puffs are a very useful and versatile item to have in your repertoire. Choux pastry is fairly straightforward to make and you can fill the puffs with all sorts of flavoured creams or ice cream. The craquelin topping that we suggest here adds an irresistible sweet crunchiness and makes the puffs almost good enough to eat unadorned!

You can double the recipe for the craquelin and choux pastry and store both in the freezer. Pipe the choux pastry out onto trays and freeze. Once frozen solid, pack the individual blobs into a plastic container and freeze until you want to bake them.

MAKES 18–20

CRAQUELIN TOPPING
65 g (2¼ oz) chilled unsalted butter, cut into small cubes
100 g (3½ oz) soft brown sugar
85 g (3 oz) plain (all-purpose) flour
pinch of fine sea salt
1 teaspoon vanilla extract

CHOUX PASTRY
70 ml (2¼ fl oz) full-cream (whole) milk
70 ml (2¼ fl oz) water
65 g (2¼ oz) unsalted butter
big pinch of caster (superfine) sugar
big pinch of fine sea salt
100 g (3½ oz) plain (all-purpose) flour, sifted
up to 260 g (9 oz) eggs (4–5), lightly whisked together (see method)

EQUIPMENT
5 cm (2 in) pastry cutter
piping bag fitted with a 2.5 cm (1 in) nozzle (optional)
water spray bottle

Make the craquelin first as it must be used from frozen. Combine the butter and sugar in the bowl of your food processor and pulse until just combined. Add the flour and salt and pulse until it clumps together damply. Pulse in the vanilla extract. Tip the dough out onto your work surface and bring together in a smooth ball. Shape into a smooth disc then roll out between two sheets of plastic wrap or baking paper to an approximate rectangle, 2.5 mm (⅛ in) thick. Use the pastry cutter to cut into discs and arrange them on a small baking tray. Freeze until required.

When ready to make your choux puffs, preheat the oven to 160°C (320°F) fan-forced/180°C (350°F). Line two baking trays with silicone baking mats or parchment paper and have the piping bag or a soup spoon to hand.

Combine the milk, water, butter, sugar and salt in a heavy-based saucepan over a medium heat. Cook until the butter melts completely, then bring just to the boil. Add the flour all at once and beat vigorously with a wooden spoon until the dough comes together as a smooth paste. Lower the heat slightly and keep beating madly for another 3 minutes, or until the paste thickens and dries and comes away from the sides of the pan as a ball. It shouldn't colour.

Tip the paste into the bowl of an electric mixer fitted with the paddle attachment and beat on low speed for 3–4 minutes to cool slightly. Now start adding the eggs. Because the actual quantity of egg required will vary, it's best to add it in four lots, beating well to incorporate after each addition. Check the consistency after adding the third addition: the dough should be smooth and satiny, something like the consistency of a stiffish cake mix, and thick enough to hold its shape when piped.

Once you've achieved the right consistency, spoon the choux pastry into the piping bag, if using, and spray your baking trays lightly with water. Pipe 3.5 cm (1½ in) rounds onto your prepared baking trays, leaving about 5 cm (2 in) between them to allow for expansion. Alternatively, use a spoon to drop little mounds of the pastry onto the tray. You should get 18–20 puffs from this amount of dough.

Place a frozen disc of craquelin on top of each one and bake in the centre of the oven for 30–35 minutes. (Don't open the oven door before the 25 minute mark.) When ready, the tops should be gorgeously crackled and golden brown and the puffs themselves should be well-risen and feel dry and sound hollow when tapped on the bottom. Make a small slit in the sides of each puff, which should release moisture and stop them going soggy. Transfer to wire racks and cool to room temperature.

When the puffs are cold, use a sharp knife to split them open and fill with your choice of ice cream or cream. Once filled, serve immediately.

See photo on page 163.

✚ SERVE WITH
Labne cream (page 26)
Middle Eastern clotted cream (page 32)
Chantilly-yoghurt cream (page 48)
any of our sorbets or ice creams (pages 55–64)
Scented orange cream (page 109)
Confit lemon cream (page 174)

FRITTERS AND PANCAKES

Doughnuts are one of childhood's great pleasures, but how many of us realise that they date back to the ancient empires of the Middle East? It's known that the Egyptians used yeast (to ferment beer and bake bread) and that early recipes for fritters – pieces of fried dough, sometimes unadorned, sometimes mixed with fruits and nuts, and soaked in milk or honey – were the forerunners of our modern-day pancakes and doughnuts. The Babylonians, Persians, Greeks and Romans all had their versions, which evolved and developed over the centuries and were eventually carried into North Africa – and ultimately Europe – by the Arabs.

Today, versions of syrup-drenched doughnuts are found all around the Eastern Mediterranean, Middle East and North Africa. Street vendors scooping these crisp golden morsels from vats of bubbling oil are a familiar sight, and *lokma*, *loukamades* and *awamat* (as they are variously known) make one of the most popular sweet daytime snacks.

Middle Eastern pancakes – generally called *ataif* – are made from yeasted batters, rather than doughs, and tend to be cooked in a crêpe pan or shallow-fried rather than deep-fried. Ataif are usually slightly thicker than Western pancakes and may be rolled around sugared nuts, soft sweet cheese or thick clotted cream. They are especially popular during celebrations and religious festivals.

Both fritters and pancakes are a great way of eking out ingredients and using up leftovers, and they are incredibly versatile. But really, it's all about the joys of hot, fried dough or batter, and the contrasting cold sweetness of a subtly perfumed syrup.

We've included some of our favourite recipes here: most use yeast (or another rising agent), which is important for texture. All are fried (in a frying pan or saucepan) except for our babas, which are baked.

Some fritters are easier to shape (or fill) with the help of a piping bag, and when it comes to deep-frying, we'd advocate using a dedicated deep-fryer or a thermometer at the very least, so you can easily monitor and regulate the temperature of the oil. It's crucial not to have your oil too hot or the fritters will brown too quickly and the centre will remain doughy and raw. If you don't have a thermometer, you can assess the temperature with your eyes (it should visibly shimmer) and by testing with a small cube of bread – see each recipe for specific timings.

ARABIC APRICOT DOUGHNUTS

Soft, fluffy doughnuts, straight from the fryer, appeal to the child in us all. They're as popular a snack in Middle Eastern countries as they are in the West, with every country having its own version. Variously known as *lokma*, *loukamades*, *luqaimat* or *awamat*, they typically come drenched in syrup instead of being glazed, sprinkled, sugar-coated or otherwise tizzed up. They are not usually filled with jam, but some Arabic doughnuts are stuffed with pieces of fruit – typically plum or apricot.

While doughnuts are usually a street vendor speciality, they are easy enough to make at home. These Lebanese awamat can be stuffed with fresh apricots in the summer months, but here we use a wonderfully tangy jam made from the dried fruit, which make them ideal as a winter treat.

MAKES AROUND 24

100 g (3½ oz) Easy apricot jam
   (page 217) or good-quality,
   chunky ready-made jam
10 g (¼ oz) dried yeast
600 g (1 lb 5 oz) plain (all-purpose)
   flour
pinch of fine sea salt
70 g (2½ oz) unsalted butter
70 g (2½ oz) caster (superfine) sugar
440 ml (15 fl oz) full-cream
   (whole) milk
195 g (7 oz) eggs (around 3)
1 egg yolk
sunflower or vegetable oil,
   for deep-frying

LEMON SYRUP
300 g (10½ oz) caster
   (superfine) sugar
20 g (¾ oz) golden syrup or mild-
   flavoured honey
100 ml (3½ fl oz) water
juice of 1 lemon
1 vanilla bean, split lengthways
   and seeds scraped (optional)

To make the syrup, combine all the ingredients in a small saucepan and heat gently, stirring from time to time, until the sugar has dissolved. Once the liquid is clear, bring to the boil, then lower the heat and simmer briskly for 1 minute. Remove from the heat and leave to cool. The syrup will keep in a sealed container in the fridge for up to 1 month.

A couple of hours before you want to make the doughnuts, put the apricot jam in the freezer, which makes it easier to work with.

Mix the yeast, flour and salt together in a large mixing bowl. Put the butter in a separate bowl.

Put the sugar and milk in a saucepan and heat gently to dissolve the sugar. Do not boil. Pour onto the butter and stir to melt. Leave until it cools to lukewarm, then whisk the eggs and egg yolk into the liquid.

Pour the liquid into the flour mixture and stir in by hand, until the batter is smooth. Cover the bowl with a tea towel (dish towel) and leave in a warm, draught-free spot for 1 hour, by which time the dough should have doubled in size.

When ready to cook, pour the oil into a heavy-based saucepan or deep-fryer to a depth of around 10 cm (4 in) and heat to 160ºC (320ºF). If you don't have a thermometer, the oil will have reached temperature when it is shimmering and when a small cube of bread sizzles up to the surface in 20–30 seconds.

Have a bowl of the syrup standing by.

Shape the doughnuts into round quenelles using two soup spoons. As you make each doughnut, use your thumb to press into the batter and stuff in a small spoonful of the frozen apricot jam. Pinch the hole to close.

Drop the doughnuts into the oil and fry for 4–5 minutes until golden brown. Move them around in the oil with a slotted spoon so they colour evenly. Monitoring the temperature is important here, as you don't want them to brown too quickly before they are cooked through.

Scoop the doughnuts out of the oil and dunk them straight into the cold syrup. Leave to soak for a few minutes before serving. They are good with a cup of coffee, or turn them into dessert by serving with ice cream.

CRUNCHY CARDAMOM FRITTERS

Versions of these delicate spiral fritters are found throughout the Middle East and Asian subcontinent. They are often luridly tinted, then dropped into a sugar syrup, where they become sticky, translucent and tooth-achingly sweet. We prefer to dust them with icing (confectioners') sugar, or even to serve them with a dipping sauce, churros-style, as we do here.

The batter holds up well, and can be made a few hours ahead of time. It even keeps well overnight in the fridge, which has the added benefit of intensifying the flavour. You can also make the sauce ahead of time as it will keep in the fridge happily for around 5 days. It will thicken as it chills, so reheat gently before serving.

MAKES 15–20

175 g (6 oz) plain (all-purpose) flour
1 tablespoon dried yeast
seeds from 30 cardamom pods, ground
  (or 1 teaspoon ground cardamom)
pinch of fine sea salt
250 ml (8½ fl oz) warm water
75 g (2¾ oz) Greek-style yoghurt
sunflower or vegetable oil,
  for deep-frying

HOT CHOCOLATE DIPPING SAUCE
160 g (5½ oz) good-quality dark
  chocolate (50–60% cocoa solids),
  chopped or broken into small pieces
80 g (2¾ oz) golden syrup or mild-
  flavoured honey
250 ml (8½ fl oz) thick (double/heavy)
  cream
100 g (3½ oz) unsalted butter
1 teaspoon ground cinnamon
pinch of fine sea salt

EQUIPMENT
piping bag fitted with a 5 mm (¼ in)
  nozzle (optional)

Sift the flour, yeast, ground cardamom and salt into a mixing bowl. Whisk in the warm water and yoghurt to form a batter. Cover with plastic wrap and leave to stand at room temperature for at least 2 hours. Alternatively, refrigerate overnight, or up to 12 hours, but bring to room temperature an hour before cooking.

To make the dipping sauce, combine all the ingredients in a saucepan and heat gently until everything softens to a smooth, molten gloss.

When ready to fry the fritters, pour the oil into a heavy-based saucepan or deep-fryer to a depth of around 10 cm (4 in) and heat to 180°C (350°F). If you don't have a thermometer, the oil will have reached temperature when it is shimmering and when a small cube of bread sizzles up to the surface in 10–15 seconds.

Pour the batter into the piping bag or into a clean plastic squeeze bottle. Pipe it into the oil in spirals, working from the centre outwards. Make the spirals as small or large as you like. Don't worry if they are not perfect – a free-form lacy effect is just as pretty. Cook for 1–2 minutes, or until the fritters have set, then use a slotted spoon to move them around gently in the oil so that they colour evenly. Once they are a rich honey colour, lift them out of the oil and drain on paper towel for a moment.

Serve the fritters hot from the fryer, with a bowl of the hot chocolate sauce for dunking.

+ ALSO SERVE WITH
  Arabic five-spice pineapple with saffron ice cream (page 18)
  Burnt orange sauce (page 36)

SHREDDED APPLE FRITTERS WITH ROSEMARY SUGAR

These knockout fritters are reprised here from our most recent book, *New Feast*. We firmly believe they merit inclusion as they proved to be so popular and, crucially, they are so easy to make and are so versatile. Serve them for brunch, an after-school treat or even dessert, accompanied by your favourite ice cream.

MAKES AROUND 20

140 g (5 oz) plain (all-purpose) flour
1½ teaspoons baking powder
30 g (1 oz) caster (superfine) sugar
pinch of ground cinnamon
½ teaspoon fine sea salt
1 large egg
140 ml (4½ fl oz) milk
3 large apples (choose a good tart-sweet variety)
sunflower or vegetable oil, for deep-frying
2 tablespoons sultanas (golden raisins), very roughly chopped (optional)

ROSEMARY SUGAR
80 g (2¾ oz) caster (superfine) sugar
¾ teaspoon very finely chopped rosemary needles

To make the rosemary sugar, mix the two ingredients together evenly and set aside.

Sieve the flour and baking powder into a mixing bowl. Add the sugar, cinnamon and salt and whisk together briefly.

In a different bowl, whisk the egg with the milk. Tip into the dry ingredients and whisk everything together well to make a smooth batter. Set aside while you prepare the apples.

Peel the apples, then cut them into halves and remove the core (this is easiest with a melon baller). Cut into 5 mm (¼ in) thick slices, then cut the slices into 5 mm (¼ in) batons.

When ready to cook, pour the oil into a heavy-based saucepan or deep-fryer to a depth of around 10 cm (4 in) and heat to 170ºC (340ºF). If you don't have a thermometer, the oil will have reached temperature when it is shimmering and when a small cube of bread sizzles up to the surface in 15–25 seconds.

Add the apple matchsticks and sultanas, if using, to the batter and mix well. Drop small spoonfuls into the oil, or use a fork. Don't worry about the fritter's shape – the more free-form, the better! Add a few more fritters to the pan, but do not overcrowd it.

Fry for around 5 minutes, turning the fritters around in the oil from time to time, until they are evenly golden brown and crisp. Use a slotted spoon to lift them onto a plate lined with paper towel to drain briefly.

Sprinkle the fritters with the rosemary sugar and serve while still warm.

RICOTTA FRITTERS WITH CHOCOLATE, ORANGE AND CANDIED PEEL

We were inspired to create these fritters by a traditional Sicilian recipe that included candied citrus peel and flower water – certainly a nod to the island's Arabic past. Unlike the original yeasted version, ours is a blissfully simple ricotta fritter. We've added chocolate, which is lovely with the citrus, and an adult splash of Grand Marnier. No need for soaking them in hot syrup, either. We like the contrasting temperature of a chilled syrup (or use runny honey) for dunking, instead.

MAKES AROUND 20

225 g (8 oz) fresh ricotta
50 g (1¾ oz) golden caster (superfine) sugar
30 ml (1 fl oz) Grand Marnier (or use orange juice)
1 egg, plus 1 yolk
zest of 1 orange
40 g (1½ oz) good-quality dark chocolate (50–60% cocoa solids), chopped or broken into small pieces
40 g (1½ oz) mixed candied citrus peel, chopped
75 g (2¾ oz) plain (all-purpose) flour
2 teaspoons baking powder
sunflower or vegetable oil, for deep-frying
icing (confectioners') sugar, for dusting
honey, to serve (optional)

ORANGE BLOSSOM SYRUP

250 g (9 oz) caster (superfine) sugar
100 ml (3½ fl oz) water
1 cinnamon stick
1 vanilla bean, split lengthways and seeds scraped
2 teaspoons orange blossom water

To make the syrup, combine the sugar and water in a small saucepan and heat gently, stirring from time to time, until the sugar has dissolved. Once the liquid is clear, bring to the boil, then lower the heat, add the cinnamon and vanilla and simmer briskly for 10 minutes. Remove from the heat and allow to cool, then stir in the orange blossom water. Chill until required. The syrup will keep in a sealed container in the fridge for up to 1 month.

Combine the ricotta, sugar, liqueur, egg and yolk and orange zest in a mixing bowl and beat until smooth. Stir in the chocolate and candied peel. Sift on the flour and baking powder and mix to combine. Cover in plastic wrap and refrigerate for 1 hour.

When ready to cook, pour the oil into a heavy-based saucepan or deep-fryer to a depth of around 10 cm (4 in) and heat to 180°C (350°F). If you don't have a thermometer, the oil will have reached temperature when it is shimmering and when a small cube of bread sizzles up to the surface in 10–15 seconds.

Form the fritter batter into round quenelles with soup spoons. Drop them into the oil in batches of 3–4 and fry for 3–4 minutes, until golden brown. Move them around in the oil with a slotted spoon so they colour evenly.

Scoop the fritters out of the oil and drain briefly on paper towel. Dust with icing sugar and serve straight away, with syrup and honey, if using, on the side for dunking.

+ ALSO SERVE WITH
Chocolate-halva ice cream (page 63)

BABY BABAS WITH CONFIT LEMON CREAM

Although rum babas might seem like rather an old-fashioned dessert, we firmly believe they should make a comeback. After all, who doesn't like boozy cakes? You can make them in little savarin ring moulds (or a large single one) – and these have the virtue of a central space, ready-made for filling – but we like the classic, rather more austere, 'bouchon' shape as we find they bake more evenly and are easier to work with. It's best to make the babas a day ahead, then leave them overnight to dry out. Although it's not absolutely critical (especially if you're feeling greedy), we do find it helps them slurp up the syrup more readily, so they become exceptionally moist and tender.

If you don't want to make the confit lemons, use a good-quality lemon curd to flavour the whipped cream instead.

MAKES 8

45 g (1½ oz) raisins (if they are a very
   large variety, chop them roughly)
30 ml (1 fl oz) dark rum or orange juice
65 ml (2¼ fl oz) full-cream
   (whole) milk
2 teaspoons dried yeast
2 teaspoons caster (superfine) sugar
200 g (7 oz) plain (all-purpose)
   flour, sifted
¼ teaspoon fine sea salt
130 g (4½ oz) eggs (around 2),
   lightly whisked
65 g (2¼ oz) soft unsalted butter,
   plus extra for greasing

RUM SYRUP
200 g (7 oz) caster (superfine) sugar
200 ml (7 fl oz) water
½ cinnamon stick
1 star anise
juice of 1 lemon
100 ml (3½ fl oz) dark rum

CONFIT LEMON CREAM
150 g (5½ oz) Greek-style yoghurt
80 ml (2½ fl oz) thick (double/heavy)
   cream
4 slices Confit lemons (page 222),
   plus extra to decorate, or 2 heaped
   tablespoons good-quality
   lemon curd
icing (confectioners') sugar
   (optional), to taste

EQUIPMENT
eight 130 ml (4½ fl oz) dariole or
   baba moulds

Combine the raisins with the rum in a bowl and leave to macerate for 30 minutes.

Heat the milk gently to blood temperature in a small saucepan. Add the yeast and sugar and whisk gently to dissolve.

Sift the flour and salt into the bowl of an electric mixer and pour in the warm, yeasty milk. Knead with the dough hook attachment for a few minutes to combine, then add the eggs in two batches, beating in well after each addition.

With the mixer on medium speed, drop in the butter in small pieces. Continue kneading for a good 5 minutes until the dough is very smooth and elastic. Tip in the soaked raisins and any residual rum and mix together evenly.

Cover the bowl with a tea towel (dish towel) and leave in a warm place for 1–1½ hours, until it has doubled in size.

Meanwhile, preheat the oven to 180°C (350°F) fan-forced/200°C (400°F). Grease the dariole or baba moulds liberally with butter.

Gently knock back the baba dough and divide it between the prepared moulds. They should be no more than half-full. Arrange them on a large baking tray, cover them loosely and leave to rise in a warm place for 20 minutes.

Once they've risen to nearly fill the moulds, bake for 3 minutes, then lower the oven temperature to 150°C (300°F) fan-forced/170°C (340°F) and bake for a further 12–15 minutes, or until they are golden brown and feel springy when lightly pressed.

Leave the babas in their moulds on the baking tray for 5 minutes before tipping them out onto a wire rack to cool completely. Cover them with a clean tea towel (dish towel) and leave them overnight to dry out. Don't panic if the babas feel rock-hard the next day. Once you immerse them in syrup, they will absorb it like greedy little sponges, becoming soft and saturated with heady spiced rum flavours.

To make the syrup, combine the sugar and water in a small saucepan and heat gently, stirring from time to time, until the sugar has dissolved. Once the liquid is clear, bring to the boil, then lower the heat, add the cinnamon stick and star anise and simmer briskly for 5 minutes. Stir in the lemon juice and rum, then tip the hot syrup into a deep container, large enough to accommodate all the babas.

Prick the babas all over with a fine skewer then drop them into the hot syrup. Leave them for 10–20 minutes, or until the syrup has been absorbed, turning them every now and then. Once all the syrup has been absorbed, transfer to a platter to serve, or refrigerate until required.

To make the confit lemon cream, gently whisk the yoghurt with the cream to form soft peaks. Finely chop the confit lemon slices and fold them in. (If using lemon curd, fold it in streakily.) Add icing sugar to taste if you must, but remember that the syrup-soaked babas are rather sweet, so what you're really aiming for here is something to provide a creamy-sharp counterpoint.

To serve, decorate each baba with extra pieces of confit lemon and serve with confit lemon cream on the side.

See photo on page 176.

+ ALSO SERVE WITH
Arabic five-spice pineapple (page 18)
Middle Eastern clotted cream (page 32)
Cream cheese ice cream (page 61)
Turkish fresh and dried fruit salad (page 212)

LEBANESE PIKELETS STUFFED WITH CRUNCHY WALNUT CHEESE

Ataif – a sort of soft and pliable Lebanese pikelet – are a favourite from Greg's childhood. There are two main ways of eating them and both have their merits. They can be served at room temperature, spread with clotted cream, jam or chopped nuts and rolled into a cone for a hand-held snack, or they can be turned into little deep-fried, cheese and nut–stuffed turnovers, doused with chilled syrup.

Here we offer a recipe for the second method, because what could be more delicious than crunchy golden pancakes with a molten cheese filling?

Local recipes use akawi cheese, a semi-hard white cheese in salty brine. By all means use this if you can source it, but remember that it needs to be soaked for at least 6 hours – preferably overnight – with several changes of water. After soaking it should be rinsed and then left to soak again in milk for 30 minutes, so you are left with only the barest residual salt tang. Here we approximate the desirable smooth texture and slight saltiness by combining fresh ricotta, mozzarella and haloumi. The results are dangerously good and we guarantee you won't be able to stop at one.

MAKES AROUND 12

2 teaspoons dried yeast
1 tablespoon caster (superfine) sugar
500 ml (17 fl oz) warm water
250 g (9 oz) plain (all-purpose) flour
1 teaspoon baking powder
pinch of fine sea salt
sunflower or vegetable oil,
　for deep-frying

ROSE SYRUP
150 g (5½ oz) caster (superfine) sugar
75 ml (2½ fl oz) water
splash of rosewater

CRUNCHY WALNUT-CHEESE FILLING
125 g (4½ oz) walnut halves
25 g (1 oz) caster (superfine) sugar
¼ teaspoon ground cinnamon
splash of orange blossom water
150 g (5½ oz) haloumi, grated and
　soaked in milk for 1–2 hours to
　remove excess salt
200 g (7 oz) fresh mozzarella, grated
200 g (7 oz) ricotta

To make the syrup, combine the sugar and water in a small saucepan and heat gently, stirring from time to time, until the sugar has dissolved. Once the liquid is clear, bring to the boil, then lower the heat and simmer briskly for 1 minute. Remove from the heat and allow to cool, then stir in the rosewater. Chill until required. The syrup will keep in a sealed container in the fridge for up to 1 month.

Dissolve the yeast and sugar in 125 ml (4 fl oz) of the warm water. Leave to stand in a warm place for 10 minutes, or until it froths.

Sift the flour, baking powder and salt into a mixing bowl. Tip in the yeast mixture and gradually add the rest of the water, whisking all the time to make a creamy, lump-free batter. Cover the bowl with a tea towel (dish towel) and leave in a warm, draught-free spot for 1 hour, by which time the batter should have become bubbly and a little elastic and have the consistency of pouring cream.

To fry the pikelets, heat a non-stick frying pan over a medium heat (there's no need to grease it). Stir the batter gently, then pour half a ladleful into the pan. Tilt it gently to spread out the batter – you're aiming for rounds about 12 cm (4¾ in) in diameter. Cook for around 20 seconds, or until little bubbles appear on the surface and it starts to dry. Check the underside: you may need to adjust the temperature so it doesn't colour too quickly. You're aiming for a pale gold tinge, not chestnut brown. Once ready, transfer to a plate and leave to cool. (Note: you are only cooking one side.) Repeat with the remaining batter, stacking the pikelets on the plate as you go.

To make the filling, first preheat the oven to 180°C (350°F) fan-forced/ 200°C (400°F). Spread the walnuts out on a baking tray and roast for 8–10 minutes, or until they are darkening and smell toasty. Rub them briskly in a clean tea towel to remove as much skin as possible. Chop finely and set aside to cool.

Once cooled, use your fingers to mix together the chopped walnuts with the sugar, cinnamon and orange blossom water evenly.

Rinse the haloumi and add to the mozzarella and ricotta. Mix to combine, then add the walnut mixture and fork it through evenly.

To fill, work with one pikelet at a time, laying the uncooked side up on your work surface. Place a chipolata-sized sausage of filling across the centre of each pancake. Fold it over and squeeze the edges together firmly. They are soft and pliable enough to stay sealed. For a super-neat finish, use a pastry cutter to trim the edges. At this stage you can cover them with plastic wrap and refrigerate up to 6 hours ahead of time.

When ready to cook the pikelets, pour the oil into a heavy-based saucepan or deep-fryer to a depth of around 10 cm (4 in) and heat to 180°C (350°F). If you don't have a thermometer, the oil will have reached temperature when it is shimmering and when a small cube of bread sizzles up to the surface in 10–15 seconds.

Fry up to six pikelets at once for around 1 minute on each side until golden.

Lift the pikelets out of the oil with a slotted spoon, allowing as much oil to drip off as possible, and drop into the cold syrup. Repeat until all are done and serve straight away. You want them to be as hot as possible, for maximum molten bliss.

See photo on page 177.

+ SERVE WITH
    Rose jam ice cream (page 57)

BERBER 1000-HOLE PANCAKES WITH DATE-LEMON BUTTER

These light and spongy semolina pancakes are a speciality of North Africa, where they are known as *baghrir*. They are often eaten during Ramadan, enjoyed warm with honey and butter. For something a bit more adventurous, we like to whip up a fruity date-lemon butter, which melts into an unctuous sweet slurry on the hot pancakes. The butter recipe makes more than you'll need, but it keeps well in the fridge or freezer and is great to have on hand as an effortless base for quick butter sauces, for adding a quick flavour hit to savoury dishes, or just to spread on your morning toast.

MAKES 12–14

125 g (4½ oz) fine semolina
125 g (4½ oz) plain (all-purpose)
    flour, sifted
½ teaspoon salt
1 teaspoon baking powder
450 ml (15 fl oz) full-cream
    (whole) milk
½ teaspoon dried yeast
1 teaspoon caster (superfine) sugar
1 large egg

WHIPPED DATE-LEMON BUTTER

50 g (1¾ oz) medjool dates
30 g (1 oz) golden caster
    (superfine) sugar
40 ml (1¼ fl oz) water
30 g (1 oz) Confit lemons (page 222),
    chopped, or 1 heaped tablespoon
    good-quality lemon curd
110 g (4 oz) unsalted butter, softened

To make the date-lemon butter, blanch the dates in boiling water for 45–60 seconds. Drain and leave them to cool for a couple of minutes. Use a sharp knife to peel away the skins, remove the pits and dice the flesh finely, then put the chopped dates into a small pan with the sugar and water. Cook for 8–10 minutes over a medium heat, or until most of the water has evaporated and you are left with a sticky paste. Remove from the heat and leave to cool.

Once cool, stir in the chopped lemon, then whisk in the softened butter. Spoon onto a sheet of plastic wrap or baking paper and shape into a log. Roll up neatly, twist the ends, tie securely and chill until required. The butter will keep in the fridge for several weeks or up to 3 months in the freezer.

Sift the semolina, flour, salt and baking powder together into a large bowl.

Warm the milk in a small saucepan to blood temperature. Stir in the dried yeast and sugar and stir until both are dissolved.

Make a well in the centre of the dry ingredients. Dribble in the milk, whisking to combine evenly and to work out any lumps. Continue adding milk and whisking until completely incorporated. Finally, whisk in the egg. The batter should be silky smooth and the consistency of pouring cream. Cover and set aside for 1 hour until it starts to bubble.

To fry the pancakes, heat a non-stick frying pan over a medium heat (there's no need to grease it). Stir the batter gently, then pour half a ladleful into the pan. Tilt it gently to spread out the batter – you're aiming for rounds about 12 cm (4¾ in) in diameter – and cook for around 60 seconds, or until little bubbles appear on the surface and it starts to dry. Check the underside: you may need to adjust the temperature so it doesn't colour too quickly. You're aiming for a pale gold tinge, not chestnut brown. (Note: you are only cooking one side.)

Serve the pancakes one at a time, hot from the pan, or stack them on a warm plate and keep in a low oven while you finish the rest of the batter. Serve topped with a thin slice of date-lemon butter.

+ ALSO SERVE WITH
    Dates in cardamom coffee (page 28)
    Middle Eastern clotted cream (page 32)
    Blackberry-nectarine compote (page 48)
    Turkish fresh and dried fruit salad (page 212)

CHESTNUT CRÊPES WITH MAPLE BANANAS

Chestnut flour is quite widely used in the Mediterranean, and we like it very much for its rounded, nutty flavour, which combines here brilliantly with the rather more Middle Eastern spicing of mahlab and fennel seed. If you omit the yeast from this recipe, you can make these as thin, French-style crêpes. With the yeast, the batter becomes light and frothy, ideal for making thicker American-style pancakes. Take your pick.

MAKES 6

60 g (2 oz) chestnut flour, sifted
100 g (3½ oz) plain (all-purpose) flour, sifted
195 g (7 oz) eggs (around 3), lightly beaten
220 ml (7½ fl oz) full-cream (whole) milk
30 g (1 oz) unsalted butter, melted, plus extra for frying
½ teaspoon ground mahlab
½ teaspoon ground fennel seeds
1 teaspoon dried yeast (optional)
pouring (single/light) cream or ice cream, to serve

MAPLE BANANAS
4 bananas
20 g (¾ oz) unsalted butter
juice of ½ lemon
½ teaspoon ground cinnamon
100 ml (3½ fl oz) maple syrup, plus extra for drizzling

EQUIPMENT
palette knife

Mix the flours together in a large mixing bowl. Make a well in the centre, add the eggs and whisk them in to form a thick paste. Dribble in the milk, whisking to combine evenly and to work out any lumps. Continue adding milk and whisking until completely incorporated. Finally, whisk in the melted butter, spices and dried yeast, if using. The batter should be silky smooth and the consistency of pouring cream.

Cover the bowl with a tea towel (dish towel) and leave in a warm, draught-free spot for 1 hour, by which time the batter should have thickened somewhat. If you are making the yeast version, it should be nicely frothy.

Preheat the oven to 100°C (210°F) fan-forced/120°C (250°F).

When ready to fry the pancakes, lightly grease a small non-stick frying pan and heat over a medium–low heat.

For crêpes, pour in around half a ladleful of batter and tilt the pan quickly so the batter just covers the base thinly. Tip out any excess. (After making a couple, you will have a clearer idea how much batter is needed.) Leave for around 1 minute, or until you see the extreme edges turning brown, then loosen with a palette knife and flip the crêpe over. Cook for around 30 seconds on the other side until lightly golden. Slide onto a plate and keep warm in the oven while you make the rest of the crêpes.

For yeasted pancakes, the batter will be thicker and spongier and will hold its shape in the pan. Pour in half a ladleful and tilt the pan gently to spread the batter out – you're aiming for rounds about 10 cm (4 in) in diameter. Cook for around 45 seconds, or until bubbles start to form on the surface. Flip the pancake over and cook for another 15–20 seconds. Keep warm in the oven while you make the rest of the pancakes.

Once your crêpes or pancakes are all made, make the maple bananas. Peel the bananas and cut into 1 cm (½ in) thick slices on an angle. Melt the butter in a frying pan. When it starts to froth, add the bananas and brown lightly on both sides. Add the lemon juice, cinnamon and maple syrup and cook for 30 seconds on a high heat, rolling the bananas around to coat evenly.

To serve, stack the pancakes with the bananas and finish with a drizzle of extra maple syrup. Serve hot with runny cream or with ice cream.

+ ALSO SERVE WITH
Salted bay-butterscotch ice cream (page 60)
Cream cheese ice cream (page 61)

HALAWAT EL JIBN

For us this recipe is bittersweet, as it reminds us of our visit to Hama, in west-central Syria, a city that has seen some of the biggest protests and bloodiest violence of recent years.

Our stay there in 2004 predated the current troubles and we went there with two aims: to see the city's iconic medieval wooden waterwheels and to taste *halawat el jibn*. Watching these delicate beauties being made was one of the highlights of our entire trip – there is a real art to stretching a vast molten mass of cheesy semolina into gossamer-thin 'pancakes'. And as is the case with many other Middle Eastern cheese pastries, the genius lies in the creamy blandness of the filling, which springs to life when doused in a perfumed syrup. We were instantly smitten. We learnt to make halawat el jibn for sentimental reasons. We hope you might be inspired to try them for their sheer deliciousness.

SERVES 8

mixed seasonal berries, to serve
    (optional)
pistachio slivers (we use Iranian),
    to garnish (optional)
1 × Lemon syrup (page 168), to serve

FILLING
500 ml (17 fl oz) full-cream
    (whole) milk
100 g (3½ oz) caster (superfine) sugar
30 g (1 oz) cornflour (cornstarch)
30 g (1 oz) rice flour (or double the
    quantity of cornflour)
240 g (8½ oz) fresh ricotta
generous splash of orange
    blossom water

DOUGH
60 g (2 oz) caster (superfine) sugar
125 ml (4 fl oz) water
200 g (7 oz) fresh mozzarella, diced
55 g (2 oz) fine semolina
splash of rosewater

EQUIPMENT
piping bag fitted with a 1 cm (½ in)
    nozzle

For the filling, put the milk, sugar and two flours into a saucepan and whisk to amalgamate. Put on a low heat and bring to the boil very slowly, whisking all the time, until the mixture begins to thicken. Turn down the heat to low and cook for 10–12 minutes, or until very smooth and stiff enough to hold a spoon upright. Whisk frequently to prevent it sticking to the base of the pan. Remove from the heat and cool for 10 minutes.

Whisk in the ricotta and orange blossom water, then cover the pan and leave to cool. Once cool, refrigerate for 2 hours, or until completely chilled and set (the consistency will be similar to choux pastry). Transfer to the piping bag.

For the dough, combine the sugar and water in a saucepan and heat gently, stirring from time to time, until the sugar has dissolved. Once the liquid is clear, bring to the boil, then lower the heat to medium. Add the mozzarella and beat with a wooden spoon or silicone spatula until the cheese has melted. Add the semolina and rosewater and cook over a medium heat for about 5 minutes, stirring vigorously all the time, until it all comes together as a smooth, soft dough.

Remove from the heat and set aside for a few minutes until the dough is cool enough to handle, but still warm.

Divide the dough into eight equal portions. Working with one at a time, roll each ball out thinly between sheets of plastic wrap. Trim to the shape of a rectangle, around 15 × 9 cm (6 × 3½ in).

Pipe the filling along one of the long edges, leaving a 1 cm (½ in) border. Use the plastic wrap to help you roll the pancake up fairly tightly. Repeat with the remaining dough and filling to make a total of eight pancakes.

To serve as a dessert, trim the ends of each completed pancake neatly, then cut them on the diagonal into six smaller pieces. Stack on dessert plates with fresh berries and pistachio slivers, if using, drizzle lightly with the lemon syrup and serve straight away.

Alternatively, serve the pancakes as a morning or afternoon treat, with a drizzle of the lemon syrup and a cup of strong black coffee.

See photo on pages 184–185.

CONFECTIONERY

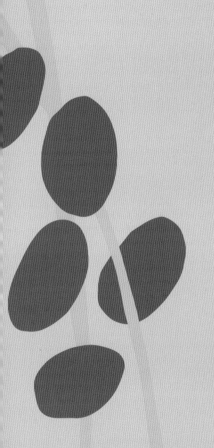

Middle Easterners have a famously sweet tooth, so it's no surprise to learn that they have a fondness for confectionery. Indeed, sweets and candies are a key part of their equally famous hospitality. It's a happy tradition in many homes to keep a large bowl of sweets on the coffee table to offer unexpected guests, and these range from hard candies to individually wrapped pieces of nougat, while in the Arabian Gulf countries you'll be offered luscious, squidgy dates, stuffed with fresh nuts, sweet cheese or perfumed almond paste.

In modern Middle Eastern cities, fancy chocolate shops are becoming as popular as they are in the West, but generally – and most likely because chocolate can be tricky in a hot climate – the tradition of confectionery there revolves around fruit (dried, candied, stuffed), nuts and sugar. Some of our favourites include nougat (or *gaz*, as it's known in Iran), fairy floss (*pashmak* or *ghazl el banet*), Turkish delight – or *lokum* – (of course!), fruit leathers and candied peels (for these, see our chapter on Preserves), crunchy nut or seed brittles, *sohan* (Persian fudge), marshmallows and dense, crumbly halva. You'll find recipes for most of these – and more – in the pages of this book. Some (stuffed dates, for instance) are exquisitely simple; others (like lokum) are more of a challenge. All are fun to tackle and would make lovely gifts for Christmas or other special occasions.

Because confectionery making is quite a specialised art-cum-science (see also our Cook's notes on page 246) there are a couple of helpful pieces of equipment you might like to invest in. Top of the list is a sugar thermometer. Indeed, we'd argue that it's pretty tricky to make many of our confectionery recipes without one. At the very least, a thermometer removes a lot of the guesswork – not to mention all that fiddling around with blobs of syrup and cold water – and will also be invaluable if you want to tackle tempering chocolate. You might also like to invest in a silicone mat, heatproof mixing bowls and a piping bag, which makes fine decoration work a breeze.

Our final tip is that, as with all technically challenging endeavours, practice makes perfect. Working with sugar is often much trickier in the summer months – especially if it's even slightly humid. So if your meringues weep and your toffee seeps, don't give up hope. It might just be the weather!

PANFORTE PETITS FOURS

Although panforte is a speciality of Siena, the use of nuts, sugar and spices are all markers of Arab influence dating from the Middle Ages, when Italian traders discovered these new ingredients – and exciting new culinary ideas – in the markets of Aleppo and Alexandria.

There are many versions of panforte, using various combinations of spices, nuts and dried fruit. Traditionally, it's made in flat cakes, which you cut into slim slices to serve, but we adore this recipe, which makes cute-as-a-button panforte petits fours and comes from our good friend and pastry chef Kate Dalziel. The recipe scales up well, so it's worth making in larger quantities to distribute as a gorgeous Christmas gift.

MAKES AROUND 44 PIECES

150 g (5½ oz) whole blanched almonds

100 g (3½ oz) whole blanched hazelnuts

150 g (5½ oz) honey

60 g (2 oz) caster (superfine) sugar

60 g (2 oz) good-quality dark chocolate (60–70% cocoa solids), chopped or broken into small pieces

120 g (4½ oz) dried fruit, roughly chopped (we like candied clementine, candied ginger, dried figs, apricots or pears)

75 g (2¾ oz) plain (all-purpose) flour

20 g (¾ oz) unsweetened (Dutch) cocoa powder, plus extra for dusting

1 teaspoon ground cinnamon

½ teaspoon ground ginger

½ teaspoon ground black pepper

finely grated zest of 1 lemon

finely grated zest of 1 orange

flavourless oil, for greasing

2 × 24 cm (9½ in) square sheets edible rice paper

icing (confectioners') sugar, for dusting

Preheat the oven to 160°C (320°F) fan-forced/180°C (350°F).

Put the almonds and hazelnuts on a baking tray, keeping them separate, and toast for 8–10 minutes, or until golden brown. Remove the nuts from the oven, but keep the oven on. As soon as the nuts are cool enough to handle, chop half of them very roughly and leave the rest whole. They should be warm when you add them to the remaining ingredients, so work quickly.

Put the honey, sugar and chocolate into a saucepan and heat gently, without stirring, until the chocolate has melted and the sugar has dissolved.

In a large mixing bowl, combine all the nuts with the dried fruit, flour, cocoa, spices and citrus zests. Tip the hot chocolate syrup into the dry ingredients and work everything together with a wooden spoon. The mixture thickens as it cools and can be hard to work.

Lightly oil your work surface with a flavourless oil and tip the panforte mixture out. Divide the mixture in half and leave it for a few minutes to cool and stiffen further – this makes it easier to work with.

Roll each portion of panforte mixture into a 24 cm (9½ in) log, about 3 cm (1¼ in) in diameter. Lift them carefully onto the sheets of rice paper and roll up tightly. Wrap in foil tightly and place on a baking tray.

Bake the panforte logs for 18 minutes, then remove from the oven and leave to cool completely in the foil on the baying trays. Don't be tempted to unwrap it, and don't worry if it feels squidgy in the centre; it firms up as it cools.

Once completely cold, store the panforte logs in their wrappings in the fridge for up to 2 months. To serve, first trim the ends from each log to tidy, then cut into 1 cm (½ in) discs; you should then get around 22 slices from each. Dust with icing sugar or cocoa as you serve.

STUFFED DATES

Dates' soft sticky flesh and dense toffee sweetness make for the perfect treat when you don't want to make actual toffee. It's an idea that is hugely popular in the Gulf states, where they really know how to use dates to their best advantage in both sweet and savoury dishes.

For date sweetmeats at their purest, simply remove the pit, slip in a roasted walnut and drizzle with a little honey. Some more adventurous suggestions follow. Each is sufficient to fill sixteen dates.

MAKES 16 EACH

16 best-quality fresh medjool
    dates, pitted

ALMOND PASTE
100 g (3½ oz) ground almonds
100 g (3½ oz) caster (superfine) sugar
orange blossom water

COFFEE MASCARPONE
1 teaspoon instant coffee
1 teaspoon boiling water
80 g (2¾ oz) mascarpone

SWEET CHEESE
20 g (¾ oz) walnut halves,
    coarsely chopped
1 teaspoon icing (confectioners') sugar
½ teaspoon ground cinnamon
½–1 teaspoon orange blossom water
80 g (2¾ oz) goat's cheese, roughly
    crumbled

CHOCOLATE-DIPPED
100 g (3½ oz) good-quality dark
    chocolate (60–70% cocoa solids),
    chopped or broken into small pieces

To make almond-filled dates, combine the almonds and sugar in the bowl of a food processor and pulse together. Dribble in orange blossom water and knead until it comes together to form a thick paste. Start with a tablespoon, and cautiously add more, if need be. Roll small, almond-shaped portions of the paste and push into each of the dates.

To make coffee mascarpone dates, dissolve the instant coffee in the boiling water and cool. Mix into the mascarpone. Spoon or pipe into each of the dates and serve straight away.

To make sweet cheese–filled dates, use your fingers to rub the walnuts with the sugar, cinnamon and orange blossom water. Fork this mixture through the goat's cheese, then put in the fridge for about an hour to firm up. Spoon into each of the dates and serve straight away.

To make chocolate-dipped dates, melt the chocolate, then dip the dates – et voilà!

See photo on page 190.

CHOCOLATE PRUNE TRUFFLES

These delectable truffles have an alluring anise flavour, but if you don't care for aniseedy things, then substitute chopped crystallised ginger. If using ginger, substitute the aniseeds for cardamom seeds and grind with sugar as described. As ever with chocolate, use the best quality you can afford. For the truffles, we find it's best to use one with no more than 60 per cent cocoa solids, as too bitter a chocolate masks the other flavours.

Keep the finish ultra-simple with a dusting of cocoa powder or, for a prettier presentation, dip them in tempered chocolate and top with a crisp little cap of kadaifi pastry.

MAKES AROUND 16

75 g (2¾ oz) good-quality prunes, such as Agen, finely chopped
50 ml (1¾ fl oz) Pedro Ximénez sherry
50 g (1¾ oz) walnut halves
200 g (7 oz) good-quality dark chocolate (50–60% cocoa solids), chopped or broken into small pieces
100 ml (3½ fl oz) thick (double/heavy) cream
1 teaspoon aniseeds
¼ teaspoon caster (superfine) sugar
zest of 2 oranges
unsweetened (Dutch) cocoa powder, for dusting

KADAIFI COATING (OPTIONAL)
50 g (1¾ oz) kadaifi pastry
2 teaspoons unsalted butter, melted

CHOCOLATE COATING
2 teaspoons unsalted butter, melted
200 g (7 oz) good-quality dark chocolate (70% cocoa solids), chopped or broken into small pieces

EQUIPMENT
sugar thermometer

See photo on page 191.

To make the truffles, first combine the chopped prunes with the sherry in a bowl and leave to macerate for at least 1 hour.

Toast the walnuts in a dry frying pan over a medium–high heat for around 5 minutes, tossing continuously, until browned and toasty smelling, then rub in a clean tea towel (dish towel) to remove as much skin as possible. Chop finely and set aside to cool.

Put the chocolate and cream in a heatproof bowl and place over a saucepan of barely simmering water, making sure the water doesn't touch the base of the bowl. Stir occasionally until the chocolate has melted. (Alternatively, put them in a microwaveable container and cook on full power in 20 second bursts until the chocolate has all but melted.) Stir to combine evenly, then leave to cool slightly.

Combine the aniseeds and sugar in a mortar and grind to a fine powder.

Stir the soaked prunes (and any liquid) into the chocolate, together with the walnuts, anise sugar and orange zest. Refrigerate until firm and cold. Once cold, use a teaspoon to scoop out even quantities of the mixture, then roll into balls. Return to the fridge while you prepare the coatings.

If using kadaifi pastry, first preheat the oven to 170°C (340°F) fan-forced/ 190°C (375°F). Loosen the kadaifi pastry and separate out the strands. Drizzle with the melted butter and rub it in gently, so all the strands are well coated. Chop into 2 cm (¾ in) lengths, scatter on a baking tray and bake for 5–8 minutes until golden. Leave to cool before using.

For the simplest finish, roll the truffles in cocoa powder. For a glossy chocolate coating you'll need to temper the chocolate by first heating, then cooling it. Put it in a heatproof bowl with the butter and place over a saucepan of barely simmering water, making sure the water doesn't touch the base of the bowl, and stir occasionally until it has completely melted. Remove the bowl from the heat and use a silicone spatula to work the chocolate gently as it cools. Once the temperature drops to 31°C (88°F) on a sugar thermometer it is ready to use.

Line a baking tray with a silicone baking mat or baking paper. Use two forks to dip the truffles into the tempered chocolate, turning gently until evenly coated. Transfer the coated truffles to the baking tray and leave to set. If adding a cap of kadaifi, then allow the truffles to cool until the chocolate is just tacky before sprinkling on the pastry shreds. Store the finished truffles in an airtight container in the fridge for up to 1 week.

CHOCOLATE MARSHMALLOWS

Middle Easterners are rather fond of fluffy foams and soft meringues. One of the most ancient foodstuffs, *natef*, is a sweet dip, similar to marshmallow fluff, that springs by some strange alchemy from the roots of the soapwort plant. And then there are marshmallow candies, which are believed to have their origins in ancient Egypt. The earliest versions were also magicked from a plant – in this instance, the mallow – which was pulped and boiled with honey into a thick concoction for medicinal use. Marshmallow candies were developed from this early recipe during the 19th century and they are now one of the most universally popular confectioneries in the world.

Modern-day marshmallows are no longer made from mallow plants, but instead are whipped into cloud-like pillows of joy from the more prosaic combination of gelatine and sugar syrup. Our version is one of the few recipes in this book that requires a truly cheffy cooking ingredient. Trimoline (invert sugar) is essential for making marshmallows, but luckily it is easy to source online. Why bother? Because the tender, melt-in-the-mouth quality is so easy to achieve at home, and in a different league to commercially manufactured marshmallows. They make killer culinary gifts, too!

MAKES AROUND 800 G (1 LB 12 OZ)

oil, for greasing
250 g (9 oz) good-quality dark
    chocolate (60–70% cocoa solids),
    chopped or broken into small pieces
425 g (15 oz) caster (superfine) sugar
130 ml (4½ fl oz) water
250 g (9 oz) trimoline
35 g (1¼ oz) gelatine leaves (see Cook's
    notes, page 243)
2 teaspoons orange blossom water

EQUIPMENT
piping bag fitted with a 2.5 cm (1 in)
    nozzle (optional)

Lightly oil two large baking trays.

Put the chocolate in a heatproof bowl and place over a saucepan of barely simmering water, making sure the water doesn't touch the base of the bowl. Stir occasionally until the chocolate has melted. (Alternatively, put it in a microwaveable container and cook on full power in 20 second bursts until the chocolate has all but melted.) Stir to combine evenly, then leave to cool slightly.

Combine the sugar, water and 10 g (¼ oz) of the trimoline in a saucepan and bring to the boil.

Soak the gelatine in cold water for a few minutes until softened. Squeeze out the excess liquid and add the gelatine to the hot syrup, stirring to dissolve completely.

Transfer to the bowl of an electric mixer along with the remaining 240 g (8½ oz) of trimoline and whisk to medium-stiff, glossy peaks. Whisk in the orange blossom water, then fold in the melted chocolate by hand.

Spoon into the piping bag. Pipe strips of marshmallow onto the oiled baking trays and leave at room temperature for at least 6 hours, or overnight, to set firm. Once set, use a sharp knife to cut into neat, plump little cylinders, varying the heights and angles if you like. (If you don't want to pipe, then tip the mixture onto a tray, cover with oiled baking paper and leave to set as one large marshmallow sheet. You can then cut it into all kinds of different shapes.)

Store the marshmallows in an airtight container until required. They will keep for up to 2 weeks in the fridge.

MINI MERINGUE KISSES

It's useful to have a meringue recipe to hand as a way of using egg whites. As a bonus, they are incredibly easy to make and keep well in an airtight container for several weeks. If you've got meringues, all you need is a splosh of cream, a scoop of ice cream or a spoonful of fruit and you've got dessert!

The following two recipes are based on the simplest and most widely known type of meringue, called French meringue. There are only two key rules to observe for success here: use good, clean egg whites (ideally not from freshly laid eggs) and spotlessly clean equipment, as any trace of yolk, grease or foreign matter will prevent them foaming. Second, add the sugar gradually – and use caster (superfine) sugar, which dissolves more readily – and make sure that each amount is thoroughly dissolved into the whites, or they may 'weep' as they bake.

You might also like to consider whether you prefer meringues that are shatteringly crisp, or that have a crisp shell but a more marshmallowy centre. For the former, as here, you'll need to cook them longer and at a lower temperature. For chewier meringues and for small pavlovas (see page 26) cook them for less time, at a slightly higher temperature.

These meringue kisses are lovely as petits fours and as a decoration for desserts (page 29) and special-occasion cakes (page 116). Serve them as is, or sandwiched with whipped cream or your favourite flavoured cream filling.

MAKES AROUND 40

90 g (3 oz) egg whites (about 2)
120 g (4½ oz) caster (superfine) sugar
½ teaspoon vanilla extract
whipped cream, to serve (optional)

EQUIPMENT
piping bag fitted with a 1.5 cm (½ in)
　　nozzle (optional)

Preheat the oven to 100°C (210°F) fan-forced/110°C (230°F). Line two large baking trays with silicone baking mats or baking paper.

Place the egg whites in the scrupulously clean bowl of an electric mixer and whisk on medium–high speed until they form soft peaks. With the motor still running, spoon in the caster sugar, a little at a time, until it is all incorporated. Increase the motor speed to high and whisk for around 3 minutes, or until the sugar has dissolved and the mixture is thick, glossy and stands in stiff peaks. Test by rubbing a little of the mix between your thumb and finger; it shouldn't feel gritty. Whisk in the vanilla extract.

Spoon the meringue mixture into the piping bag. To create neat meringues, hold the piping bag vertically above the baking tray. As you pipe, lift the nozzle straight up to form a tiny peak. Aim to pipe a range of sizes, ranging from 2 cm to 3.5 cm (¾ in to 1½ in) in diameter. You should easily fit 20 on each tray.

If you don't want to pipe, then spoon the mixture onto the prepared baking trays in small, even-sized dollops.

Bake the meringues for 90 minutes, then turn off the oven, prop the oven door slightly ajar with a wooden spoon and leave the meringues undisturbed for around 2 hours until completely cold.

If not using immediately, store the meringues in an airtight container for up to 2 weeks. You can sandwich them with cream just before serving.

+ ALSO SERVE WITH
Pomegranate-lime jelly (page 29)
Turkish coffee petits pots (page 40)
Lebanese love cake (page 116)

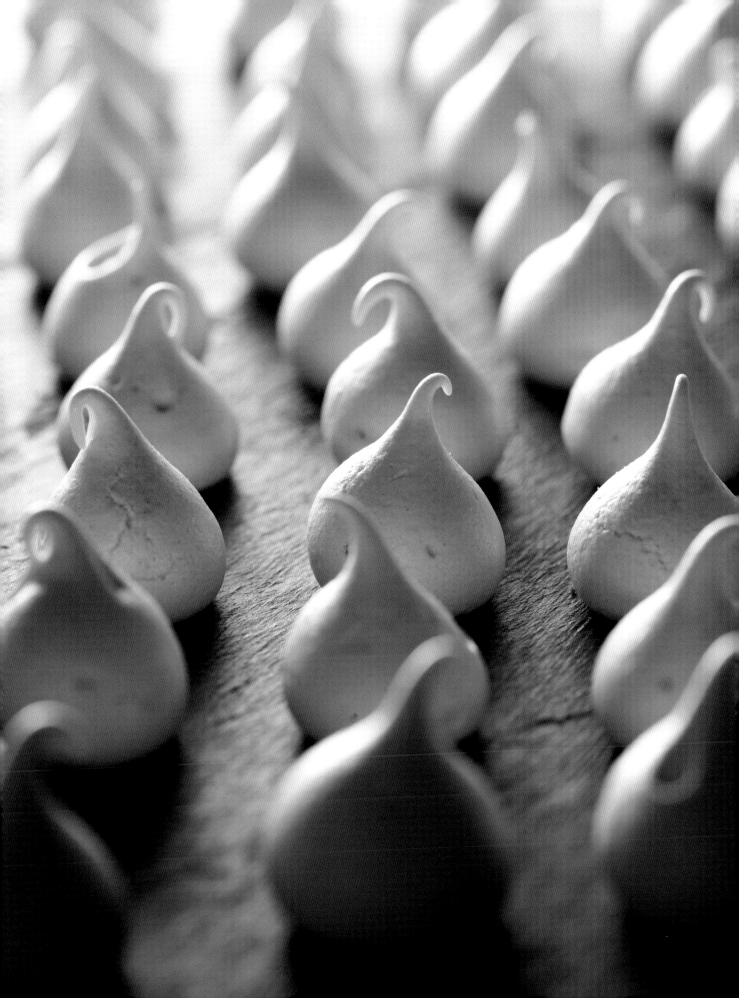

COFFEE MERINGUES

There are numerous ways to flavour a basic plain meringue, but we particularly like this coffee-flavoured version. They are even better when sandwiched with a cardamom–orange blossom flavoured mascarpone filling.

MAKES 16–18 MEDIUM MERINGUES TO SANDWICH TOGETHER

90 g (3 oz) egg whites (about 2)
100 g (3½ oz) caster (superfine) sugar
1½ teaspoons instant coffee dissolved in 2 teaspoons boiling water

ORANGE BLOSSOM MASCARPONE FILLING

160 g (5½ oz) mascarpone
seeds from 8 cardamom pods, ground (or ¼ teaspoon ground cardamom)
2 teaspoons honey
½ teaspoon orange blossom water

Preheat the oven to 100°C (210°F) fan-forced/110°C (230°F). Line two large baking trays with silicone baking mats or baking paper.

Place the egg whites in the scrupulously clean bowl of an electric mixer and whisk on medium–high speed until they form soft peaks. With the motor still running, spoon in the caster sugar, a little at a time, until it is all incorporated. Increase the speed to high and whisk for around 3 minutes, or until the sugar has dissolved and the mixture is thick, glossy and stands in stiff peaks. Test by rubbing a little of the mix between your thumb and finger; it shouldn't feel gritty. Fold in the coffee briefly with a rubber spatula, so the mixture is streaky and marbled, rather than thoroughly amalgamated.

Dollop small, freeform spoonfuls of meringue on the prepared baking trays, around 8 per tray.

Bake the meringues for 90 minutes then turn off the oven, prop the oven door slightly ajar with a wooden spoon and leave the meringues undisturbed for around 2 hours until completely cold.

If not using immediately, store the cold meringues in an airtight container for up to 2 weeks. When ready to use, whisk the filling ingredients together, then sandwich between two meringues.

+ ALSO SERVE WITH
Labne cream (page 26)

QUINCE TURKISH DELIGHT

There's no escaping the fact that home-made Turkish delight, or *lokum*, is labour intensive. But there's also no escaping the fact that its availability in Western countries tends to be limited to a few predictable flavours – rose or vanilla being the usual suspects. And don't get us started on that lurid pink chocolate-coated offering. It's all a far cry from the Eastern promise of the harem.

Our visits to Turkey over the years have opened our eyes to the true delights of lokum – and myriad versions of the stuff are everywhere there. Flavours range from saffron to cinnamon, quince to coffee, mulberry to mastic; it comes in cubes and fat little logs, can be studded with nuts or dates, is drenched in sugar, rolled in coconut or sprinkled with dried rose petals.

Our recipe here, for a tart-sweet quince lokum, is based on a traditional one, but uses shop-bought quince paste as a shortcut to flavour. If you're keen to attempt it, you'll need patience and a strong stirring arm, but the reward is a versatile jewel-like confection, whose delights extend from your after-dinner coffee to use as a garnish for all kinds of desserts, cakes and cookies.

MAKES 36–40 PIECES

oil, for greasing
800 g (1 lb 12 oz) caster
    (superfine) sugar
1.25 litres (42 fl oz) water
1 teaspoon lemon juice
125 g (4½ oz) cornflour (cornstarch),
    plus an extra teaspoon for dusting
½ teaspoon cream of tartar
200 g (7 oz) ready-made membrillo
    (quince paste), cut into tiny dice
200 g (7 oz) icing (confectioners')
    sugar, for dusting

EQUIPMENT
sugar thermometer

Lightly oil a 30 × 25 × 3 cm (12 × 10 × 1¼ in) baking tray and line it with baking paper.

Put the sugar into a large, heavy-based pan with 375 ml (12½ fl oz) of the water and the lemon juice and bring to the boil, stirring occasionally to dissolve the sugar. Keep at a brisk simmer.

Meanwhile, combine the cornflour and the cream of tartar in a large mixing bowl and gradually incorporate the remaining water, ensuring there are no lumps.

As soon as the syrup reaches 116°C (240°F) on a sugar thermometer, whisk in the cornflour mixture – if it seizes up into clumps, don't panic, just keep whisking until it smooths out.

Lower the heat to the barest simmer and cook for around 2 hours. You'll need to be stirring as often as you can bear it to ensure it doesn't stick to the bottom of the pan and burn. The mixture will gradually thicken and become translucent, while the colour will deepen to a soft amber hue.

Eventually, the mixture will be thick enough for you to draw distinct lines on the bottom of the pan with your spoon. At this point, add the quince paste and stir everything in evenly. Pour into your prepared baking tray, smooth the surface and leave to set at room temperature.

Mix the icing sugar and a teaspoon of cornflour together.

Turn the lokum out of the tray and peel away the baking paper. Cut into 2 cm (¾ in) cubes and roll in the icing sugar mixture before serving with strong black coffee. Store at room temperature – and this is one time when you won't be needing an airtight container as that causes it to weep. A tin or a wooden or cardboard box is ideal.

SALTED GINGER TOFFEES

Fabulous chewy toffees with a double hit of ginger heat. If you don't have a sugar thermometer, we'd like to think that this recipe (and the following liquorice caramels) might persuade you to get one. It's not that you can't make candies and confectionery without one, but really, why faff about with bowls of iced water and blobs of hot sugar syrup when this simple, inexpensive and readily available piece of kitchen equipment removes all the guesswork?

For optimum chew, store the toffees in the fridge as they will be softer if left in a warm environment.

MAKES AROUND 500 G (1 LB 2 OZ)

170 ml (5½ fl oz) thick (double/heavy) cream

100 g (3½ oz) fresh ginger, thinly sliced

¾ teaspoon sea salt flakes (ideally fleur de sel), plus extra for sprinkling

60 g (2 oz) unsalted butter, cubed and at room temperature, plus extra for greasing

200 g (7 oz) caster (superfine) sugar

160 g (5½ oz) golden syrup or dark corn syrup

40 g (1½ oz) crystallised ginger, chopped

EQUIPMENT
sugar thermometer

Lightly butter a small baking tray. Line it with foil or baking paper (sufficient to overhang the edges, which makes it easier to lift the toffee slab out) and butter this as well. Sit on a wire rack.

Put the cream into a small saucepan and bring just to the boil. Remove from the heat, add the sliced ginger and leave to infuse for 30 minutes.

Strain the mixture through a sieve, pressing to extract as much of the infused cream as you can. You'll lose some of the volume, but don't worry. Return the cream to the pan, together with the salt and half the butter. Bring back to the boil, then remove from the heat and set aside.

Combine the sugar and golden syrup in another saucepan and heat gently, stirring from time to time, until the sugar has dissolved. Once the liquid is clear, bring to the boil, then lower the heat and simmer briskly until it reaches 155°C (310°F) on a sugar thermometer.

Remove from the heat and stir in the ginger-infused cream. Don't panic if it bubbles ferociously. Continue stirring until it all comes together as a smooth, shiny, homogeneous caramel, then return to the heat and cook to 135°C (275°F), which is the soft crack stage. Turn off the heat and stir in half the crystallised ginger and the remaining butter.

Pour the hot toffee into the prepared baking tray, spreading the ginger out evenly, and leave to cool on the wire rack for 20 minutes. Sprinkle with the remaining ginger and extra sea salt flakes and leave for at least 2 hours, or until completely cold.

Once cold and firm, lift out the slab of toffee and invert it onto your work surface. Peel away the foil or paper and use a knife dipped in boiling water to cut the toffee into small squares or your choice of shape. Layer between sheets of greaseproof paper and store in the fridge in an airtight container for up to 1 month.

See photo on page 200.

LIQUORICE CARAMELS

Another blissful use for our new favourite ingredient, liquorice powder. These soft, chewy caramels make a wonderful gift, and be warned that if you *don't* give them away, you may well eat them all yourself.

MAKES AROUND 500 G (1LB 2 OZ)

170 ml (5½ fl oz) thick (double/heavy) cream

¾ teaspoon sea salt flakes (ideally fleur de sel), plus extra for sprinkling

60 g (2 oz) room temperature unsalted butter, cubed, plus extra for greasing

2½ tablespoons liquorice powder (we use Lakrids fine powder), or to taste

200 g (7 oz) caster (superfine) sugar

160 g (5½ oz) golden syrup or dark corn syrup

½ teaspoon black food colouring gel

EQUIPMENT
sugar thermometer

Lightly butter a small baking tray. Line it with foil or baking paper (sufficient to overhang the edges, which makes it easier to lift the caramel slab out) and butter this as well. Sit on a wire rack.

Combine the cream, salt and half the butter in a saucepan and bring to the boil. Remove from the heat and set aside.

Mix the liquorice powder together with a couple of tablespoons of the hot cream mixture and whisk until dissolved and smooth. Set aside.

Combine the sugar and golden syrup in another saucepan and heat gently, stirring from time to time, until the sugar has dissolved. Once the liquid is clear, bring to the boil, then lower the heat and simmer briskly until it reaches 155°C (310°F) on a sugar thermometer.

Remove from the heat and stir in the cream mixture. Don't panic if it bubbles ferociously. Continue stirring until it all comes together as a smooth, shiny, homogeneous caramel, then return to the heat and cook to 130°C (265°F), the hard ball stage. Turn off the heat and stir in the black food colouring, reserved liquorice liquid and remaining butter.

Pour the hot caramel into the prepared baking tray and leave to cool on the wire rack overnight.

Lift out the slab of caramel and invert it onto your work surface. Peel away the foil or paper and use a knife dipped in boiling water to cut into small squares or your choice of shape. Layer between sheets of greaseproof paper and store in the fridge in an airtight container for up to 1 month.

PERSIAN BUTTER FUDGE

This wickedly buttery cardamom-scented fudge – *sohan* – is from the city of Qom, about an hour south of Tehran, and is famous all around Iran. It is super sweet and very addictive.

MAKES AROUND 650 G (1 LB 7 OZ)

15 saffron threads (we use Iranian)
2 tablespoons boiling water
500 g (1 lb 2 oz) caster (superfine)
    sugar
100 g (3½ oz) golden syrup or
    dark corn syrup
60 ml (2 fl oz) water
300 g (10½ oz) unsalted butter,
    roughly diced
2 teaspoons ground cardamom seeds
50 g (1¾ oz) pistachio slivers
    (we use Iranian)
dried rose petals, to garnish (optional)

EQUIPMENT
sugar thermometer

Line a large baking tray with baking paper.

Lightly toast the saffron threads in a dry frying pan over a medium heat for about 30 seconds. They must be crisp and dry, but be careful not to let them burn. Cool slightly before crushing to a powder. Mix the saffron powder with the boiling water and set aside to infuse for 1 hour.

Combine the sugar, golden syrup and measured water in a heavy-based saucepan and melt over a low heat, stirring from time to time. When the sugar has dissolved, increase the heat and cook for 10–15 minutes until it begins to colour golden. Whisk in the butter, cardamom and liquid saffron and cook for a few minutes more until it colours an even butterscotch colour and reaches 118°C (245°F) on a sugar thermometer.

Pour onto the paper-lined tray and use a spatula to smooth it out as thinly as you can. Sprinkle on the pistachio slivers and rose petals, if using, pressing them gently into the surface of the fudge.

Leave it to cool completely before breaking into random-size pieces. Store in an airtight container in the freezer for up to 1 month.

SAFFRON GLASS

As our Iranian friend Ali Taheri likes to say, tea is everything in Iran; without it, nothing functions. It is generally served sweetened or with a dish of roughly hewn lumps of sugar, which are lodged between the teeth to sweeten the tea as it is drunk. Some sophisticated venues offer gorgeous saffron-tinted sugar wafers instead. And whether or not you like your tea sweetened, there's something rather decadently blissful about letting them melt slowly on your tongue into a saffron syrup.

MAKES AROUND 15

25 saffron threads, or more if you love saffron (we use Iranian)
2 tablespoons boiling water
200 g (7 oz) caster (superfine) sugar

Line a large baking tray with a silicone baking mat or baking paper and have another sheet to hand.

Lightly toast the saffron threads in a dry frying pan over a medium heat for about 30 seconds. They must be crisp and dry, but be careful not to let them burn. Cool slightly before crushing to a powder.

Mix the saffron powder with the boiling water and set aside to infuse for 1 hour.

Combine the sugar and saffron water in a small saucepan and heat gently, stirring from time to time, until the sugar has dissolved. Once the liquid is clear, bring to the boil, then lower the heat and simmer briskly for 8 minutes to form a deep golden caramel.

Working quickly, spoon four or five small rounds of caramel onto the prepared baking tray. It sets hard quickly, so you really need to work fast. Place the second sheet of paper on top and use a rolling pin to roll into thin 'glass' wafers. Repeat with the rest of the caramel, replacing the baking mat or baking paper sheets as necessary. (Alternatively, and more simply, pour the hot caramel onto the baking mat or sheet, top with another sheet of paper and roll it thinly. Leave to cool and, once hard, break into shards of varying sizes.)

Once completely cold, store in an airtight container between layers of baking paper. The saffron glass will keep for up to 1 week.

Variation

For saffron sugar, put pieces of saffron glass into a food processor and blitz to a fine vibrant yellow powder. Use for garnish.

SUGARED NUTS

Nuts and sugar are a sublimely versatile combination and, to our mind, an indispensable part of any dessert table.

CANDIED NUTS

These are whole nuts coated in a crunchy layer of crisp caramelised sugar. Use the same technique with your favourite nut, then add salt, herbs or spices to vary the flavours.

MAKES AROUND 450 G (1 LB)

150 g (5½ oz) caster (superfine) sugar
60 ml (2 fl oz) water
300 g (10½ oz) blanched nuts
    (hazelnuts or almonds are our
    favourites)

EQUIPMENT
sugar thermometer

Line a baking tray with a silicone baking mat or baking paper.

Combine the sugar and water in a heavy-based saucepan and heat slowly to dissolve the sugar, stirring from time to time. Once the syrup is clear, increase the heat and bring to a rolling boil. Cook for around 5 minutes until it reaches 110°C (230°F) when measured with a sugar thermometer. This is the thread stage – the syrup falls from a spoon in a long thread.

Add the nuts to the pan. The oils coming out of the nuts will soon make the syrup seize and crystallise, but don't panic. Keep stirring (which can become hard work) until the crystallised sugar slowly redissolves to a caramel and deepens to a chestnut brown. This will take 10–15 minutes.

One the caramel is completely clear and liquid again, pour onto the prepared baking tray and use a silicone spatula or fork to separate the nuts out. Leave to cool and harden.

Store in an airtight container for 1 week.

See photo on pages 208–209.

Variation
For a different, rather more rustic, funky effect, tip the nuts out onto the baking tray while the sugar is still crystallised, and before it reverts to caramel.

PRALINE

Pulverise your candied nuts and you have praline! The best technique is to bash them with a rolling pin into varying sized chunks or coarse, sandy crumbs. Alternatively, blitz in a food processor to a fine powder. Use praline to add texture and crunch to iced cakes, smooth creamy desserts and ice cream. You can also fold praline into whipped cream, mousses and custards. Pralines can be stored in the freezer and used as required.

See photo on pages 208–209.

BRITTLE

Another variation on the nut-sugar theme, brittles are thin sheets of nut- or seed-studded hard sugar candy. Most of us are familiar with peanut brittle (one of the most popular American confections) while in the Middle East, brittles are more likely to be made with pistachios, pine nuts, pumpkin or sesame seeds.

Eaten on their own, brittles are a delicious treat, and they are always well received as a homemade culinary gift. Break your favourite brittle into varying sized shards for brilliant – and stunningly attractive – garnishes for desserts.

Brittles are slightly more complex than candied nuts and praline as they include extra ingredients, such as butter (for richness), liquid glucose (or corn syrup) to guard against crystallisation, and bicarbonate of soda (baking soda) for aeration. Recipe variations (and the end result) abound, but this is our go-to favourite, which works well with all different nuts and seeds.

MAKES AROUND 750 G (1 LB 11 OZ)

340 g (12 oz) shelled nuts or seeds
400 g (14 oz) caster (superfine) sugar
125 ml (4 fl oz) water
110 g (4 oz) unsalted butter
80 ml (2½ fl oz) liquid glucose
   (or light corn syrup)
½ teaspoon bicarbonate of soda
   (baking soda)
sea salt flakes

EQUIPMENT
sugar thermometer

Preheat the oven to 170ºC (340ºF) fan-forced/190ºC (375ºF).

Spread the nuts in a single layer on a baking tray and bake for 8–12 minutes (it will depend on the nut; seeds will only need 5 minutes or so) until they are golden brown and smell toasty. Stir them around halfway through the baking time so they colour evenly.

Turn the oven down very low to keep the nuts warm while you prepare the caramel. Line another baking tray with a silicone baking mat or baking paper.

Combine the sugar, water, butter and liquid glucose in a heavy-based saucepan and cook on a medium heat until the sugar dissolves, stirring from time to time. Increase the heat and cook for around 10 minutes until the mixture is a golden caramel colour and registers 160ºC (320ºF) on a sugar thermometer. This is the hard crack stage.

Remove the pan from the heat and stir in the bicarbonate of soda, which will make it foam and bubble. Working quickly, stir in the warm nuts and immediately pour the mixture onto the prepared baking tray. Use a spatula to spread it out as thinly as you can. Sprinkle with salt and leave to cool completely, which will take around 30 minutes.

Break into shards and store in an airtight container for up to 1 week.

See photo on pages 208–209.

Optional extras (add with the bicarb)
- spices (cinnamon, cardamom, ginger, mahlab, chilli flakes)
- citrus zest (lemon, lime, orange, grapefruit)
- flavours (vanilla, almond, peppermint, flower waters)
- dried flower petals, chopped rosemary

PRESERVES

Preserving is about capturing the bounty of one season, then releasing it into another. When you open a jar of apricot jam on a cold mid-winter's morning, you once again experience the flavours – the smells, sights, sounds and, most of all, the joy – of a hot summer's day. These poetic notions are born of necessity, of course. Conserving produce when it's abundant and storing it up for leaner months is not merely good housekeeping but can be literally life-sustaining. And there are still many parts of the world where this imperative endures.

The simplest method of preserving fruit in hot Middle Eastern countries is, unsurprisingly, to dry it out in the sun until the moisture, which provides the medium for food-spoiling bacteria, has evaporated. It's hard to replicate this in colder climes, but an oven on a low setting gives a good result, too – see our fruit wafers and leathers.

Sugar is also an effective preserving agent, something that ancient civilisations knew well. The earliest methods used honey, but all forms of sugar have an osmotic effect, drawing water out and creating an inhospitable environment for microorganisms. There are several ways of using it to preserve foods. Desiccated or boiled fruit can simply be packed in sugar: crystallised citrus peels and root ginger are classic examples of this technique. Fruits can also be cooked or stored in a thick sugar syrup – confit citrus and spoon fruits use this approach – while Persian *sharbats* (and modern day cordials) tweak this method to produce sweet fruit drinks (see our Drinks chapter, pages 228–239).

Jams, jellies and other fruit preserves involve boiling fruit initially, to reduce the water content, then adding sugar to prevent bacterial growth. There are a few key things to know to achieve the perfect jam. It's essential to sterilise all jam-making equipment: you can run things through a dishwasher cycle, boil them for 10 minutes, or put them in an oven at 150°C (300°F) for 15 minutes. Fill while still hot and seal tightly. Some low-pectin fruits need a boost from powdered pectin, although we prefer to add a high-pectin fruit into the mix. It definitely helps to warm the sugar before adding it to the fruit as it reduces the cooking time, resulting in a fresher-tasting jam.

As for equipment, a large casserole or saucepan will do in place of a preserving pan, but you'll need a funnel, a ladle, muslin (cheesecloth) (for jellies), and lidded glass jars. We'd also strongly recommend a sugar thermometer, to use in conjunction with the wrinkle test.

TURKISH FRESH AND DRIED FRUIT SALAD

Fresh fruit salads are popular all around the Middle East, but this dish was inspired by the myriad *hoşafs* that we've encountered on our travels around Turkey. Hoşafs are light and fragrant dried fruit salads, and they are a crucial way of preserving the summer's bounty (apricots, grapes, figs, prunes and so on) through the winter months. As well as being offered as dessert, they are often served icy cold as a refreshing and moistening element alongside savoury pilafs, borek and pasta dishes.

Here we combine fresh and dried fruit (as well as a rather non-Turkish splash of apple brandy) in a delicate syrup, which makes a quick and easy topping for ice cream, yoghurt or your breakfast cereal.

Most of these dried and candied fruits are available from Middle Eastern stores or good specialist food stores.

SERVES 6–8

4 dried apricots, cut into 1 cm
 (½ in) dice
2 dried peaches, cut into 1 cm
 (½ in) dice
1 candied clementine, cut into 1 cm
 (½ in) dice
60 g (2 oz) sultanas (golden raisins)
60 g (2 oz) dried muscatel raisins
4 cm (1½ in) piece fresh ginger,
 peeled and thinly sliced
1 ripe pear, cut into 1 cm (½ in) dice
1 ripe peach, cut into 1 cm (½ in) dice
1 ripe plum, cut into 1 cm (½ in) dice
60 g (2 oz) walnut halves, coarsely
 chopped

AROMATIC SYRUP

250 g (9 oz) caster (superfine) sugar
175 ml (6 fl oz) water
50 ml (1¾ fl oz) Calvados or
 any brandy
½ cinnamon stick
2 cloves
4 cardamom pods, lightly crushed
1 long strip orange peel, all pith
 removed
1 small strip lime peel, all pith
 removed

To prepare the syrup, combine the sugar, water and Calvados in a saucepan and heat gently, stirring occasionally, until the sugar dissolves. When the syrup is clear, add the spices and citrus peels, then increase the heat and bring to the boil. Lower the heat and simmer gently for 2 minutes.

Add the dried fruit and sliced ginger to the pan and simmer for 2 minutes. Stir in the fresh fruit and walnuts and simmer for 1 more minute, then remove from the heat and leave to cool completely.

Transfer to an airtight container and refrigerate until ready to use. The compote will keep for a few days in the fridge.

Serve chilled, at room temperature, or gently warmed through.

+ ALSO SERVE WITH
Middle Eastern clotted cream (page 32)
Chantilly-yoghurt cream (page 48)
Cream cheese ice cream (page 61)
Baby babas (page 174)
Berber 1000-hole pancakes (page 181)

APRICOT SPOON FRUITS

We were introduced to spoon fruits in Turkey, where we were offered tiny, intensely green and almost translucent figs, along with coffee and an accompanying glass of water. This common custom is part and parcel of the region's hospitality. Spoon fruits are also popular on the breakfast table, served with thick, creamy yoghurt or soft flatbreads and white cheese.

All sorts of fruits, nuts and flowers are preserved in this way, but apricots are one of our favourites because of their floral tang and the way they tint the syrup a lovely amber colour. A really thick syrup is important to hold the fruits in suspension.

MAKES ENOUGH FOR A 1 LITRE (34 FL OZ) JAR

500 g (1 lb 2 oz) granulated sugar
300 ml (10 fl oz) water
1 kg (2 lb 3 oz) apricots, halved and pitted
juice of 3 limes

EQUIPMENT
sugar thermometer
1 litre (34 fl oz) sterilised preserving jar

Gently heat the sugar and water in a saucepan, stirring occasionally, until the sugar has dissolved. Once the liquid is clear, bring to the boil, then lower the heat and simmer briskly for 10 minutes.

Add the apricots to the syrup and cook for 5 minutes, until just barely tender. Remove the pan from the heat, cover with a lid and set aside for 24 hours.

The next day, lift the apricots out of the syrup into a bowl. Heat the apricot-scented syrup until it reaches 110°C (230°F) on a sugar thermometer. Add the lime juice to the syrup and skim away any surface scum.

Return the apricots to the pan and gently stir them to coat thickly with the syrup. Ladle into a large sterilised preserving jar (see page 211) and seal while hot. Keep in your pantry (or another cool dark place) for up to 3 months and refrigerate after opening.

WILD FIG PRESERVE WITH GINGER AND ORANGE

This lovely breakfast preserve is halfway between a jam and a spoon fruit. We use tiny wild Iranian figs, which must be simmered gently to maintain their shape rather than collapsing down to a jammy muddle.

Small dried wild figs are available from Middle Eastern food stores and good provedores.

MAKES ENOUGH FOR 3 × 225 ML (7½ FL OZ) JARS

500 g (1 lb 2 oz) small dried wild figs
400 g (14 oz) granulated sugar
1 cinnamon stick
2 tablespoons finely diced crystallised ginger
500 ml (17 fl oz) orange juice
juice of 1 lemon

EQUIPMENT
sterilised preserving jars

Cover the figs with boiling water and leave for 20 minutes to soften. Drain well and tip into a heavy-based saucepan, along with the remaining ingredients.

Heat gently, stirring from time to time, until the sugar has dissolved. Once the liquid is clear, bring to the boil, then lower the heat and simmer gently for 40–50 minutes, or until the figs are tender and the syrup coats the back of a spoon thickly. Stir regularly and skim from time to time to remove any frothy scum that rises to the surface.

Ladle into sterilised preserving jars (see page 211) and seal while hot. Keep in your pantry (or another cool dark place) for up to 1 year and refrigerate after opening.

RHUBARB, ORANGE AND GINGER JELLY

Iranians are very fond of rhubarb, and it has particular significance for the Zoroastrian religion, which has it that the human race emerged from the rhubarb plant! Rhubarb has an affinity with both orange and ginger, and the apples are included to bump up the pectin content. It makes for a lovely amber-hued jelly.

MAKES AROUND 2 × 225 ML (7½ FL OZ) JARS

800 g (1 lb 12 oz) rhubarb stalks, trimmed and roughly chopped
2 apples, coarsely chopped
75 g (2¾ oz) fresh ginger, thinly sliced
juice of 2 oranges, squeezed out halves reserved
1.5 litres (51 fl oz) water
785 g (1 lb 12 oz) granulated sugar (approximate weight)

EQUIPMENT
jelly bag
sugar thermometer
sterilised preserving jars

Put the rhubarb, apples and ginger into a large saucepan. Add the squeezed out orange halves and water and bring to the boil. Lower the heat and simmer gently for 1–1¼ hours until very pulpy. Remove from the heat and allow to cool, then ladle into a jelly bag suspended over a large container and leave to drain overnight.

The next day, preheat the oven to 150°C (300°F) fan-forced/170°C (340°F) and line a small roasting tin with foil. At the same time, put a couple of saucers in the freezer to chill.

Add the orange juice to the collected liquid, then weigh the mixture and return it to the cleaned out pan.

Measure out three-quarters that weight of sugar – this should be around 785 g (1 lb 12 oz) – pour it into the prepared roasting tin and warm in the oven for 10 minutes. (This makes it dissolve much more easily, resulting in a clearer jelly.)

Tip the warmed sugar into the pan with the fruit juices and heat gently until the crystals have all dissolved, stirring every now and then to help it along. Increase the heat to a rolling boil, skimming away any scummy froth that rises to the surface. Cook until it reaches the setting point, which will take 50–60 minutes. It's easy to determine if you have a sugar thermometer (at 105°C/220°F), but it's useful to do the wrinkle test as well. Dollop a small spoonful onto one of the cold saucers and return it to the fridge to cool for a few minutes. It has reached setting point if it forms a wrinkly skin when you push your finger across the surface. If it hasn't set, continue boiling and repeat the test at 5-minute intervals.

Once the jelly reaches setting point, remove the pan from the heat, skim away any remaining froth and leave to settle for 10 minutes. Skim again, if necessary, then ladle into sterilised preserving jars (see page 211) and seal while hot. Keep in your pantry (or another cool, dark place) for up to 1 year and refrigerate after opening.

ROSE PETAL JAM

One of the most iconic Middle Eastern jams, it's not just enjoyed for breakfast but dolloped on top of yoghurt and rice puddings, served with ice cream and used to fill all manner of biscuits and cakes. Rose petals don't contain any pectin, which means the resulting jam is much more liquid than fruit jams – but to us, this only increases its appeal.

You need intensely fragrant, completely organic unsprayed blooms to make this jam. The darker the colour of your rose petals, the more intensely pink the jam.

MAKES AROUND 3 × 225 ML (7½ FL OZ) JARS

250 g (9 oz) organic unsprayed rose petals, preferably
    red or dark pink with a strong perfume
juice of 2 lemons
600 g (1 lb 5 oz) granulated sugar
600 ml (20½ fl oz) water

EQUIPMENT
sterilised preserving jars

Wash the rose petals gently and put them into a large mixing bowl with the lemon juice and 200 g (7 oz) of the sugar. Use your hands to gently massage the sugar into the petals. Leave overnight to macerate.

The next day, combine the water and the remaining 400 g (14 oz) of sugar in a large saucepan and heat gently, stirring from time to time, until the sugar has dissolved. Once the liquid is clear, add the rose petal mixture and bring to the boil. Lower the heat slightly and simmer briskly for around 30 minutes, or until the syrup thickens slightly to a silky loose-jam consistency.

Ladle into sterilised preserving jars (see page 211) and seal while hot. Keep in your pantry (or a cool, dark place) for up to 1 year. Refrigerate after opening.

EASY APRICOT JAM

A useful and easy 'jam' to have on hand for various cakes, pastries and doughnuts (page 168), or to dollop on yoghurt. It's made with dried apricots, giving it year-round appeal. And because it's closer to a compote than a cooked jam (albeit a very thick and sticky one), there's no messing around with setting points and sterilised jars, and you can simply store it in the fridge.

MAKES AROUND 400 G (14 OZ)

300 g (10½ oz) good-quality dried apricots,
    coarsely chopped
75 g (2¾ oz) golden caster (superfine) sugar
strips of peel from 1 orange
juice of ½ lemon
few sprigs of thyme
juice of 2 oranges
1 tablespoon orange blossom water (optional)

Put the chopped apricots in a small saucepan and add enough water to just cover. Add the sugar and strips of orange peel. Heat gently to dissolve the sugar, then bring to the boil. Lower the heat and simmer for 45 minutes, stirring from time to time, or until the pieces of apricots are very tender and the syrup has reduced. Add the lemon juice and thyme. Simmer for 15 minutes until the syrup has reduced further and the apricot flesh looks plump and sticky.

Remove from the heat and leave the apricots to cool. Fish out the orange peel and thyme sprigs and discard. Tip into a food processor along with the orange juice and orange blossom water, if using, and whiz to a smoothish purée (the level of chunkiness is up to you). Transfer to an airtight container and refrigerate for up to 2 weeks.

ROSE-LIME MARMALADE

This is a twist on one of Lucy's all-time favourite childhood breakfast preserves: Rose's lime marmalade. Back then, limes seemed impossibly exotic, but nowadays they are widely available in supermarkets at all times of the year. The vibrant green colour of this marmalade is irresistible and – dare we say it – our version is less sweet and more refreshing than its inspiration, while the rosewater adds a lovely perfume that complements the sharpness of the fruit brilliantly.

MAKES AROUND 4 × 225 ML (7½ FL OZ) JARS

625 g (1 lb 6 oz) limes (around 10)
750–800 g (1 lb 11 oz–1 lb 12 oz)
    granulated sugar (approximate
    weight)
75 ml (2½ fl oz) rosewater

EQUIPMENT
muslin (cheesecloth)
preserving pan
sugar thermometer
sterilised preserving jars

Cut the limes in half and squeeze them, reserving the juice separately. Put the lime halves into a bowl, cover them with cold water and refrigerate overnight. This helps soften the skins and makes the fruit easier to work with. Refrigerate the juice, too.

The next day, drain the limes and use a teaspoon (or your fingers) to scrape out the pulp and membranes from each half. Chop the pulp and membranes roughly and tip onto a square of muslin (cheesecloth), then tie into a small bag with string.

Cut the limes in half again and shred the skins very finely lengthways.

Put the shreds into a large preserving pan together with the muslin bag (tie this to the handle of the pan so you don't lose it). Add enough water to the reserved lime juice to make up the volume to 2 litres (68 fl oz) and add it to the pan. Bring just to the boil, then lower the heat and simmer gently, uncovered, for around 2–3 hours, or until the lime shreds are very tender and translucent.

Towards the end of the 2 hours, preheat the oven to 150°C (300°F) fan-forced/170°C (340°F) and line a small roasting tin with foil. At the same time, put a couple of saucers in the freezer to chill.

Once the lime shreds are soft, remove the pan from the heat, fish out the muslin bag and set it aside. Weigh the fruit and liquid, then return it to the pan.

Measure out the same weight of sugar – this should be around 750–800 g (1 lb 11 oz–1 lb 14 oz) – pour it into the prepared roasting tin and warm in the oven for 10 minutes. (This makes it dissolve much more easily, resulting in a clearer marmalade.)

Tip the warmed sugar into the pan with the fruit and liquid and heat gently until the crystals have all dissolved. Stir every now and then to help it along. Once the sugar has completely dissolved, squeeze the muslin bag over the pan to extract as much of the jelly-like juice as you can; this is the source of pectin, which will make the marmalade set.

Stir briefly, then increase the heat to high and bring the mixture to a rapid boil, skimming away any frothy scum that rises to the surface. Because limes have a high pectin content, the setting point for this marmalade can be reached surprisingly quickly. It's easy to determine if you have a sugar thermometer (at 105°C/220°F), but it's useful to do the wrinkle test as well. After about 5 minutes of brisk boiling, dollop a small spoonful onto one of the cold saucers and return it to the fridge to cool for a few minutes. It has reached setting point if it forms a wrinkly skin when you push your finger across the surface. If it hasn't set, continue boiling and repeat the test at 5-minute intervals.

Once the marmalade reaches setting point, remove the pan from the heat, skim away any remaining froth and leave to settle for 10 minutes. Skim again, if necessary, then stir in the rosewater.

Stir gently to distribute the shreds evenly, then ladle into sterilised preserving jars (see page 211) and seal while hot. Keep in your pantry (or another cool, dark place) for up to 1 year and refrigerate after opening.

PRESERVED CITRUS

Much of citrus fruits' zing comes from the zest – the very outer layer of the skin – which is where most of the flavour compounds are found. There are various ways of preserving citrus zest to create fabulous flavour hits to enliven your food. Here we showcase two techniques – drying and preserving in syrup – each of which has its own merit. The third recipe, for confit citrus slices (page 222), is different yet again because it includes the entire rind – pith and all – as well as some of the flesh, and the resulting flavour is even more complex.

DRIED CITRUS PEEL

The simplest method of preserving citrus peel is just to dry it out. Dried orange peel is used particularly extensively in Persian cooking, and in Iran it is easy to find in spice bazaars. It can be tricky to find elsewhere, but is simplicity itself to prepare at home. The method below uses an oven, although we've also been known to dry strips of citrus on a sunny windowsill or on top of radiators (which perfumes the room beautifully). An old-fashioned airing cupboard also works well.

MAKES AS MUCH AS YOU LIKE

your choice of citrus fruit (Seville oranges, clementines and tangelos are our favourite)

Preheat the oven to 120°C (250°F) fan-forced/140°C (275°F). Using a sharp knife or vegetable peeler, pare the peel away from the thick white pith as thinly as possible. Carefully slice away any pith that lingers, then cut the strips of peel into 10 cm (4 in) lengths. Arrange on a baking tray and dry in the oven for 15–20 minutes. Store in an airtight container. It keeps well for several months.

CANDIED CITRUS ZEST

A quick method of preserving citrus zest, which makes a fabulous garnish and a surprisingly moreish snack. We decorate cakes with a tangle of citrus strips or chop them finely for adding to mousses, ice creams and nut stuffings for sweet pastries. As a bonus, the syrup can be sharpened up with an extra squeeze of juice and used in fruit salads, cake icings or in cold summer drinks. We find it's particularly useful to splash around in our favourite cocktails.

Use any citrus you like, but remember that very bitter fruit, like grapefruit, need to be blanched more times.

MAKES AS MUCH AS YOU LIKE

your choice of citrus fruit
caster (superfine) sugar
water

Use a sharp knife or vegetable peeler to pare the peel away from the pith as thinly as possible. Carefully slice away any pith that lingers, then cut into fine julienne strips.

Put the strips of zest in a saucepan and cover with cold water. Bring to a vigorous boil then immediately tip into a sieve to drain and rinse under cold running water.

Repeat this blanching process several times (grapefruit peel needs to be blanched five or six times). After the final blanching, set the peel aside to drain and air-dry for a few minutes.

Weigh the peel then set aside. Measure out double that weight of both sugar and water and combine in a medium saucepan. Heat gently until the sugar dissolves. Bring to the boil, then lower the heat to a simmer. Add the shredded peel and simmer very gently for 30 minutes (grapefruit can take up to 2 hours) until the zest is soft and translucent.

Cool in the syrup, then transfer to a jar with a lid. Make sure the zest is completely submerged in syrup or it may crystallise. If this does happen, transfer to a saucepan and heat gently until the sugar redissolves. The zest keeps well for several months.

Variation

For sugared zest, after cooking, remove the zest from the syrup with a slotted spoon and spread it out as loosely as you can on paper towel to dry for around 1 hour. Sprinkle liberally with sugar and leave to set. Store the sugared strips in an airtight container for several months.

CONFIT CITRUS

These translucent slices of syrupy citrus make exquisitely pretty decorations for all kinds of cakes and desserts. As well as being intensely sweet-sour, with a back-note of bitterness, their chewability means added texture, too. They can easily become habit-forming, and you may well find yourself looking for excuses to eat them. The recipe below is for confit lemons, but works with other citrus fruits too. Some of our favourite are ruby grapefruit, tangelo and clementine.

MAKES AROUND 400 G (14 OZ)

2 large unwaxed lemons
425 ml (14½ fl oz) water
110 g (4 oz) caster (superfine) sugar

Using a very sharp knife, trim the ends from one and a half lemons and cut crossways into 3 mm (⅛ in) slices. (Reserve the remaining half.) Carefully remove the pips, then transfer the lemon slices to a saucepan and cover with cold water. Bring to a gentle boil, then lower the heat and simmer for 3 minutes. Drain and repeat.

Add the measured water to the pan together with the sugar. Heat gently, stirring to dissolve the sugar, then return the lemon slices to the pan. Bring to a simmer, cover the surface with a circle of baking paper to keep the lemon slices submerged and simmer very gently for 45 minutes. Test to see if the lemon skins are tender; if not, continue cooking for a further 10–15 minutes, or until they are.

Use a slotted spoon to carefully lift the lemon slices into a shallow lidded container.

Measure the syrup and, if necessary, simmer to reduce it to 125 ml (4 fl oz). Remove the pan from the heat and stir in the juice from the reserved lemon half. Pour the syrup onto the lemon slices; ideally, they should be fully submerged. Cover and leave overnight before using. They will keep well in an airtight container for several months.

DRIED APPLE WAFERS

Removing the moisture content from fruit (see opposite) is a simple and effective way of preserving it for use in the cold winter months, and it has the added effect of intensifying the flavour. In Middle Eastern countries, hot summer sunshine is the ideal drying medium. If you live in a colder climate then you will need to use your oven, or a dehydrator, if you have one. The method used here is relatively quick and surprisingly effective – and the technique works equally well with apples and pears. No, the plastic wrap won't melt in the oven, and it prevents the apples from sticking to the tray. Once cooked, they magically slip off.

Be warned: you will find these fruit wafers are pretty moreish. They make a nice crunchy snack and a lovely (and relatively healthy) lunchbox treat. We love to use them as garnish (page 129) or as an addition to a cheeseboard.

1 large granny smith (or bramley)
   apple
1–2 tablespoons icing (confectioners')
   sugar

Preheat the oven to 80°C (175°F) fan-forced/100°C (210°F). Wrap two flat baking trays in plastic wrap.

Use a mandoline or a very sharp knife to slice the apple as thinly as possible. Work in towards the core, then turn the fruit around and slice the other side. Work briskly to avoid the apple discolouring (although these sharp green varieties don't oxidise too much).

Lay the apple slices out on the prepared baking trays in a single layer, with no overlaps, then sift on the icing sugar in a thin even layer.

Bake for around 1 hour, until the apple slices are just slightly coloured and are super-crisp. Remove them from the oven and use a small spatula to remove them from the tray. Once they are completely cold, store them in an airtight container for up to 1 week.

FRUIT LEATHERS

All around the Middle East you see vast sheets of fruit leather drying in the hot sunshine: plums, grapes, apple, mulberries and apricots are all popular. If you're lucky enough to live somewhere with guaranteed sunshine, then try that method; otherwise, you can achieve a similar result by drying trays of fruit purée in the oven. Our favourite leathers are apple, plum and apricot, but you can apply the same principle to most fruit. They make a terrific lunchbox snack, but are also good to snip into tiny shapes as a garnish.

MAKES 2 SHEETS FRUIT LEATHER

600 g (1 lb 5 oz) granny smith apples (around 4), (or use the same weight of pears, plums or apricots)
200 ml (7 fl oz) water
60 g (2 oz) granulated sugar
2 tablespoons lemon juice
1 teaspoon ground cinnamon

Preheat the oven to 80°C (175°F) fan-forced/100°C (210°F).

Line two 40 × 30 cm (16 × 12 in) baking trays with silicone baking mats or baking paper.

Combine the ingredients in a large saucepan and heat gently to dissolve the sugar. Bring to the boil, then simmer for around 15 minutes until the apples start to break down and the liquid has mostly evaporated.

Transfer to a food processor and blitz to a very smooth purée. Pour onto the baking mat and use a spatula to spread it out very thinly. Bake for 4–5 hours, or until the fruit has dried to a paste and is no longer sticky.

Remove from the oven and tip the baking mat out onto your work surface. Allow to cool for a few minutes then peel away the baking mat to reveal your sheet of pliable 100 per cent fruit leather. To store, roll into a long tube and cut into snack-sized portions for using as a lunchbox treat. Alternatively, store as a flat or folded sheet in a large zip-lock bag and cut into shapes to use for garnish as needed. Keeps for up to 6 months.

CRYSTALLISED FLOWERS

Roses grow in many parts of the Middle East, where they are adored for their beauty and intoxicating perfume. They are used with abandon in the kitchen, in varying forms: Iranian cooks like to sprinkle dried petals onto pilafs and puddings; in the Maghreb, tiny rosebuds are used in spice mixes for both sweet and savoury dishes; in Lebanon and the Gulf countries they are particularly fond of rosewater – and nearly every country has a tradition of rose petal jam (page 217).

Although it is increasingly easy to find dried rose petals to scatter over your Middle Eastern desserts (and savoury dishes) it is very simple to crystallise your own at home. And for something a bit different, the technique translates to other edible flowers (try violets, pansies, primroses, lavender or cornflowers) and soft herb leaves, too.

1–2 organic unsprayed roses in full
    bloom (about 20 petals)
1 egg white, whisked to a light froth
50 g (1¾ oz) caster (superfine) sugar

EQUIPMENT
tweezers

Carefully pick the petals from the roses, taking great care not to bruise or tear them. Select small, unblemished petals.

Have two bowls lined up on your work surface, one containing the whisked egg white, the other the sugar.

Working one at a time, hold a petal on one forefinger and use the other to lightly brush it all over with egg white, then drop it gently into the bowl of sugar. Once you have coated several petals with egg white, tumble them gently in the sugar so they are evenly coated, but take care not to touch them too much with your fingers. Use a small pair of tweezers to pick the petals out of the sugar and transfer them to a wire rack. It's best to hold them at the base, as even the slightest touch can dislodge the sugar and egg white, leaving them patchy. Once you've completed a few, you will work out the method that works best for you.

Leave the petals alone for 12 hours to dry completely. They harden as the sugar and egg white sets. Store the crystallised petals between sheets of baking paper in an airtight container. They will keep for several months.

DRINKS

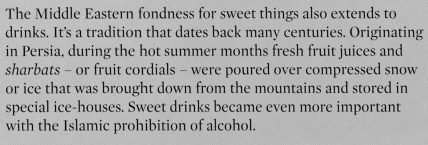

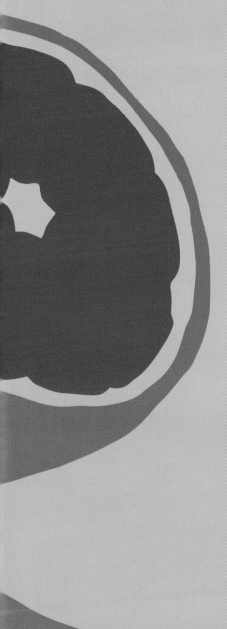

The Middle Eastern fondness for sweet things also extends to drinks. It's a tradition that dates back many centuries. Originating in Persia, during the hot summer months fresh fruit juices and *sharbats* – or fruit cordials – were poured over compressed snow or ice that was brought down from the mountains and stored in special ice-houses. Sweet drinks became even more important with the Islamic prohibition of alcohol.

To this day, in many Middle Eastern cities, wandering drinks vendors are a common sight in the old quarters and souks. They announce their arrival with jingling cymbals, wear distinctive traditional garb and carry heavy, ornate urns on their backs. There's a real skill to dispensing the drink – liquorice, tamarind and lemonade are all popular – from over their shoulder and into the waiting receptacle.

Other sweet drinks are served from mobile carts or small shopfronts. Depending on the season, you'll find freshly pressed orange, pomegranate or watermelon juices, tangy hibiscus tea or milky sahlab. In Iran, distilled infusions are also popular, and they're not just made from fruit, but also from a vast and intriguing variety of herbs, spices and blossoms.

The need to rehydrate, refresh and restore is even more vital when the fasting period of Ramadan falls during summer. There are some regional variations, but universal favourites are *jallab* (made from grape molasses, dates and carob), *amar al din* (made from apricot paste), *erk el-sous* (liquorice) and *tamar Hindi* (a sour-sweet tamarind infusion).

The other significant cold drink in Middle Eastern countries is diluted yoghurt (called *ayran* in Turkey, *dugh* in Iran and *lassi* on the Indian subcontinent). This is often served plain or salted, as a kind of digestif alongside kebabs, but in some regions sweet versions are also popular.

When it comes to hot drinks, these are also drunk sweet, by choice, and are offered not merely as refreshment, but as a cornerstone of Middle Eastern hospitality. There are some regional variations. In the Maghreb and Iran, tea is king: in Morocco, Tunisia and Algeria, it is infused with mint, while in Iran it may be flavoured with cinnamon, saffron or rose petals. In Lebanon and Syria, coffee is generally preferred – often cardamom-scented – while in the Gulf states and Turkey, tea and coffee are equally popular. Simplest of all, and one of Greg's favourite drinks, is a soothing café blanc – or *kahwa beida* in Arabic – which is merely hot water flavoured with orange blossom water and sweetened to taste.

IFTAR JALLAB

Jallab is an immensely popular molasses drink from the Middle East, made from carob, dates, grape and rosewater. Some brands are even smoked with incense! Jallab is diluted with water, poured over crushed ice and garnished with pine nuts and raisins. It's drunk by the gallon during Ramadan, as a post-fast Iftar refresher. You'll find jallab syrup in Middle Eastern grocers.

SERVES 6–8

250 ml (8½ fl oz) jallab syrup
1.25 litres (42 fl oz) water
1 tablespoon rosewater
40 g (1½ oz) pine nuts
30 g (1 oz) golden raisins, roughly chopped

Pour the jallab syrup into a jug, then add the water and rosewater and mix thoroughly. Pour into chilled glasses over crushed ice and sprinkle over the pine nuts and chopped raisins to serve.

BLOOD ORANGE JUICE WITH ORANGE BLOSSOM ICE

We're especially fond of blood orange juice, which has a lovely tartness (not to mention a glorious colour), but this floral ice works with any citrus juice. You might like to ring the changes with clementine, ruby grapefruit or regular freshly squeezed sweet orange juice.

SERVES 4

1 litre (34 fl oz) blood orange juice or other citrus juice, chilled
strips of citrus peel, to decorate (optional)

ORANGE BLOSSOM ICE
200 ml (7 fl oz) water
100 ml (3½ fl oz) lemon juice (about 1½ lemons)
1 tablespoon orange blossom water
various small flowers (jasmine, orange blossom, rose petals, herb flowers), plus extra to decorate (optional)

For the orange blossom ice, stir the water, lemon juice and orange blossom water together and pour into ice trays. Add the flowers, if using, and freeze.

To serve, pile the orange blossom ice into long glasses and pour over the blood orange juice. Garnish with extra flowers or strips of citrus peel, if you like.

GINGER-LIME CORDIAL

A fabulously zippy cordial with a spiky-hot hit of ginger. This cordial makes a refreshing summer drink when diluted with sparkling or still water and garnished with mint sprigs and extra lime wedges. It also serves as a terrific base for summer cocktails.

Don't discard the ginger itself. Pat it dry on paper towel and add to lemon pound cake batter or your favourite biscuit dough. You can even turn it into a sort of cheat's crystallised ginger by drenching it in caster sugar and storing it in a jar to use as garnish.

MAKES AROUND 500 ML (17 FL OZ)

225 g (8 oz) fresh ginger, peeled
400 g (14 oz) caster (superfine) sugar
500 ml (17 fl oz) water
juice of 2 limes

EQUIPMENT
sterilised bottle

Slice the ginger thinly, then chop into smallish pieces. Put it into a medium saucepan, along with the sugar and water, and heat gently, stirring occasionally until the sugar has dissolved. Bring to the boil, then lower the heat and simmer for 50–60 minutes.

Remove from the heat and leave to cool slightly, then strain the syrup through a fine-mesh sieve (reserving the ginger pieces) and stir in the lime juice. Pour into a sterilised bottle and seal (see page 211). When completely cold, store in the fridge. It will keep for up to 3 months without losing its intensity.

Serve on crushed ice and top up with sparkling water, your favourite lemon soda or fancy tonic water.

ROSE SYRUP

A sweetly perfumed syrup that makes a lovely chilled summer drink. Serve with lime segments, crushed ice, and still or sparkling water.

MAKES 600 ML (20½ FL OZ)

400 g (14 oz) caster (superfine) sugar
250 ml (8½ fl oz) water
1 tablespoon lemon juice
75 ml (2½ fl oz) rosewater
few drops of grenadine (optional, for colour)

EQUIPMENT
sterilised bottle

Put the sugar and water into a saucepan and heat gently, stirring occasionally, until the sugar dissolves. Add the lemon juice and bring to the boil. Simmer for 10 minutes without stirring. Skim off any froth from the surface. Add the rosewater and grenadine, if using. Stir and simmer for a further 2 minutes.

Remove from the heat and cool slightly, then pour into a sterilised bottle and seal (see page 211). When completely cold, store in the fridge. It will keep for up to 3 months without losing its intensity.

To serve as a refreshing summer drink, mix 1 part syrup with 3 parts chilled water or soda water. Top with ice and serve straight away.

SOUR MINT SYRUP

This Persian mint sherbet – *sharbat-e sekanjebeen* – features an ancient combination of sugar and vinegar and is believed to be the inspiration for old-fashioned English fruit-vinegar cordials. It makes a wonderfully reviving summer drink, but make sure you choose a good-quality, mild-flavoured vinegar, and not one you slosh on your fish and chips.

MAKES 400 ML (13½ FL OZ)

350 g (12½ oz) caster (superfine) sugar
400 ml (13½ fl oz) water
160 ml (5½ fl oz) apple cider vinegar
juice of 1 lemon
12 mint sprigs

EQUIPMENT
sterilised bottle

Combine the sugar and water in a heavy-based saucepan over a low heat, stirring until the sugar has dissolved. Increase the heat and simmer for 10 minutes. Add the vinegar, lemon juice and mint sprigs and simmer for a further 5 minutes. Remove from the heat and leave to cool. When completely cold, fish out the mint and transfer to a sterilised bottle (see page 211). Seal and store in the fridge for up to 3 months.

To serve as a refreshing summer drink, mix 1 part syrup with 3 parts chilled water or soda water. Top with ice and serve straight away.

AYRAN

Yoghurt drinks – known variously as *ayran*, *dugh*, *lassi* or *tan* – are immensely popular throughout the Eastern Mediterranean, Middle East and India, both on their own and at the dinner table. In Iran and Turkey they are considered the *only* accompaniment to kebabs because their sharpness cuts through the grease of the grilled meat and refreshes the palate.

While yoghurt drinks are often served salty, rather than sweet, they are equally delicious flavoured with fruit or sweet spices. You might not want to serve the following versions with your chicken shawarma, but they make lovely summer coolers and refreshing rechargers at Iftar (the post-sunset meal) during the fasting month of Ramadan.

SERVES 4 EACH

AYRAN BASE
500 g (1 lb 2 oz) plain yoghurt
250 ml (8½ fl oz) ice-cold water (still or fizzy)
100 ml (3½ fl oz) thickened (whipping) cream (optional, but makes for a frothier, creamier drink)
couple of handfuls crushed ice

HIBISCUS SUGAR
1 teaspoon dried hibiscus flowers
1 tablespoon icing (confectioners') sugar

LIQUORICE
1–2 tablespoons sweet or salty liquorice syrup (we like Lakrids)

HONEYED MANGO
1 mango, flesh puréed smoothly
2 tablespoons mild runny honey
¼ teaspoon ground nutmeg

SAFFRON
1–2 generous pinches of saffron threads (or to taste)
1 tablespoon boiling water
1 tablespoon runny honey

EQUIPMENT
blender

To make hibiscus sugar ayran, pound the hibiscus flowers to a powder with the icing sugar. Sieve to remove any bits, then set aside.

Combine the yoghurt, water, cream (if using) and crushed ice in a blender and whiz until very light and frothy. Serve in tall chilled glasses with some extra ice and a sprinkling of hibiscus sugar.

To make liquorice ayran, add the liquorice syrup to the ayran base ingredients. Whiz until very light and frothy and serve in tall chilled glasses with extra ice.

To make honeyed mango ayran, add the mango purée, honey and nutmeg to the ayran base ingredients. Whiz until very light and frothy and serve in tall chilled glasses with extra ice.

To make saffron ayran, steep the saffron threads in the boiling water for 30 minutes (or longer, for maximum vibrancy). Warm the honey gently, then stir it into the base recipe, together with the saffron liquid. Whiz until very light and frothy and serve in tall chilled glasses with extra ice.

HIBISCUS ICED TEA

In Middle Eastern countries they understand that hot drinks are more refreshing than cold. Although iced tea is a Western invention, Greg liked the idea of playing around with the concept, using an infusion of dried hibiscus flowers as a base and perfuming it with orange blossom water.

You'll find dried hibiscus flowers in Middle Eastern delis, specialist food stores and good tea shops.

SERVES 6–8

1.5 litres (51 fl oz) water
120 g (4½ oz) dried hibiscus flowers
30 ml (1 fl oz) lemon juice
100 g (3½ oz) caster (superfine) sugar
1 vanilla bean, split lengthways and seeds scraped
1 teaspoon orange blossom water, or to taste
orange slices, to garnish (optional)

Heat the water in a large saucepan. As soon as it boils, add the dried hibiscus flowers and take the pan off the heat. Leave to steep for 10–15 minutes.

Once steeped, pour through a fine-mesh sieve into a large jug. You want to make sure no flower sediment comes through, so line the sieve with muslin if necessary.

Add the lemon juice and caster sugar and stir vigorously to dissolve the sugar. Scrape in the vanilla seeds and add the bean too. Refrigerate for at least 1 hour, or up to 6 hours. Before serving, fish out the vanilla bean and save it to perfume your sugar canister.

When ready to serve, stir in the orange blossom water. Pour into chilled glasses over crushed ice and garnish with slices of orange, if using.

APPLE-MINT TEA

From Turkey to Tehran, and right across to North Africa, tea is usually drunk hot and sweet. This hybrid recipe combines some of the region's favourite flavours – Turkish apple and Moroccan mint – and finishes with the classic Arabian garnish of pine nuts. For our taste, the apple juice provides sufficient sweetness, but add extra sugar if you like. Serve in attractive glasses with your favourite wafer biscuit.

SERVES 6

500 ml (17 fl oz) water
1 teaspoon good-quality black tea leaves
60 ml (2 fl oz) clear organic apple juice
1 pink lady apple, cut through the core into 2 mm (1/8 in) slices
1 lime, cut crossways into 2 mm (1/8 in) slices
1 bunch mint, washed
20 g (¾ oz) pine nuts

Bring the water to the boil in a medium saucepan, then tip onto the tea leaves in a warmed ceramic bowl. Stir in the apple juice. Add most of the apple and lime slices and most of the mint, reserving some of each to garnish. Cover the bowl and leave to steep for 10 minutes.

Once steeped, strain the tea back into the saucepan and bring it back to the boil. Tip into a teapot and add the reserved fruit slices and mint sprigs.

Serve in little glasses, and garnish each with a few pine nuts.

SPICED ARABIC COFFEE

Arabic coffee, as enjoyed in the Gulf States, is typically served without sugar, as a foil to sweet biscuits or pastries. It is infused with a variety of spices and, to a Western palate, can be something of an acquired taste as it is both bitter and rather thin. Our version uses dark-roast coffee (use your favourite blend) and is rich, warm and spicy. Add sugar, to taste, if you like. A dollop of softly whipped cream makes it extra indulgent.

MAKES 6–8 SMALL CUPS

6 level tablespoons freshly ground dark-roast coffee
1/8 tablespoon saffron powder (or around
   10 saffron threads)
1/4 teaspoon ground ginger
1/4 teaspoon ground cardamom seeds
1/8 teaspoon ground cloves
1/8 teaspoon freshly ground black pepper
1/8 teaspoon freshly grated nutmeg
500 ml (17 fl oz) water
sugar, to taste
softly whipped thick (double/heavy) cream,
   to serve (optional)

EQUIPMENT
Cafetière (French press)

Mix the ground coffee with all the spices then tip into a cafetière.

Bring the water to the boil. Pour half of the boiling water onto the spiced coffee grounds and leave to sit for 30 seconds. Stir gently, then add the rest of the water. Leave to brew for 3–5 minutes.

Press the plunger all the way down and serve the coffee immediately in small cups. Add sugar, to taste, and whipped cream, if desired.

SPANISH HOT CHOCOLATE

This unctuous, thick and rich Spanish-style hot chocolate bears no resemblance at all to the super-sweet thin hot chocolate you find in most English or Australian cafes, and is all the better for it. During the winter, prepare the cinnamon-scented ganache ahead of time and store it in the fridge for up to a month, just ready for when the need arises. You can easily scale the recipe up for a chocolate-obsessed family.

MAKES AROUND 400 G (14 OZ)

80 g (2¾ oz) good-quality dark chocolate
   (50–60% cocoa solids), roughly chopped
40 g (1½ oz) golden syrup
50 g (1¾ oz) unsalted butter
235 ml (8 fl oz) thick (double/heavy) cream
1 teaspoon ground cinnamon
simmering full-cream (whole) milk, to serve

Combine the ingredients in a small saucepan and heat gently until everything has amalgamated to a smooth, glossy sauce. Remove from the heat and leave to cool completely. Transfer to a lidded jar or plastic container. Store in the fridge until the desire for hot chocolate strikes. It will set to a firm ganache.

Heat the milk to a simmer in a small pan and use a balloon whisk to work to a gentle froth. Pour into a warmed mug or Irish coffee glass and add a generous tablespoon of chocolate ganache. Stir briskly to melt the chocolate and serve straight away.

COOK'S NOTES

Ingredients

BUTTER

We use good-quality unsalted butter for its cleaner, fresher flavour. It's not that salt can't be a good counterpoint to sweet dishes, but it's preferable to add it yourself, so you can control the quantity. While butter is best stored in the fridge, it is really important to note the specified temperature called for in a particular recipe. Some require chilled butter (for rubbing into crumbles or whizzing into pastry). Others (cake and cookie batters, for instance) call for softened butter – which means nicely squidgy and pliable, rather than melting or liquid – so it will cream (blend in) readily with other ingredients.

Melted butter and its sophisticated cousins, clarified butter and *beurre noisette*, are called for in batters and recipes when liquid ingredients are combined and then added to dry ones. To melt butter, cut it into cubes so it melts evenly, and do it gently, to avoid burning.

Clarified butter is indispensable in Middle Eastern pastries and desserts and is favoured because it has a mellow flavour and a high burning point. It is made by skimming off the milk solids from melted butter, resulting in a clear yellow liquid. It's worth making in reasonably large batches as it keeps in the fridge for several months. Commercially available ghee is a similar product and can often be substituted for clarified butter in our recipes.

To make clarified butter, cut 500 g (1 lb 2 oz) unsalted butter into small cubes, put in a small saucepan and melt over a medium–low heat. Use a large spoon to skim away the froth as it rises to the surface. Remove the pan from the heat and leave for around 5 minutes to settle. Skim off any more froth so you have as clear a layer of yellow fat as possible. You'll also see a milky residue (the milk proteins) at the bottom of the pan. Carefully pour off or spoon up the clarified butter, leaving the milky solids behind. The butter will set hard in the fridge. Many pastry recipes require it to be melted gently before using.

Brown butter is also called burnt butter or nut butter (from the French, *beurre noisette*). It is made in a similar way to clarified butter, but taken to the point where the moisture content evaporates, it starts to foam and the milk solids turn brown. It results in a lovely toasted nut flavour, and is traditionally used in French cake batters, such as madeleines and financiers.

Compound butters help to jazz things up. To make, simply add herbs, spices or other sweet additions to butter, roll into a log and chill, then cut into slices for a lovely quick-and-easy sauce. (See page 181 for our Whipped date-lemon butter recipe.)

CHOCOLATE

It might seem obvious, but it's important to use the type specified in a recipe. While the range of chocolates available nowadays can be overwhelming, for cooking we find that there's generally no need to opt for a pricey single-origin variety – the subtleties of flavour tend to be obscured by other ingredients in a recipe. That being said, it's important to use the best quality you can afford, with a high ratio of cocoa solids to sugar. In professional environments, the chocolate of choice comes as chips or pellets (*callets*), which melt evenly and are easy to work with. You can buy these online, but for home cooking, you can use bars of chocolate and chop them as directed in each recipe. Store chocolate in a cool, dark place for up to a year. Don't refrigerate unless the weather is very hot, and bring to room temperature before using.

Dark chocolate varies hugely in the amount of sugar and cocoa solids it contains, so check the label. Generally speaking, the higher the percentage of cocoa solids, the pricier the chocolate, but remember that anything above 70 per cent will be very dark and very bitter. In our recipes, we favour two strengths of dark chocolate: for a good all-round, pleasingly rich flavour, we use a chocolate containing 50–60 per cent cocoa solids, while for something a bit edgier, we will choose 60–70 per cent.

Milk chocolate has a milder, sweeter flavour than dark chocolate because it contains milk solids as well as sugar.

White chocolate, technically speaking, isn't chocolate at all, as it's made from cocoa butter (not cocoa solids), which is combined with milk solids, sugar and vanilla. It has a distinctive (and not universally popular) vanilla-sweet taste, but we find it can make for a pleasing counterpoint to sharp, fruity flavours.

Cocoa powders are generally mixed with a boiling liquid to release their chocolatey flavour. As with solid chocolate, powders contain varying amounts of cocoa solids and sugar, and, as a result, the intensity of flavour also varies. Choose a good-quality brand for the best result. We generally favour Dutch-processed cocoa (also called 'alkalised') as it tends to be less acidic, with a rounder, smoother flavour.

CITRUS

Greg shares the Lebanese love of sour, so a life without citrus is unthinkable. Lemon, orange and (to a lesser extent) lime are all popular in the Middle Eastern dessert kitchen. In all citrus fruit the essential oils contain the citrus flavour, and these are mainly located in the very outer layer of the peel, which is known as the zest. Use a designated zester, microplane grater, vegetable peeler or very sharp knife to remove the zest in strips or shreds, always making sure you avoid the bitter white pith. Sometimes, when using strips of peel, you may need to pare away any residual white pith. At other times, you may need to blanch the peel several times in boiling water to reduce the bitterness.

COFFEE

In the Middle East, coffee is usually flavoured with cardamom or other spices, like saffron, cinnamon and cloves, and it is almost always served sweet. We use these flavour combinations in several of our recipes (see pages 28 and 40). It's not always essential to go to the trouble of brewing up espresso; instant coffee granules are often an expedient choice and very successful substitute.

CREAM

There are many different types of cream available, and what you will have access to depends on whereabouts in the world you live – the quality and flavour can vary wildly. While there are often no direct equivalents, broadly speaking, the way cream is used depends on its fat content, and whether it can be heated or whipped.

Pouring (single/light) cream has a fat content of around 18 per cent. It is used for pouring over desserts (or adding to coffee). It can't be whipped and tends to curdle when boiled. The closest US equivalent is half-and-half.

Thickened (whipping) cream has a fat content of around 35 per cent and can be heated. It can be served as a runny pouring cream, but can also be whipped. It is not quite as stable as whipped double cream and will collapse if not used straight away. Australian thickened cream contains gelatine.

Thick (double/heavy) cream has a fat content of around 48 per cent and is extremely versatile. It makes a decadent treat for pouring and can be heated to make rich custards. It can also be whipped to make an unctuous filling for cakes, tarts and buns. When whipping double cream, it's best only to take it to the soft-peak stage. If you take it too far (which is easy enough to do) it becomes stiff and grainy. There is no direct US equivalent to double cream; heavy cream or heavy whipping cream are the closest substitutes.

Crème fraîche originates from Normandy in France. Traditionally, it's made from unpasteurised milk, which is left to age so that natural bacteria thicken it and give it a slightly sour tang. Modern-day versions are made from pasteurised milk to which a bacterial culture is added. Crème fraîche is increasingly widely available in UK and Australian supermarkets and we are particularly fond of it. While it's high in fat, at roughly 40 per cent, the sour flavour offsets the richness. It is thick enough to dollop onto desserts, and can be heated (although half-fat versions tend to split).

Clotted cream is the richest cream available, at around 55 per cent. It comes from the English West counties, Devon and Cornwall, and is made by heating cream to concentrate it, and then leaving it to stand. The butterfat rises to the surface and forms a thick, yellow crust. There is a Middle Eastern equivalent, called *ashta* (page 32).

Sour cream is made from single cream, which is soured by adding a culture. It has a fat content of 18 per cent and can't be whipped. It has a rich tangy flavour.

DRIED FRUIT

Drying fruit so it can be enjoyed out of season is a popular preservation method in the Middle East. We use dried fruits in many of our recipes – apricots, apples, cherries, currants, dates, figs, peaches, pears, prunes and raisins are all favourites. They are not to be confused with glacé or candied fruits, which are preserved in sugar. Dried fruits are also favoured during Ramadan – their concentrated sugars provide an instant energy hit at the end of a fasting day. Store dried fruit in a cool, dry place and once a packet is open, keep in an airtight container.

EGGS

We urge you to use the freshest, best-quality eggs – which is to say free-range at the barest minimum – not just for ethical reasons, but because they have a superior flavour and texture, which will produce the best results in baking as well as in eating.

In the sweet kitchen, measurements can be critical for a successful outcome. Eggs come in various sizes/grades, and these are not consistent between countries. Often, they are not even consistent within a particular size/

grade. Our recipes were mainly tested in the UK, where eggs come as small, medium, large and very large. For our recipes, we use large eggs, which weigh between 63–73 g (2.2–2.6 oz) out of the shell. Straight away, potential problems are clear as this difference is likely to be magnified with each egg used.

To avoid regional differences and size variations, for our recipes we give weights, rather than a number of eggs. We'd recommend acquainting yourself with the weight of the eggs you use – the grading systems are different in Australia and the US – so you know the approximate weight of a whole egg (unshelled), the white (which comprises about two-thirds of the unshelled weight) and the yolk (one-third). It is then a reasonably straightforward exercise to calculate how many you will need for a specified weight in a recipe.

Because eggshells are porous, it's best to store them separately from other strongly flavoured foods. If you keep your eggs in the fridge, then bring them to room temperature before using because if they are too cold, you run the risk of the batter splitting. As a quick fix, you can sit the whole eggs in a bowl of hot (not boiling) water for 5 minutes. If, like us, you find you are often left with a surplus of egg whites, store them (properly labelled) in small zip-lock bags in the freezer for when you feel like whipping up a pavlova.

Egg wash Either a whole egg or egg yolk, beaten with a little water (or sometimes milk), and brushed onto pastry and dough to give a lovely shine when baked.

FLOUR
When baking cakes, we always recommend sifting flour – often twice – to remove clumps and to help aerate it.

For the cakes, pastries and puddings in this book we generally use **plain (all-purpose) flour**, which is a fine-textured, standard flour that is available everywhere. It is milled from winter wheat that produces flour with a protein content of around 10 per cent, which is lower than the higher protein – stronger – flour needed for making bread. Plain flour is ideal for most general cooking, including cakes, biscuits, pastries and sauces.

Self-raising flour is plain flour that has added raising agents – usually baking powder – and is designed for baking cakes. Baking powder is a combination of bicarbonate of soda (baking soda) (alkaline) and cream of tartar (acid), and it reacts with liquid to produce carbon dioxide bubbles which are captured in the batter during the baking. It's easy enough to make self-raising flour yourself by sifting 2 teaspoons of baking powder with every 150 g (5½ oz) plain flour.

Sometimes we call for **cake or sponge flour**, which is milled from a slightly softer flour than general plain flour, and is particularly suitable for sponge cakes.

FLOWERS
Both fresh and dried flowers are used abundantly in Middle Eastern desserts. They are scattered on as a garnish *au naturel*, crystallised (page 226), turned into jams (page 217), made into cordials and distilled into flower waters (see below). Dried petals are available from Middle Eastern stores and some supermarkets. If using fresh flowers, make sure they are free from insecticides.

FLOWER WATERS
For many thousands of years, Middle Easterners have made liberal use of flower waters both in and out of the kitchen. They are made from distilled petals, often as a by-product of making oil for the perfume industry. As well as making a fragrant hand wash, they are used in syrups for drenching pastries, cakes and milk puddings, they are sprinkled over fruit salads, and used to perfume refreshing drinks and sherbets.

The best known in the West are rosewater and orange blossom water. The general rule of thumb is to use rosewater with red fruits and orange blossom with yellow fruits. However, they are often used interchangeably, and even together. We strongly recommend buying the best-quality flower waters you can afford (the artisanal Mymouné brand from Lebanon is our absolute favourite, with Cortas coming in second) as they have a much more concentrated flavour. Use judiciously: a few drops is often all you need to add a pleasing floral note.

GELATINE
Gelatine comes in powdered and leaf form, and in many different brands/strengths. Problematically, there is no standardised approach to the setting properties of each, and one can't simply be substituted for another.

We always choose leaf gelatine over powdered, because we find the latter has a discernible smell and flavour and doesn't always dissolve readily. Gelatine leaves used in commercial kitchens come in several different strengths, but these vary between countries (variously described as bronze, silver, gold, platinum and titanium). From our recipe testing, we've determined that the two commonly available supermarket products Costa Fine Leaf (in the UK) and Mackenzie's gelatine leaves (in Australia) are sufficiently similar to be interchangeable. As a rule of thumb, we find that one small sheet is sufficient to set 100 ml (3½ fl oz) liquid to a soft, easy-to-turn-out set, or to set 125 ml (4 fl oz) to a wobbly, serve-in-a-glass set. If you don't have access to either product, then our best suggestion is to follow the instructions on the packet. You will first need to see how many leaves are used in a particular recipe and estimate the quantity of liquid this will set. Then check what the manufacturer of your product recommends in terms of the amount of leaf or powder to set that amount of liquid. As with many culinary techniques, it's usually worth doing a test run to ensure future success.

To use leaf gelatine, it first needs to be 'bloomed': softened in a little cold water. When using multiple sheets, be sure to jiggle them about in the water so they are separate and don't clump together. Once the leaves have softened and become slippery (don't leave them too long, or they will dissolve) lift them out and squeeze them gently to extract any excess water. Add the gelatine to the liquid that is to be set (which must be hot). As the liquid cools to below 4°C (40°F), the gelatine will set it firm.

LABNE

This is a wildly popular, delectably creamy strained yoghurt product – like a tangy, soft cheese spread – that's found all across the Middle East. It's made by hanging yoghurt in a bag until the whey drains away. In Middle Eastern countries, you can easily buy commercially produced labne, but it's easy to make yourself at home.

For 500 g (1 lb 2 oz), spoon 1 kg (2 lb 3 oz) natural yoghurt into a clean muslin (cheesecloth) square or tea towel (dish towel). Tie the four corners of cloth together to form a hanging bag and suspend it from a wooden spoon over a deep bowl (we often hang it from the kitchen tap, as long as the weather isn't too warm). Allow it to drain for 6–72 hours; the longer the time, the firmer the result. Bear in mind that thicker Greek-style yoghurts have already been strained, so they will take less time to firm up. If you like, swirl in various flavourings before you strain it: honey, saffron, vanilla seeds, flower waters and spices all make lovely additions.

LIQUID GLUCOSE

We use this clear, viscous syrup in many of our sorbet recipes. It improves the texture, making it smooth, creamier and less crystalline. You can substitute corn syrup if you live in the US, for much the same result.

LIQUORICE

We've developed a bit of an addiction to liquorice. We've always been partial to the confectionery (especially the hard, salty Scandinavian kind), but recently we've begun using liquorice powder in our desserts and adding liquorice syrup to, well, just about everything. (Drizzle some onto yoghurt to make a quick-and-easy midweek dessert – you'll see what we mean.) We recommend the Danish brand Lakrids. It can be purchased direct from the company, from online suppliers or specialist food stores.

MILK

We always use full-cream (whole) milk, with a fat content of around 4 per cent, as we prefer its flavour and consistency. You can substitute lower fat milk, although the resulting flavour won't be quite as creamy.

MOLASSES

As distinct from the dark treacly product refined from sugarcane or beet, Middle Eastern molasses are made from intensely reduced fruit juices, and are wildly popular as a natural sweetener. In their simplest form, they're combined with sparkling or still water or yoghurt to make refreshing non-alcoholic drinks (see pages 229 and 230), or mixed with tahini paste to make a dip or spread for toast. Pomegranate, grape, date and carob are the most widely available, although so far only pomegranate has been embraced in Western countries. Each has its own distinctive flavour.

NUTS

Another indispensable ingredient in the Middle Eastern dessert kitchen. A wide variety of nuts are grown in the region and are available in abundance in local markets. In Western countries, fresh nuts can be hard to source. Because of their high oil content, it's important to buy nuts from a reputable supplier that has a brisk turnover, as they can quickly turn rancid if not stored correctly. They come in various forms: raw (skins on), blanched (skins off), roasted, whole, flaked, slivered and ground.

Our favourite nuts for garnish are almond flakes (both raw, and fried in butter to golden toastiness), and vivid green Iranian pistachio slivers. Almonds, hazelnuts, pistachios and walnuts all make popular fillings for cookies and pastries when finely ground and combined with spices and sugar. We also like to use ground nuts in cakes, where they contribute moisture and texture, as well as their own unique flavour. We store nuts in the freezer, where they'll keep happily for up to 6 months.

PASTRY

Middle Eastern sweet pastries, such as baklava, are usually made from paper-thin translucent sheets of filo (the North African equivalent is brik or warqa), which bakes to a super-crisp, flaky crunch. Others use kadaifi (a fine, shredded pastry), while small nut or fruit–stuffed pies – like sweet borek – tend to use more resilient, specific pastry doughs, often made with semolina. Because our pastry repertoire reaches into European-style tarts and pies – albeit with an Oriental twist – we also use puff pastry, a range of shortcrust pastries and choux pastry. See page 135 for additional information and tips on how to use each of these. *See also* Blind baking (page 246).

SALT

We use fine, free-flowing sea salt in our recipes, as it disperses readily. Good-quality table salt will do just as well. When salt is required as a garnish, we use sea salt flakes, as their larger crystals are attractive, contribute texture and have a fine flavour.

SEEDS

We use different varieties of seeds in our dessert recipes – often toasted to maximise their flavour: sesame, pumpkin and sunflower are favourites. *See also* tahini (below).

SPICES

Middle Eastern cooks are dab hands with spices and use a wide variety in savoury and sweet dishes. We use all the usual suspects – allspice, cardamom, cinnamon, cloves, fennel, nutmeg, peppercorns, saffron, star anise, vanilla and so on – available in most supermarkets. Other more unusual spices include mastic (the resinous gum from a type of acacia tree with a subtle pine flavour) and mahlab (made from ground cherry kernels), which you may have to source from a Middle Eastern grocer or specialist online supplier. As a general rule, for maximum freshness and flavour, we usually buy spices whole and grind them individually, as required in a recipe. If you do buy ready-ground spices, we'd recommend buying them loose and in small quantities from a supplier with a large turnover.

SUGAR

Sucrose, to give it its technical name, is refined from sugar cane and sugar beet, and is the most widely used sweetener of modern times. We use various kinds of sugar (and indeed other sweeteners, such as honey, fruit molasses, maple syrup, golden syrup and treacle) in our recipes. Each has its own flavour and properties, so it's best to use whichever is specified in a recipe.

We mostly use **caster (superfine) sugar**, as the finer grains dissolve more easily than granulated sugar. If you only have granulated sugar to hand, blitz it in a food processor for 15–20 seconds. We frequently substitute golden caster sugar, which is made from unrefined raw cane sugar, and has a richer, more caramelly flavour.

Some of our recipes call for **brown sugars** – soft light brown, soft dark brown and muscovado – which are more strongly flavoured still. They are hydroscopic, meaning they retain moisture in baked items, so prolong their lifespan. They have a tendency to dry out to rock-hard lumps in your pantry, so should always be tightly wrapped and sealed in an airtight container. A slice of bread or apple, or a piece of damp kitchen paper, can be tucked into your sugar container overnight to re-soften it.

Icing (confectioners') sugar is a powdered sugar that is mostly used to make icings (frostings) and for dusting on as a final flourish. Nearly all icing sugar is mixed with a little cornflour (cornstarch) to keep it free-flowing, but it still tends to get hard and lumpy with age and should always be sifted before using.

Flavoured sugar There are many ways to jazz up the flavour of plain sugar. Cinnamon and vanilla sugars are classics (you'll find the suggestion of storing scraped-out vanilla beans in your sugar canister throughout our recipes), but we also like to add grated citrus zest, finely chopped herbs or other ground spices to create all sorts of different flavour boosts. (See page 42 for one of our favourites, Star anise sugar.)

Sugar syrups are a cornerstone of the Middle Eastern pastry repertoire and endless versions trickle through the pages of this book, variously flavoured with spices, citrus zests and flower waters. It's well worth knowing how to make a simple, unflavoured stock syrup base recipe too.

To make around 500 ml (17 fl oz), combine 250 g (9 oz) caster (superfine) sugar and 250 ml (8½ fl oz) water in a saucepan. Heat gently, stirring from time to time, until the sugar has dissolved. Once the liquid is clear – and only then – bring to the boil, then simmer briskly for 5 minutes. Remove from the heat and allow to cool. The syrup will keep in a sealed container in the fridge for up to 1 month.

TAHINI AND HALVA

Tahini is a thick paste made from ground sesame seeds that is often mixed with yoghurt to make a sauce, or with jam or molasses to spread on bread (the Middle Eastern equivalent of peanut butter and jelly, perhaps?). The crumbly confectionery known as halva is also made from ground sesame seeds. Both make a surprisingly pleasing contribution to our dessert repertoire.

YOGHURT

Considered a staple in Middle Eastern and Eastern Mediterranean countries, yoghurt is eaten on a daily basis and is made into a refreshingly sour drink in these hot climates. Yoghurt in the region is almost always the plain, unsweetened, full-fat type, and is served on its own, as an accompaniment to grills and kebabs, soups and stews, and alongside pastries and cakes. We always use full-fat yoghurt with a fat content between 3.5 and 5.5 per cent for its creamier flavour and richer consistency. We also like traditional Greek or Greek-style yoghurts, which are strained for an even richer result. *See also* labne (page 244).

Techniques

BAIN-MARIE (OR WATER BATH)

This technique is used for delicate dishes (such as custards and some cheesecakes) that require gentle, even heat. It typically involves sitting the dish in a roasting tin half filled with hot water – some cooks also recommend placing it on a cardboard piece as an extra insulating layer. The water temperature doesn't rise above 100°C (210°F) and provides a moister, more constant cooking environment than the fiercer, drying heat of your oven.

BLANCHING

Some raw nuts and fruits require soaking in boiling water for a few minutes to help remove the skins. Blanching in one or several changes of boiling water is also used with some citrus fruits to remove any bitterness from the skins.

BLIND BAKING

Most tart recipes require a pastry shell to be partially – or completely – cooked before the filling is added. The uncooked, chilled tart is lined with baking paper and weighted with baking beads (or raw rice or pulses) which help stop the base from puffing up as it cooks, and help set the shape. The shell is baked for 15–20 minutes, until the pastry is dry and sand-coloured. At this point, the paper and beads are removed and the tart can be filled with a raw custard mixture and baked until this is set. Otherwise, the empty shell can be returned to the oven for a further 5–10 minutes, or until it is firm, dry and golden brown. This cooked tart shell, once cooled, can be filled with fresh fruit, whipped cream or crème pâtissière.

CARAMEL

Caramel is sugar that is cooked until it melts, then gradually darkens and browns until at around 174°C (345°F) it develops complex, buttery, toasty toffee aromas and flavours. Dry caramel is mainly used for making pralines and for decoration. It is quicker to make – and is simpler if you just want a small quantity – but can be tricky as it can burn at the edges before uniformly melting. Scatter 100 g (3½ oz) sugar in an even layer over the base of a heavy-duty saucepan or small frying pan. Put over a medium–low heat and wait until it starts to liquefy around the edges. Shake the pan gently (but never, ever stir) to encourage this process and, with luck, by the time all the sugar has melted, it will have transformed into a rich reddish-gold caramel. Continue to cook until it darkens, but before it burns (it's a fine line), then take off the heat and use immediately before it sets hard. Wet caramel includes water with the sugar

(in varying ratios), so it cooks more slowly. It is less prone to burning, but can sometimes crystallise and become cloudy. Crystallisation can occur for various reasons: if a rogue speck of something gets into the pan, for instance, or sometimes by stirring. We would always make wet caramel for larger quantities and the simplest method is to put sugar into a pan with just enough water to dampen it all over. Then heat gently to dissolve the sugar completely, without letting it boil. Have a jug of cold water and a heatproof pastry brush standing by and use it to lightly brush the sides of the pan, should any crystals form. Swirl the pan gently, rather than stir, and use straight away.

Caramel sauce is made by adding cream with caramel, while butterscotch also includes butter. We are huge fans of fruit caramel sauces, made by adding fruit purées. This technique works well for different kinds of fruit – plum, blackberry, peach, orange and apple are some of our favourites – and has the effect of capturing and preserving the flavour of the fruit. See pages 35, 36 and 65.

CONFECTIONERY

When you cook sugar syrup (see page 245), its physical transformation from crystal to liquid is the basis of all confectionery making. It passes through various stages, each of which has its own properties, and you will need a sugar thermometer for the best results. Thread stage is reached at around 110°C (230°F), and is appropriate for making standard syrups. It falls from a wooden spoon in a long thread, or a little cool syrup will stretch into a thread between the thumb and forefinger. With further cooking, small dollops of syrup are dropped into cold water to test. Initially, a pliable ball forms which can be squeezed to asses its degree of firmness. The soft ball stage is reached at around 115°C (240°F). The firm ball stage is reached at around 122°C (250°F) and is required for soft caramels and toffees. At around 130°C (265°F), it forms a hard ball, which is ideal for harder toffee and nougat. At the subsequent soft and hard crack stages, the syrup forms threads which are initially pliable and then brittle, and are correspondingly necessary for making hard nougat and toffee (taffy) and butterscotch (soft crack) and hard candy and brittle (hard crack).

ICE BATH

Fill a sink or large bowl with ice and water and that's an ice bath. It's used to bring down the temperature of something quickly – a pan of custard for instance – and to stop it cooking any further.

MELTING CHOCOLATE

This is a bit of an exercise in patience as it's best to do slowly. The change from solid to liquid occurs within a narrow temperature range and it is easy to overheat and burn the cocoa solids. Additionally, any rogue moisture droplets can cause chocolate to 'seize' into a lumpy, grainy consistency, so make sure your equipment is bone-dry.

The most reliable way to melt chocolate is over a pan of simmering water. Chop the chocolate into small, even pieces, no larger than 1 cm (½ in). Put into a heatproof bowl. Sit this over a saucepan of barely simmering water, making sure the water doesn't touch the base of the bowl. Stir occasionally until the chocolate has completely melted. Alternatively, put chopped chocolate into a microwaveable container and cook on full power in 20 second bursts until the chocolate has all but completely melted, stirring between each session. Milk and white chocolate should be microwaved at 30 per cent power.

Some recipes call for melting chocolate with a liquid. Always bring the liquid to the boil first, then pour it over the chopped chocolate and leave it to melt almost completely before stirring gently.

MERINGUE

Meringues are one of the simplest desserts to master, comprising only two ingredients: egg whites and caster (superfine) sugar. When whipped together and cooked, a kind of alchemy occurs, setting the thick glossy mass of foam into sweet, airy clouds that melt on the tongue. Depending on *how* you combine these two ingredients and cook them, the outcome will be quite different: another kind of magic!

Simplest, and most recognisable, is **French meringue**, which is made by whisking egg whites and sugar into snowy peaks and then baking in the oven. It is used to make little kisses, shells and pavlovas, is combined with nuts for dacquoise and folded into various batters to make sponge fingers, cakes and soufflés. To make French meringue, start whisking the whites at low speed, which helps develop structure and volume. Increase to medium–high speed and, once they reach a stiffish foam (about four times the starting volume), add the sugar gradually, making sure each quantity is thoroughly dissolved before you add more to prevent the meringues 'weeping' in the oven. Test for graininess by rubbing a small amount between your fingers. Keep whisking until the whites are stiff and shiny. When you lift the whisk, the mixture should hold firm peaks. Immediately shape and bake the mixture – it will break down if not used straight away.

Italian meringue is made by trickling boiling sugar syrup into egg whites as they are whisked. This causes the whites to puff up and 'cook', and results in a very smooth-textured meringue, which needs no further cooking and can be used as a topping for tarts, in sweet icings (frostings) and as a base for some mousses and ice creams (see page 57). It is virtually indestructible, and can be kept for several hours in the fridge.

Swiss meringue is a complex cooked meringue loved by pastry chefs, but is not used in the recipes in this book.

When **whisking egg whites**, bear in mind the following: older egg whites aerate better than super-fresh ones. Whites whisk up more easily, and the sugar dissolves more readily, at room temperature. Separate your eggs cleanly to ensure there's not even a speck of yolk, and make sure all your equipment is spotlessly clean – the smallest trace of fat can lead to whisking disaster.

PROVING DOUGH

Proving, or rising, dough is the process of resting it to allow the yeast to ferment and leaven the dough. There is generally a first rise, when the dough is allowed to double in size, and then a subsequent proof before baking. It's important not to over-prove, or your dough runs the risk of collapsing. Follow the recipe guidelines in respect of temperature and rising times: most recipes recommend a warm environment, but some call for a slower rise in a cooler environment – even the fridge – overnight.

SIFTING

We encourage you to sift dry ingredients at least once, sometimes twice. Not only does sifting remove clumps (crucial with icing/confectioners' sugar), but it helps to separate and aerate the particles, ensuring maximum lightness. When combining multiple dry ingredients (flour, salt, baking powder, cocoa powder, spices and so on), sift them together for even distribution.

SKINNING, TOASTING AND GRINDING NUTS

To remove the skins from raw, whole nuts, blanch them in boiling water for a few minutes, which makes the skins slip off easily. To remove the skins from walnuts, it's easier to roast them for 8 minutes or so in a hot oven until browning. Tip the hot nuts into a clean tea towel (dish towel) and rub briskly to remove as much skin as you can.

In fact the flavour of skinned nuts is often improved by toasting them in a dry frying pan or by roasting them. Scatter them on a baking tray in an even layer and roast for 6–8 minutes until they are browning and smell toasty. Stir or shake the tray once or twice to help them colour evenly. Allow to cool before using.

Although you can buy ready-ground nuts easily enough, the flavour will always be better and fresher if you grind them yourself, and this is easy enough to do in small batches in a food processor. Whiz in short bursts to achieve a fine, free-flowing, uniform texture, similar to breadcrumbs. Be careful not to overprocess as they will become oily or, worse still, turn into nut butter. We often add a few spoonfuls of sugar to the processor while blitzing them, as it absorbs some of the oil.

TEMPERING CHOCOLATE

The process of slowly heating and cooling chocolate to specific temperatures so that the fats crystallise uniformly and when it hardens it has a polished, glossy consistency and 'snaps' when broken. (Untempered melted chocolate has a dull, streaky appearance by contrast.) The technique is primarily used in high-end chocolate making, to line moulds for filled chocolates, and for coating truffles. (See our recipes on pages 85 and 192.)

There are several tricksy techniques using marble slabs or elaborate machines to help the professional chocolatier with tempering, but it's perfectly possible to do at home with small quantities. For this 'seeding' method, chop the chocolate evenly, then put it into a heatproof bowl, reserving a quarter of the amount. Sit the bowl over a saucepan of barely simmering water, making sure the water doesn't touch the base of the bowl, and stir occasionally until it has completely melted. (Specifically, dark chocolate should reach a temperature of 45°C/115°F on a sugar thermometer.) Remove the bowl from the heat and add the reserved chocolate pieces. Use a silicone spatula to work it in gently. Once the temperature drops to 31°C (88°F), it is ready to use. To temper milk and white chocolates, heat and cool to 2°C (36°F) lower.

Other

EQUIPMENT

Cakes, pastries and desserts require little more than the usual *batterie de cuisine*: weighing scales and measuring spoons, mixing bowls, an electric mixer and/or food processor, a fine-mesh sieve, microplane grater, metal and silicone spatulas, spoons and whisks, sharp knives and chopping boards. But see also the opening of each chapter for more specific equipment.

MEASURING

We'll tackle this thorny issue head-on and state that, for us, weighing scales are one of the essential pieces of equipment in any kitchen. Measuring solid ingredients in cups is unfortunately wildly inaccurate (measure a cup of flour and weigh it ten times and you'll get ten different results). This matters somewhat in general cooking, but can be crucial for pastries, cakes and desserts. We do appreciate that habits can be hard to break, but we would strongly encourage everyone to invest in a set of weighing scales. Not only are they quicker and easier to use, but you'll be rewarded by more consistent, better results.

When it comes to measuring liquids, volume is fine, as long as you are completely accurate. We suggest you use a measuring jug (measuring cups differ between countries).

We use the metric system for measuring, but provide imperial conversions too. Modern weighing scales will measure in both systems (another reason to give them bench space), so use whichever system you are more comfortable with; just don't switch between the two.

OVEN TEMPERATURES

All ovens are different (yes, they really are!) and the best advice we can give you is to invest time in getting to know and understand your own. Just like people, ovens have their own particular and peculiar quirks: they have hot (and cool) spots, and at times they may need 'finessing'. This is a roundabout way of saying that, rather than slavishly following the guidelines provided in our recipes, you may also need to exercise common sense. If a cake appears to be browning too fast, then you may need to slightly lower the temperature or cover it with foil. And don't be afraid of tweaking a recipe if, for instance, dishes are consistently taking more (or less) time to cook.

Idiosyncrasies aside, there are some general principles to observe. Always preheat your oven for at least 20 minutes before baking. Set the oven temperature according to the recipe, remembering that fan-forced (convection) settings are around 20°C (68°F) hotter than conventional oven temperatures.

Unless otherwise stated, position your item in the centre of the oven, to allow for proper circulation of air. Sometimes you may find you need to swivel the tin or tray, to ensure even baking; do this carefully and swiftly, after two-thirds of the baking time has elapsed. And if you are baking multiple items – two trays of biscuits, for instance – then set them on racks just above and below the centre and swap them around halfway through the cooking time.

INDEX

ACKNOWLEDGEMENTS

An awful lot of cakes and puddings were consumed in the making of this book. Thank you, first and foremost, to George, for whom no offering was ever too much. He undoubtedly ate more desserts than was good for him, but always remained enthusiastic in the face of the onslaught. (And yes, it's good getting back to 'normal' eating again.)

SUQAR is the result of several year's of experimenting and testing and a number of people have helped us, both with recipe ideas and with actual cooking. We'd like to thank Joelle Bou Khalil, Kate Dalziel, Hend Hassan Mohammed, Virginia Hodgkinson, Amal Malouf and the Riachi family for their invaluable help with testing, and for providing accurate and detailed information about many Middle Eastern desserts and techniques. You are all inspirational.

Lucy also wants to say a big thank you to the Bridge Babes – Zara, Sue V de V., Lynne, Jacque, Shereen, Sue M., Ros, Mandy and Julie – who endured the weekly sweet offerings with such fortitude. Your comments and advice were generously offered and so gratefully received. Thanks, too, to Patrick and Freddy Duffy who always handled leftovers with such gusto.

For providing accommodation, feeding us and generally looking after and supporting us during our Melbourne visit, Greg thanks his brother, Geoff and sister-in-law, Amal, and Lucy thanks Stephen Fair. (And Stevie, thanks, too for the loan of your wheels: we literally couldn't have made it anywhere without them.)

A huge thank you to the team that worked on the photoshoot. Lindsay Harris was a tireless tracker of ingredients, as well as a huge help in the kitchen. Clare Duncan and Brooke Payne – you are both cooking legends. Thank you for always remaining cheerful in the face of a ridiculous schedule and ridiculous chef demands. Thank you for caring about the food, for always giving more than is asked of you, and for being such a joy to work with.

That SUQAR looks and feels so strikingly lovely is due in large part to designer Daniel New. We really couldn't be any happier. And if the text reads well, it's down to Simon Davis, genius editor. Thank you for always enhancing our words (often so cleverly) and for providing such insightful, considered advice throughout.

Enormous thanks, too, to photographer Alan Benson and food stylist Caroline Velik, who are jointly responsible for the gorgeous images. You are trusted old friends and we love working with you. Thank you both for being so patient and unflappable and for your seemingly boundless creativity in the midst of the chaos.

And so, to other trusted friends. We've been working with our publisher, Hardie Grant, for nearly 20 years now and while the team has grown and evolved, you still provide the same wonderful support and encouragement that has allowed the two of us to grow and evolve as cookbook authors. Thank you, in particular, Julie Pinkham and Jane Willson for believing in us and for prodding us along. And finally, deep and heartfelt thanks to Anna Collett, without whom (it really feels) nothing would have happened at all! We've been so lucky to have such an organised, thorough, tireless and dedicated project editor on our side. Thank you for wanting to make SUQAR as perfect as possible. What more could one ask for?

Hardie Grant Books (Melbourne)
Building 1, 658 Church Street
Richmond, Victoria 3121

Hardie Grant Books (London)
5th & 6th Floors
52 54 Southwark Street
London SE1 1UN

hardiegrantbooks.com

A catalogue record for this
book is available from the
National Library of Australia

SUQAR

ISBN 978 1 74379 413 5

10 9 8 7 6 5 4 3 2 1

Publishing Director: Jane Willson
Managing Editor: Marg Bowman
Project Editor: Anna Collett
Editor: Simon Davis
Design Manager: Jessica Lowe
Designer: Daniel New
Typesetter: Hannah Schubert
Photographer: Alan Benson
Stylist: Caroline Velik
Home Economists: Lindsay Harris, Brooke Payne, Clare Duncan
Production Manager: Todd Rechner
Production Coordinator: Tessa Spring

Colour reproduction by Splitting Image Colour Studio
Printed in China by Leo Paper Product. LTD